Learning to Grow

A spiritual guide to your year in Israel

Rabbi Gamliel Shmalo

KODESH PRESS

Learning to Grow
A Spiritual Guide to Your Year in Israel
© Gamliel Shmalo 2016
978-0-9978205-2-2

The Publisher extends its gratitude to Rabbi Yeshayahu Ginsburg for his help with this project.

Published & Distributed by
Kodesh Press L.L.C.
New York, NY
www.KodeshPress.com
kodeshpress@gmail.com

To my dear parents

Thank you for giving me the support,
vision, and room to grow.

למהנז

ידעתני בטרם תצרני   וכל עוד רוחך בי תצרני

In fresh and engaging style, Rabbi Shmalo, an eminent educator, weaves together a rich tapestry of thoughtful Torah-based insights, ranging from the practical to the profound. I highly recommend this book for all those who seek to fully embrace the opportunities for spiritual growth which are integral to the Israel yeshiva experience.

— Rabbi Elchanan Adler, Rosh Yeshiva, RIETS, Yeshiva University

This book will be an important tool in the development of the deeply intelligent, growth-oriented student throughout his time in yeshiva or seminary, and beyond. Rabbi Shmalo's novel ideas are rooted in ancient sources, peppered with practical applications and real-life anecdotes which enable true integration of his conceptual gems. Sharing from his heart, mind, and personal experience, Rabbi Shmalo forms with his reader the warm student-teacher relationship necessary for the transmission of life-developing wisdom.

— Rabbi Yehoshua Styne, Machon Shlomo, Educational Director, Meor Israel

Rabbi Shmalo helped my wife and I make the commitment, navigate the challenges, and reap the inestimable rewards of learning for a year in Israel. It was the best decision that we ever made and one that would not have been made without his encouragement.... Rabbi Shmalo once shared a parable about a man who traveled through Europe by train. Content with the narrow view from his cabin window, he never bothered to disembark and explore. It is debatable whether or not this man ever really traveled.

Reading this book will help you immerse yourself in the spiritual landmarks of our heritage and experience your time in Israel to the fullest. As such, it is essential reading for anyone preparing to embark on such a journey.

Alexander Perlman is from New York City. He received a BA in Philosophy at Binghamton University. He currently works as a Media Manager for Univision.

Leah Enowitz is from San Diego. She received a BFA in Interior Design at Pratt Institute. She currently works as an Associate Designer for Tiffany and Company.

Table of Contents

Foreword

by Rabbi Beryl Gershenfeld
Rosh Yeshiva, Machon Shlomo, Machon Yaakov

Humans yearn to create. They yearn to grow. Healthy people are not satisfied with merely existing, but yearn to develop, actualize, and express their own unique potential in a creative manner.

What awakens this desire? Why is this a unique expression of being human? Rabbenu Yonah (*Shaarei Avodah* 16) links this desire to grow to the most essential root of our humanity—the reality that we are all made in the image of God. Man wants to express himself as God expressed Himself: "Just as God is a Creator of worlds; similarly man should be a creator of worlds."

During the last thirty years a new norm has developed which expresses this yearning. Every year thousands of Jewish students travel to Israel to live and study Torah in a new iteration of mankind's essential desire to grow. In Western society during the 18th and 19th centuries, wise students classically responded to this desire by embarking on a grand tour of Europe. Today, Jewish young adults and adolescents sense that in our diaspora, where institutions too often fail to nourish the roots of our shared humanity, every individual must be proactive in crafting a life of meaning, morality, and greatness. They understand that "If they are not for themselves," their culture will not be for them. Their society will not help them grow.

These yearnings are deep and foundational. They are not just expressions of youthful, footloose fancy to travel. The echo is clear as one generation of students tells the next that "My year in Israel was the best year of my life! You too should spend a year growing in Jerusalem." What began as a pilgrimage of a few unique individuals has become a well-traveled path of thousands of young Jewish souls.

Anyone who has begun an exercise plan, started a diet, or tried to learn a new sport has quickly realized, "All beginnings are difficult" (Exodus 19, Rashi). Surprisingly, to grow in any meaningful way is not natural. Man—surrounded by a world that grows, flourishes, and blossoms "naturally"—finds it confusing and awkward that his own growth is not "natural"; it requires considerable wisdom and exertion. The anomaly is expressed in the Biblical creation narrative. In Genesis, all of nature is created by God's word without introduction or dialogue. However, man's creation is preceded by God making a decision and verbalizing His intention: "Let us make man in Our image..." (*Bereshis* 1:26). Only after this preamble does God then create man. Similarly man's growth is not natural. For man to grow, he must first gather wisdom and make a decision. For individuals to develop and become mature expressions of their deepest roots, they need to "learn to grow"; they need to find wisdom, and they need to find a mentor.

My wife's grandfather, Rav Shimon Schwab, once described the difficulty of his first day in the Mir Yeshiva in Europe and the life-lessons that his *rebbe* taught him. Rav Schwab, then a young *bachur*, entered the famed *beis midrash* of Mir with great excitement. As he settled himself before his *shtender*, he couldn't get comfortable. He was used to learning in different yeshivas where learning occurred at desks and where emphasis was placed on studying many sources enabling one to understand the *gemara* from a variety of perspectives. But in the Mir, there simply wasn't room for all of his *sefarim* on the small *shtender*. He organized them this way and that way; he left some *sefarim* on his lap and a few dangling dangerously off the side of his *shtender*, but he was uncomfortable... he couldn't even begin to learn. He couldn't get comfortable and he felt ill at ease even before opening the Talmud. Just as he was considering these difficulties, the great spiritual leader of the Mir Yeshiva, Rav Yeruchem, appeared in front of him. Rav Schwab jumped to his feet, grabbing the *sefarim* on his lap and holding the dangling *sefarim* on his *shtender* so they wouldn't fall. He remembered feeling awkward and embarrassed. Rav Yeruchem looked at him for what seemed like an eternity. He wanted Rav Schwab to internalize the absurdity of his present posture.

Rav Yeruchem then explained, "At the Mir we focus on learning the *gemara*, Rashi and Tosfos; not on studying the other *sefarim* [*acharonim*] that you have brought to the *beis midrash*. Put the other *sefarim* away and now you will be able to begin studying."

A great mentor had enabled Rav Schwab to confront the difficulties of growth, to understand the awkwardness he was feeling, and to explain a new path of growth. This is the crucial role of mentors in all generations—they know the impediments along the new path, they can empathize with the student's awkwardness and help them understand the sources for their discomfort, and finally they can illuminate paths for growth.

Rabbi Shmalo's mission in his book *Learning to Grow* is to provide this vision and assistance for students seeking to grow and make their year in Jerusalem the best year of their lives!

Rabbi Shmalo is a great mentor for this mission because he has lived his "year of growth" for several decades. As one reads this book of a great mentor, one senses he is still also a student whose greatest desire is to continue understanding and integrating the depths and breadths of God's beautiful world. Rabbi Shmalo has learned in the most classic *batei midrashim* of Jerusalem and studied in the academic world of Hebrew

University. He has grappled with texts of all hues and colors—Talmud, *Shulchan Aruch*, classical philosophy, *musar*, Chasidus, and Kabbalah. He is a great and dynamic teacher who has shared his Torah with Jews of all backgrounds, whether Charedi or Modern Orthodox; whether religious or secular; whether young or old. If one is searching for a mentor who is a man for all seasons and a man for all Jews Rabbi Shmalo is such a person.

But, as with all growth, after being informed by the head, one needs inspiration from the heart. Rabbi Shmalo's abilities to find diamonds of exciting, enriching growth even in dustbowls of boredom is exhilarating. Rabbi Shmalo's advice from Kelm turns the necessary evil of a ten-hour airplane flight to Israel into a journey of growth and connection. Since reading Rabbi Shmalo's book, whenever I board a plane I hear his advice chirping in my ear and penetrating my heart. The physical journey is accompanied by an ethical one.

The desire to grow is our deepest human urge. But growing is difficult and it needs to be learned; for that we need wisdom and a wise, sensitive mentor. Rabbi Shmalo's book provides us with such a mentor's head, heart, and hand. "Beginnings are difficult," but as Chazal state, "ends are soft... and sweet" *(Zohar Tetzaveh* 187).

Shouldn't we begin?

Beryl Gershenfeld
August 2016

Acknowledgements

I arrived in Israel in 1988, and it was then, at Machon Shlomo, that I discovered the kinds of ideas at have ultimately found expression in this book. As I moved from yeshiva to yeshiva, and from one side of the desk to the other, I continued to collect thoughts and impressions, and to develop those impressions into classes, articles and chapters. I write these words of acknowledgment in 2016, almost thirty years after having entered yeshiva, and a full twenty years after I started teaching Torah at Michlalah and Ohr Yerushalyim. In short, I've been working on this book, knowingly or not, for almost my entire adult life. Naturally, I've accumulated a great deal of "acknowledgment debt," which can't be repaid in these few pages.

Of course, I owe my greatest debt to my parents. From the youngest of ages, they taught me in love and by example, the central importance of my Jewish identity, a pride in my heritage, and a profound connection to Israel. As I explored and developed these aspects my identity, in ways sometimes similar and sometimes different from theirs, they continually supported and encouraged me, generously providing me opportunities to continue to learn, grow, and ultimately teach. Mom and Dad, thank you for empowering me. May you be blessed, and may your children and grandchildren always be a source of pride.

I cannot overstate the influence of Rabbi Beryl Gershenfeld's teachings on this book. His students will recognize several broad themes and many particular insights that have made Rabbi Gershenfeld one of the master teachers of his generation. Rabbi Gershenfeld's late father-in-law, Rabbi Yaakov Rosenberg, *zt"l*, founded Machon Shlomo together with Rabbi Gershenfeld in the mid-eighties, and Rabbi Gershenfeld continues the mission of quietly producing some of the most refined, well-balanced, and responsible *b'nei Torah* in the yeshiva world. In many ways, this book is a very modest tribute to them and the work for which they stand, a modest effort to share some of their educational approach with the broader yeshiva world.

The influence of Rabbi Meir Triebitz on this book is less explicit but no less profound. Whatever skills I might have as a creative thinker, as a lover of Torah, and as a pursuer of truth have been nourished, shaped, and refined by Rabbi Triebitz. Indeed, he personifies these qualities, and to whatever degree they have found expression in this book, I and my readers are deeply indebted to him, his instruction and his friendship.

My earliest teacher of Torah, Morah Kaylee Frager, has been a lifelong friend since I was in her second-grade class at the Westchester Day School. Rabbi Chaim Goldwicht, *zt"l*, the legendary Rosh Yeshiva of Kerem B'Yavneh expanded my mind in *midrash*, *middot*, and *de'ot*. Rabbi Zvi Kushelevsky inspired me with his love of learning and dedication to his life-mission as a teacher. I am unqualified to comment on his obvious mastery of Talmud; I am qualified to write that I was and remain awestruck by his lessons. Rabbi Yaakov Warhoftig helped me develop my anchor in *halachah* while he presided over (and continues to guide) perhaps the most diverse group of rising *talmidei chachamim* in Jerusalem at Beit Ariel. In person, in print, and on tape, Rabbis Shlomo Wolbe, *zt"l*, and (YBH"LH) Moshe Shapira illuminated my mind and nourished my soul. The unique Torah of each of these model teachers has found expression in my own teaching and in this modest book.

Rabbi Chaim Pollack of Michlalah Jerusalem College, and Rabbis Moshe Chaim Sosevsky and Shmuel Wagner of Yeshivat Ohr Yerushalyim

Acknowledgements

trusted me with their students, providing me with the laboratories in which I was able to develop my thoughts deliberately and rigorously for a full decade. I thank them and all my students for allowing me to participate in their "year in Israel" again and again, and to play some role in this most magical time of their lives. I thank Rabbi Ephraim Karnarfogel and Dean Karen Bacon of Yeshiva University's Stern College for Women, for giving me a second decade to continue teaching (and learning from) the idealistic women of Stern, many of whom return from their year in Israel inspired and apprehensive as they try to keep that magic alive in our more prosaic twenty-first-century America.

As young students, I often discussed the ideas in these chapters with my dear friend and *baal musar*, Daniel Michaels, and with Rabbis Dovid Schoonmaker, Eli Pielet, Ephraim Epstein, and Mattis Rosenbloom. I have grown personally through our friendships which I continue to cherish. Now of Yeshivat Yishrei Lev, Rabbi Pielet was a regular sounding-board and early advocate for this project. He generously and carefully read through the entire manuscript and his many comments have improved this book significantly. Alec Goldstein of Kodesh Press had faith in this work when I was ready to surrender and added the polish that only an experienced editor can. Many thanks. Of course, only I can take responsibility for the final product.

I have spent the past thirty years in one idealistic learning community after another. The endless flow of creative Torah ideas shared by teachers, community rabbis, colleagues, friends and neighbors has shaped my worldview and—in one way or another—this book. My thanks to Rabbis Reuven Leuchter, Avraham Edelstein, Yitzchak Berkovitz, Pinchas Auerbach, Moshe Stav, Mendel Blachman, Dovid Peleg, Menachem Deutch, Moshe Dov Harris, Jeremy Kagen, Yirmiahu Cowan, Zev Rudman, Menachem Nissel, Meir Tamari, Elchanan Adler, Meir Goldwicht, Yosef Edelstein, Yehuda Sarna, Yehoshua Styne and Aharon Cohen. Thanks to Rabbis Dovid Refson, Moshe and Rachel Chalkowski, and Dovid and Zahava Kass of Neve Yerushalayim. Special thanks to my partner of ten years in Meor NYU, Aharon Dovid Eisemann – the inimitable and indefatigable Rabbi E – my personal Rebbe in Ahavas Yisroel, and to Yaakov Steinberg of Meor for making the impossible happen.

Any work of this sort requires *siyata d'shmayia* on many levels. My relationship with the Almighty is too personal for me to condense it into an "acknowledgment"; I can, however, acknowledge the vessel that has contained the greatest of divine blessings, and that is my family. After all, the Sages teach that the divine presence only settles on families, and if I have felt the hand of God lead me in life, I can only attribute that to my family that is, or that would one-day-be. To my sons and daughter, Yitzchak, Menachem, Elazar, Yonah, Akiva, Elisha, and Avigail: thank you for being such active participants in our Shabbos table discussions, for enjoying hiking, for keeping me honest, for embracing our shared mission of idealism and personal growth, for caring for each other, and for being so much fun. Special thanks to Yitzchak, Menachem, and Yonah for reading and commenting on parts of this book, to Elazar for stimulating discussion that provoked my thoughts and improved my teaching, to Akiva who has embraced the project of personal growth which is at the heart of this book, and *mazel tov* to Elisha and Avigail on this year of their bar and bat mitzvah.

Lastly, most importantly, to the one who brings the *shechina* into my home and life every day, to my dear wife Mahnaz. Ultimately this work, *Learning to Grow*, has been a self-help book for the author: as much auto-biographical as educational. A great deal of my own journey towards Torah was a search for you, and much of my growth in Torah has been to remain worthy of you. This book has ended, but may the Almighty guide us, as you and I continue to write chapters in our own growth together.

Gamliel Shmalo

August 2016

Preface

My "year in Israel" began in the fall of 1988. I had graduated college that spring and, having become excited by the power of Torah to effect change, both personally and globally, I set out to learn and grow, as much as possible, as fast as possible. I had not grown up observant, so my Hebrew literacy was poor, and I knew that I had a lot of tough ground to cover. But I had learned how to analyze dense texts, having done well in philosophy and sociology at the University of Pennsylvania. Indeed, it was at Penn that one of my professors, the brilliant Philip Rieff, encouraged me to take Judaism seriously, considering his own field of sociology to be moribund. He also considered the Western world in desperate need of a moral and ethical recalibration. I looked at my own life and felt much the same.

The plan was to spend a year in Israel and then to return to the US, possibly to study towards some rabbinic degree at Yeshiva University, where I now teach. But I fell in love with Israel in general, and the Torah of Israel in particular. One year at Machon Shlomo in Jerusalem's Har Nof neighborhood studying under Rabbis Beryl Gershenfeld and Meir Triebitz was not enough. So one year turned into a second year. Then, wanting to deepen my connection to Israeli society and the Hebrew language, I spent a third year at Yeshivat Kerem B'Yavneh where I was exposed to one of the greatest masters of Midrash of his generation, Rabbi Chaim Goldwicht.

Learning to Grow

The Gulf War struck in January 1991. This was a strange war, because the Israeli army had to sit on its hands while the United States worked to disarm the Iraqi Scud missiles that were slamming into Tel Aviv. Together with friends who were both serious young Torah scholars and also soldiers in the Israeli army, I felt like the *yeshivot* were the spiritual front lines, pumping morale into the country and spiritual energy into the world. It was a time of national unity, and some would argue it was a time of open miracles. In any case, that year helped seal my identity as an observant Jew and my commitment to a life in Israel.

I felt privileged to have studied under master teachers, and I expressed my admiration by aspiring to some of their wisdom myself—to understand Torah deeply and to teach it to others. I felt drawn to the purity and intensity of the great Jerusalem *yeshivot*, and was honored to sit in the *beit midrash* and hear the lectures of Rabbi Zvi Kushelevsky for two years, seeing up close what that level of learning is all about. Halfway through my five year rabbinic program at Bayit VeGan's Beit Ariel, I started teaching at Jerusalem's Michlalah College for Women and then, in parallel, at Yeshivat Ohr Yerushalyim in Moshav Beit Meir.

For ten years I taught several classes each day at Michlalah and Ohr Yerushalyim to idealistic students who were first experiencing adulthood, away from home, confronted with inspiring Torah and a sense of responsibility for the future trajectory of their own lives. Like you, most of these students were trying to get the most out of their "year in Israel." To help guide them, I drew on the lessons I had learned from some of the greatest educators on the planet.

My own year in Israel finally ended eighteen years after it began, when I returned to the United States with my Iranian-born wife and my Israeli-born children. I returned to a new professional challenge, serving as the Director of Education for Meor at New York University, and teaching Jewish philosophy at Yeshiva University's Stern College for Women. My students are similar to those in Israel, insofar as they are eighteen- to twenty-one-year-old men and women, but they are from very different backgrounds and study in a very different settings, and I could not be more excited.

In other words, I can't seem to get away from the intensely dynamic years of discovery that you are now entering. Whether I sit on one side of the desk as a student, or the other side of the desk as a teacher, there is no doubt in my mind that your age and your stage of life are pregnant with huge potential, possibility, and responsibility. These are blessings that must not be squandered; this is a year that will affect the trajectory of your entire life.

All too often, students bumble through their year in yeshiva or seminary with little direction, certainly picking up useful skills and inspiring ideas along the way, but with little context with which to approach the year actively and deliberately. There is an easy solution for that. Because every year has a similar rhythm, and although each student is certainly an individual, I have found that every student can benefit by being aware of the common themes and opportunities that emerge as Elul passes into Tishrei and Tishrei gives way to Marcheshvan and the long winter begins.

The themes that I will bring to your attention stem from the tradition of the *musar* movement founded by Rabbi Yisrael Salanter, as developed by teachers like Rabbis Eliyahu Dessler and Shlomo Wolbe. My teacher Rabbi Beryl Gershenfeld taught me a great deal of this book's contents, and even what he did not teach me explicitly is informed by the spirit of his wisdom. Just so that you understand where I'm coming from: Rabbi Gershenfeld learned from, among others, Rabbi Shlomo Wolbe and Rabbi Moshe Shapira. Rabbi Wolbe was a student of Rabbi Yeruchom Levovitz, the disciple of the Alter of Slabodka and the *mashgiach* of Mir; Rabbi Shapira grew up in the house of Rabbi Eliyahu Dessler, who himself learned in Kelm. Ultimately, this work is informed, if only indirectly, by Slabodka and its vision of *gadlut ha-adam*—the essential, hidden greatness of the human image, and by the focus and emotional sensitivity of Kelm. This modest work, therefore, has very immodest ambitions: it is your guide to greatness during your year in yeshiva or seminary and beyond.

In developing my approach to teaching, and in developing the chapters that follow, I have been influenced, to the edge of plagiarism, by works like Rabbi Dessler's *Michtav me-Eliyahu* and Rabbi Wolbe's *Alei Shur*. The latter, tellingly, is subtitled "an attempt to guide a son of our generation as he enters into the world of Torah, and through the stages of his ascent." *Alei Shur* is a masterwork from which I have grown personally and from which I have drawn. It is also in Hebrew and was first published in 1963. So while I urge you to read it—to learn it!—I also recognize that in both language and idiom, it and similar works may be somewhat inaccessible to you.

So I humbly offer to you, son or daughter of a new generation, the chapters that follow. Some of it is indeed old wine in new vessels, and some of it is the product of my own reflections as I thought about what was helpful to me as I was challenged, and struggled, and ultimately thrived and flourished during my protracted "year in yeshiva." I have taught these ideas for almost twenty years, to both young men and young women, to students with a significant background in Jewish learning, and to students who only recently discovered that they are Jewish. The most important factor they had in common was a self-confident willingness to explore their own strengths and their own weaknesses in order to change and grow.

One of the things I wish I had when I first got to yeshiva was some introduction to the more important personalities my teachers kept quoting. Like some of my students, I also made the mistake of referring to the Vilna Gaon as "Rabbi Gaon" (if you don't get it, you will certainly appreciate this book). It took too long for me to get oriented and understand the dates, traditions and relative importance of the various sages who were being cited. So as I introduce new ideas, I will also introduce the rabbi who said it and give a short biographical blurb about him (and sometimes a picture).

I also want you to view this book as not just a user-friendly guide to personal growth, but also as a window into texts that will continue to enrich your understanding of Judaism for the rest of your life. To that end, I will not only translate reasonable chunks of seminal texts, I will also quote the original in offset boxes. As you become more comfortable with the language, please take advantage of the original texts, notice how my translations are—like any translation—something of an interpretation, and try to uncover a richness in meaning beyond what I can bring in English.

Lastly, please discuss these chapters with your teachers. For Torah to be translated into true personal growth it must be personalized, and your teachers and rabbis can help you do that in a way no book can. One of the reasons that oral law was forbidden to be written, by design, is that the oral method of instruction forced the student to have a living relationship with a mentor. So while I don't know whether this book will be the "first word" on any subject, I certainly hope it will not be the last. Your teachers may disagree with the usefulness of some of these ideas for you; they may disagree with my interpretations entirely. That is as it should be. In Torah there are few easy answers and even fewer easy applications. The world is complex and life is a process of discovering truths about yourself and that world that are not always intuitive. It is through that process, hand-in-hand with our prophetic tradition, that you can find greatness and fulfillment.

Welcome to Israel!

Chapter 1

The Flight

נושא בעול עם חברו (פרקי אבות ו, ו)

Flights to Israel, especially on El Al, are a unique ethnic experience. Don't expect the trip to be stuffy, cold, and anonymous. This is not British Air to London. In fact, the cabin might seem more like a family reunion. Unless some computer error seated you in the business section, bring food. To share. Don't be surprised if some neighboring passenger asks you to pass a tray of smoked fish to a relative in a different aisle. And if you taste a bit as it goes by, most likely your distant cousins will feel only flattered.

On the other hand, they might very well be shocked and offended.

Family reunions are like that.

You will notice the children, especially the babies. When I was young and single I found the kids unbelievably annoying. There is always a good possibility of being stuck for eleven hours at 30,000 feet next to an infant with an ear ache. Infants are not known for courtesy, and any one of the many babies on board will not hesitate to keep an entire 747 awake because of a tickle in the back of his throat. How, I wondered in my innocent youth, could anyone so inconsiderately impose his brats on an entire transcontinental flight?

The Flight

Then I became a father and realized that this is what real life is all about. People have children and some of our best people have many children. And they travel, often by air. The kids act like kids and the babies act like babies, and the parents do their best, which is not always enough. No one (seriously) expects children to be checked like luggage. The first time I flew with my own children, they were one-year-old twin boys, and my eyes begged for mercy from every intolerant countenance. My years of being annoyed had come full circle: now I was the reluctant villain.

Your job on the flight is to be nice to the kids and not to act like one. For many of you, this will be your first time away from home. That's why so many parents cry at the airport. A continent away from Mom and Dad, you will be experiencing the greatest independence that you have yet known. But independence in Jewish terms does not just imply freedom from externally imposed demands; it implies an adult responsibility to care for others. One of the reasons why religious parties in Israel opposed an Israeli "Bill of Rights" is because rights don't bring people together.

Rights make certain that I don't violate your space and that you do not violate mine. Rights demand that my kid not scream in your face high above the Atlantic. Jewish morality, on the other hand, is built upon a system of *obligations*. I don't steal your mobile phone or your house or your sleep because I am obligated not to. But I am also obligated to act towards you in a positive way. I have an obligation to save your life and protect your property and to treat you with respect and dignity. These are positive, community-building actions and attitudes that cannot be imposed through a system of rights.

The parents of the cranky child have an obligation to try and calm him. And believe me, they want to. But you also have an obligation to act with more than just tolerance. Your job is to "share the burden with your friend," as formulated by the Rabbis in *Pirkei Avot*. This, they teach, is one of the forty-eight virtues through which Torah is acquired; and given that you are on your way to Israel to acquire Torah, you might as well begin carrying the burden now. To tell you the truth, I can think of few places where you can do this better than in air travel.

Let's look at this objectively. You are young, strong, relatively well-fed, and rested. You have a couple of heavy bags, but not more than you can manage. And when you put them on the floor, they tend to stay put. The hypothetical young couple next to you at check-in is moving to Israel with their infant, a two-year-old and a four-year-old. This means that they may have maybe fifteen bags. Their baby is up half the night, every night, and the two-year-old may still be in diapers (you will find out quickly if seated next to them on the flight) and is constantly on the move. This means that they are sleep-deprived and have trouble dealing with all their stuff.

Help them. Carry a bag; read to the four-year-old. The alternatives are tuning out to some music on your headphones and staring blankly into space. I honestly suggest scanning the crowd to see if someone needs some help getting a piece of carry-on luggage or stroller onto the plane. The young and healthy often don't realize how many others would appreciate an extra hand. I didn't until I started traveling with my own brood, and then it was pretty much too late for me to be of use to anyone. As a young father I once had to fly to the United States and back by myself. It was Swissair via Zurich to Cincinnati, so the flight was not quite as ethnic as it could have been, but still I was able to help one very pregnant woman with a carry-on, and that felt good.

The same thing goes for baggage claim. For many economic, social, and political reasons that are way beyond the scope of this book, people tend to bring more stuff to Israel than to any other destination on the planet. The result is that baggage claim at Ben Gurion Airport can be utter pandemonium. After a long flight, people can't wait to rush through customs, and I've seen passengers nearly trampled as others pushed through the crowd to haul their bags off the conveyor belt.

Again, your job is to be part of the solution, not part of the problem. Help the elderly retrieve their luggage. Don't push. Ever. (Yes, even if it means letting your bag take yet another lap around the carousel.)

On the flight itself there isn't so much carrying that needs to be done. You can be helpful by just being nice to the parents of the kid sitting behind you as he keeps kicking the back of your chair. Of course, you can point out to them that the kicking is going on, but nicely, and with the understanding that it may well be completely out of their control. "Peek-a-boo" is a game almost every two-year-old enjoys; use it to entertain and to be entertained.

At 30,000 feet, perhaps the biggest challenge is simply not to offend others. There was a case a couple of years ago when a whole group of students on their way to the same yeshiva found themselves together on a particular flight. I once read that a single locust is like a nice sweet grasshopper when alone; only in a group do locusts change—physiologically—and become a destructive swarm. Apparently these yeshiva guys were part locust. Fine young men when apart, but in a group, particularly under the influence of alcohol, they became the least violent of international terrorists. When the stewardesses finally refused to supply them with booze, they simply took out their own and the party got even rowdier. These boys didn't actually ditch the plane in the sea or hijack the flight to Entebbe, but they did make the Israeli news that night. They abused the passengers and vomited everywhere and got themselves into a legal mess.

I modestly suggest that you avoid this kind of behavior.

Although this example is extreme, others are much more common. For example, prayer. Once, after I had been in yeshiva for several years, a professor of mine came to lecture at the Hebrew University in Jerusalem. He was an older, very dignified scholar, Jewish, very respectful of the tradition and those who guard it, but not religious himself. We spent a great amount of time together that summer and at one point he described his disappointment with the behavior of some religious people he had encountered. He told me about his flight to Israel. Being old and infirm, he was given a seat on the aisle, right near one of the plane's exits where there was plenty of leg room. As the plane flew east and the sun began to rise over the horizon, a group of men congregated and began to pray next to the exit, right in front of his seat. I remember clearly the way he described, calmly and analytically, in detached and exquisite detail, how one man would bow low, bending at the knees and the waist, imposing his rump only inches away from the good professor's nose.

Rabbi Moshe Isserles (the "Rema," 1520–1572) wrote *Ha-Mappah* (lit., "the tablecloth"), an inline commentary on the *Shulchan Aruch* (lit., "the set table"), which became the basis for Ashkenazi *halachah*. He was born and lived in Krakow, Poland, where his synagogue still stands.

"Remuh Synagogue, 40 Szeroka street, Kazimierz, Krakow, Poland" by Zygmunt Put.

This too should be avoided. The passengers on the plane have paid for the right to enjoy their seats unmolested by the overly pious. Use your judgment when joining a *minyan* on a flight. If it might come at the expense of another passenger, pray in your seat. I have recited the *Shemoneh Esrei* (which is almost always said standing) sitting in my seat so that I wouldn't have to wake the passenger sitting next to me. On the other hand, you should never be reluctant to pray or put on *tefillin* just because you might be embarrassed to engage in practices that might appear "odd" to others. In his glosses to the very first law in the *Shulchan Aruch*, Rabbi Moshe Isserles (the Rema) writes that we must often be brazen in our observance of *halachah*. So although we must avoid bothering others in our observance or anything else, we should never be ashamed to do our own thing.

A friend's father told me that he once flew from Fiji to Papua New Guinea on business. As the time came for the morning prayers he stood and he went to the back of the plane to put on his *tefillin*. The stewardess saw him slowly tying the unfamiliar black boxes to his head and arm. Immediately afterwards he began to sway while speaking softly, yet audibly, in a strange language. Looking concerned she hurried to the cockpit only to return a few moments later with a message from the captain: the Jewish businessman would have to stop transmitting immediately. The signals might garble the plane's navigational equipment.

I don't think you have to worry about this sort of reaction on El Al. But, unfortunately, the justified displeasure of my former professor is all too common.

A Deeper Look at "Carrying the Load"

I assume that you are not coming to Israel just for the great nightlife; if you grew up near any large North American city, you are better off just staying put. Find one of the many émigrés from Israel in your community and ask them, since that may be one of the reasons that they moved to the U.S.

I also assume that you are not coming to Israel just for the academic excellence that our yeshivas and seminaries offer. Not because we are not academically excellent; we are, but that is only one piece of the puzzle. I hope that your real motivation for coming is to take advantage of the special insight that Jewish tradition teaches on becoming a better person.

Learning to Grow

A couple of hundred years ago many Jews learned Torah for the intellectual thrill of it. The result was people with big heads and little hearts, people for whom the religion was more an intellectual exercise than a system that makes humanity more divine. Normative Judaism responded in several ways to this deviation in spiritual focus. One reaction was the Chasidic movement, which emphasized an ecstatic and individualistic relationship to spirituality. Another reaction was Rabbi Yisrael Salanter's Musar movement, which emphasized the development of ethical greatness in people. Much of what I intend to express in this book is drawn from this latter tradition.

> **Rabbi Yisroel Lipkin** (1810–1883, called "Rav Yisroel Salanter" since he learned under Rabbi Yosef Zundel of Salant) was the father of the Musar movement and a famed rosh yeshiva. He brought deep psychological insight to his teachings, alluding to the subconscious decades before Freud, and emphasizing the need to understand our own biases and motivations. His students included Rabbi Eliezer Gordon, (the Rosh Yeshiva of Telz), Rabbi Simcha Zissel Ziv Broida (the Alter of Kelm), and Rabbi Yitzchak Blazer (a leader of the Slabodka Yeshiva).

The Musar movement draws attention to man's unique position as the center of creation. The entire universe was created to challenge us and help us come closer to God by coming closer to ethical perfection. If so, Rabbi Yisrael taught, certainly man's perfecting himself should be one of our main focuses of study. Just as we study the Torah and we study the world, just as we study Talmud and law and Tanach, so too should we study ourselves.

Know Yourself, By Yourself

The Talmud in the Tractate *Shabbat* (63b) quotes the following verse: "Rejoice, young man, during your childhood, and let your heart be pleasant during the days of young manhood. And follow the ways of your heart and the sight of your eyes. Yet know that God will bring you to judgment for all these things" (*Kohelet* 11:9).

The verse is as difficult to understand as it is poetic. The Talmud cites the explanation of Reish Lakish, who certainly had an interesting "young manhood" as a pirate. He believed that King Shlomo, the author of

תלמוד בבלי מסכת שבת דף סג/ב

אמר רב הונא מאי דכתיב (קהלת יא ט) שְׂמַח בָּחוּר בְּיַלְדוּתֶיךָ וִיטִיבְךָ לִבְּךָ בִּימֵי בְחוּרוֹתֶךָ וְהַלֵּךְ בְּדַרְכֵי לִבְּךָ וּבְמַרְאֵי עֵינֶיךָ וְדַע כִּי עַל כָּל אֵלֶּה יְבִיאֲךָ הָאֱ-לֹהִים בַּמִּשְׁפָּט? ... רֵישׁ לָקִישׁ אמר עד כאן לדברי תורה מכאן ואילך למעשים טובים

פירוש רש"י

עד כאן לתורה - שמח בתלמודך, למוד משמחה ומטוב לב, והלך בדרכי לבך להבין מה בלבך לפי ראות עיניך:

מכאן ואילך למעשים טובים - ודע כי על כל אלה על כל מה שלמדת סוף ליתן את הדין אם לא תקיים:

Kohelet, is encouraging us to spend our unencumbered youth in the joys of Torah study. Then, as he grows older and must turn to the practicalities of life, he should express his earlier study by doing good works. "Up to here —Torah; from here on—good works!" We see from this passage that Torah study will best develop into ethical excellence—good works—if it engages the heart joyfully. Therefore, it is important that you find sweetness in your learning.

Reish Lakish's reading of the verse seems to bother Rashi. True, the first part of the verse may be a call to learn Torah with a happy heart, but what is the meaning of "and follow the ways of your heart and the sight of your eyes"? Rashi interprets this to mean, "Understand what is in your heart, according to what your eyes see." Reish Lakish says only that you should learn Torah, yet Rashi is forced by the verse to understand that there are two parts to learning Torah: the objective Torah that is external to you, and the subjective way that you relate to and internalize that Torah. After all, if our goal is more refined behavior, we have to not just learn the Torah intellectually; we need to internalize it emotionally. And we can't do that unless we know ourselves.

And ultimately, we can only know ourselves by ourselves. "Understand what is in your heart, according to what your eyes see." Your parents, teachers, and friends can all act as a mirror for you to learn about yourself, but at the end of the day, it's all up to you. What's amazing is that this study—the study of the self—is also called Torah.

> **דרשות המהר"ל - דרוש על המצות**
>
> שם תורה הונח על המצות שנתן הש"י על ידי משה. ולא נקראו בשם מצות, אף שהיה שם זה ראוי יותר באשר הם מצות מאתו ית'. מפני כי לשון מצוה שייך בציווי הבא ממי שלא יבקש שידע המצטוה ענין הציווי ומהותו רק כל תכליתו לשתהא ציוויי נעשית, והש"י רחקו מחשבותיו מזה בתתו המצות לישראל וחפץ שידעו ויבינו כל ענין המצוה, ולכך נקראו תורה לשון הוראה שמורה דברים השכליים שבהם והחכמה. ובאולי תאמר א"כ היה ראוי לקרותם חכמה שאין לך חכמה יותר מזה, והכתוב העיד (דברים ד) ראה למדתי אתכם חקים ומשפטים וגו' ושמרתם ועשיתם כי היא חכמתכם ובינתכם וגו'. אין הכוונה בתורה שנתן הש"י החכמה לבדה, רק שיא מורה לאדם המעשה אשר יעשה, מה שאין בזולת מהחכמות, שאין כוונת תכליתם על המעשה רק עצם החכמה בלבד, אבל התורה צריכה לשניהם להבין החכמה שבמצותי' ולעשותם על פי הידיעה ההיא.

This should not be surprising to anyone who understands why the Torah is called "Torah." The Maharal of Prague in various writings explains that our most holy book is not referred to as "the book of wisdom" because wisdom alone can be dry and theoretical; "Torah" comes from the word *horah*, which means practical instruction that we need to express in action. On the other hand, the Torah is not referred to as "the book of commandments," which would emphasize practical application—because God also wanted us to study His law and understand it; "The Book of Commandments" alone would deemphasize the intellectual component. The word "Torah" therefore comprises both the intellectual study and the practical application. Reish Lakish taught that we cannot hope to apply the study of God's commandments in a healthy and natural way unless we study ourselves as well.

The Alter of Kelm on "Sharing the Load"

This study of the self is rigorous and demanding, even if it seems foreign to the Western academic tradition. Much of Rabbi Yisrael Salanter's life was a mission to convince his contemporaries that this study is authentically Jewish and should be taken seriously. One of Rabbi Yisrael's closest students was Rabbi Simcha Zissel Ziv Broida (1824–1898), often referred to as the Alter of Kelm, after the great yeshiva he founded in the modest Lithuanian city of that name. What Rabbi Yisrael taught to his disciples, the Alter of Kelm built into the curriculum of an entire yeshiva. And one of the most important principles that the Alter repeatedly discussed with his students was this idea of "carrying the burden with your friend."

And rightly so. An attitude of helping one another is the cement that binds people together and creates the environment of healthy camaraderie—the glue of any good institution. This is the mind-set that allows marriages to flourish. It enables parents to guide children in a way that is not preachy or manipulative. It empowers teachers to become more than disinterested conduits of desiccated skills. It excites professors to truly "profess" ideas, and not just lecture dry facts. It creates a dynamic corporate culture in which workers are encouraged to innovate, even if this means risking occasional failure.

Most immediately, it enables students to come together as an ethical community to acquire Torah. This is an attitude that deserves attention. You should actually *work* on trying to cultivate it, to make it part of your character. And there is no better place to start than on the plane.

Learning to Grow

I also feel that it is such a basic attitude that it belongs in the front of this book. The collected lectures of the Alter of Kelm begin with this lesson. The second lecture as well. And the third and the fourth.

I want to share with you a couple of the Alter's insights about how to acquire this basic spirit of "carrying a burden with your friend." In short: what is going to motivate you to help the people on your flight to Israel (or in your yeshiva, or your seminary, or your family), enthusiastically and naturally, today, tomorrow, and forever?

The Alter writes that, like in most ethical work in which we try to acquire basic virtues, action is an important component. Kindness is habit-forming; beneficence is addictive. This will be explored at greater length in chapter 13, but for now please note that one of the best ways to become a great person is to consistently try to act like a great person. Good actions have a way of dripping into the heart to be assimilated into a well-developed personality, making the next action that much more subtle and natural. (A caveat: this works for immoral actions as well—corrupting one who would otherwise be morally admirable.) The trip to the airport can be viewed as a visit to an ethical gymnasium: it's a place to exercise greatness. Each crying baby, each couple with too much baggage, is another station; each work-out makes you stronger, and prepares you for yeshiva.

And you will need it there. As powerful as this attitude is in any social environment, you could still study other disciplines successfully without much concern for others and their burdens. You can be a social island, a pariah, and still learn to be a good lawyer or businessman—perhaps even a physician. But without a concern for others, you will never achieve a satisfying understanding of Torah. After all, the Torah was given to the Jewish people only when we became a nation, and even then, only when we were united in spirit, "as one man with one heart" (Rashi to *Shemot* 19:2).

The Flight

As great as the patriarchs were, the Torah was not revealed to them, since they were only individuals. Even Moshe, the humblest of men, the greatest of the prophets, only perceived what he did because he was acting on behalf of the nation. There he was on Mount Sinai for forty days and nights, without eating or sleeping, talking to God and learning the Torah from His own lips (whatever that means). Moshe had achieved an understanding that was superhuman, and God considered him worthy of dwelling in the community of the angels. But as soon as the nation committed the sin of the golden calf and was therefore no longer deserving, God commanded him, "Get down! I have only given you this greatness because of them" (Rashi to *Shemot* 32:7).

The Torah is universal. God created the Torah before He created the world. The Torah therefore transcends any individual perspective and any particular time. The only way to relate to the Torah is somehow to get outside of our own narrow visions of reality and to see other perspectives. You have to be able to hear what your teachers say and what your friends believe. You have to relate to the thousand-year-old opinions of Rashi and Rambam, the two-thousand-year-old opinions recounted in the Mishnah, the three-thousand-year-old messages of the prophets, and the four-thousand-year-old wanderings of the patriarchs. You have to transcend yourself by seeing others in their lives with their needs and burdens, and you have to care. Because if you can't connect to them, you can't connect to their Torah. And if you can only hear your individual "Torah," you can't get any of it.

This connection between the Nation of Israel and the Torah of Israel is something that I hope you are able to experience this year, particularly in the Land of Israel. When you arrive in Israel you will find a thriving society with tremendous achievements and tremendous potential. There are daunting problems as well. The Arab-Israeli conflict is just one "burden" that you can help your brothers and sisters carry. Israel society is also struggling under social burdens no less troubling. Unemployment, spouse and child abuse, drug and alcohol abuse, and senseless death in traffic accidents are some of the more unfortunate parts of modern Israel. How can you help? For one, I am confident that your Torah study will help attach our people to its sources of blessing. The light of the Torah not only illuminates those who study it directly; it shines on and brings redemption to the Jewish people in general, and through us, the world. The more you realize that the Torah has this power, and the more you care to bring its healing forces into a very infirm world, the more powerful your study becomes.

If you are reading this chapter in the month of Elul, and I hope you are, then you should already have sensed how much this attitude of concern and willingness to "carry the burden" with those around you can help prepare for Rosh Hashanah, the Day of Judgment. Many of Rosh Hashanah's most central prayers focus on the ideal of a world-perfecting revelation of God's kingdom.

As we pray for redemption, we should reflect on the Exodus, the template for all future redemptions. In many ways, the Exodus began when young Moshe, the prince of Egypt, came down out of his palace to share in the suffering of his brothers. In the second chapter of *Shemot*, Rashi comments that Moshe "placed his eyes and heart to feel their pain." In doing so, Moshe risked, and ultimately lost, the wealth and power of the Egyptian throne; but his concern for others compelled him to act. At the end of that same chapter, the verse says, "And God saw the children of Israel and God knew." Rashi again comments, "'And God knew': He placed His heart on them and did not divert His eyes." The parallel is obvious and the lesson is striking: when we help shoulder the burdens of others, God responds by shouldering the burdens of us all. And God has big shoulders.

Have a great flight. Use it well.

Chapter 2

Welcome to Yeshiva

The Month of Elul: What's in It for Me?

In both the United States and the State of Israel, a child must, by law, receive an elementary school education. Even if it were not a law, almost all parents would require their children to go to school. I suspect you weren't given the choice whether or not to go to elementary school or high school. Almost all of my students report that their parents insist that they go to college as well.

On the other hand, spending a year in an Israel yeshiva is generally perceived as optional. Neither the U.S. government, nor the government of Israel, obligates an intensive year of Torah study, and even parents who encourage their kids to go learn Torah for a year rarely insist on it. A kid who is driven to start college right after high school is usually—and rightly—allowed that choice. As a rabbi, I naturally feel that a year of Torah study is essential; but I also believe in free will, and I know that religious coercion is almost always counter-productive. So the options are left open, and the choice is yours.

This means that for you, this year's educational experience is totally voluntary, the product of your own initiative and decision. And it may well be the first completely voluntary educational experience of your life. Let's examine the choice that you made.

There are, after all, many reasons *not* to come to an Israeli yeshiva. Firstly, you are stalling, if only temporarily, your studies and career plans. Your Israeli dorm will not compare to the comforts of home. And the food is, well, institutional. So precisely in light of the downsides, I believe that the choice to study in yeshiva for a year is a clear example of an adult decision, asserted by a healthy, adult mind. Let me explain myself.

In my opinion, the three defining traits of adulthood are: the ability to make sacrifices of short-term comfort for long-term pleasure; the ability to choose a way of life based on independent rational thought; and the ability to accept responsibility for one's actions. We can see that these are unique adult attributes if we reflect for a moment on children, because everyone knows that kids have problems dealing with these three areas.

1. Children like short-term pleasure and quick fixes.

In my son's elementary school, the younger students are not motivated to learn because of the nobility of an informed life. Rather, they are motivated by the candies and praise that the teachers dole out to the kids who do the work and get the answers right. Only adults are interested in the long-term pleasures of an enlightened life. I remember visiting San Diego's SeaWorld on a family vacation. There, large fish (mammals, actually) do terrific stunts for a few handfuls of sardines and mackerels. Kids aren't so different.

2. Children make few reasoned decisions.

Little kids have passionate desires for trivial matters that can be emphasized with shouts and tears. Go reason with a five-year-old about the virtues of a colorful lollipop in the supermarket check-out line. As the child grows, rational discussion becomes more and more possible and is, in fact, an important part of a child's education. The parent's mode of argument should not only train a child to avoid lollipops; it should also train him to be, quite literally, reasonable. This is a daunting task, since this aspect of immaturity is seldom completely outgrown. Most of advertising plays upon the kid in each of us to motivate an impulse purchase based on anything but reason. Peer pressure, passion, and whim are the main engines that drive immature desire.

3. Children find it very difficult to accept blame and responsibility.

I was once visiting the home of a teacher of mine on Shabbat. Halfway through lunch, one of his young sons exited the bathroom in a fit of real anger. It seems that the family usually removed the roll of toilet paper before every Shabbat and replaced it with tissues that had already been cut, so that no one would have to tear toilet paper on Shabbat. This Shabbat they had forgotten to remove the roll and the child tore off a piece of toilet paper out of habit. Rather than accept blame himself, he accused his parents, "you made me get an *aveirah*." I just loved that (age appropriate) childish formulation, according to which: an *averiah* isn't an action, but rather it something that one passively "gets"; and he "got" one not as a result of his own action, but as a result of his parents' mistake.

In contrast, your decision to come study in Israel this year was a very adult decision for exhibiting the very opposite of these three child-like traits:

1. You've been willing to sacrifice the comforts of home in general and the United States of America in particular in order to participate in something quite idealistic, with mostly long-term reward. The study of ancient Aramaic and medieval Jewish philosophy rarely translates into instant pleasure, and this is certainly true for students (like I was) who need to expend a large percentage of their mental energy just to understand what the words mean. Nevertheless, like any good businessman, you have recognized that a big investment up-front is always necessary for a big return in the future. True, your Israeli mattress is the width of a dime, and the *cheder ochel* schnitzel is more breading than meat, but if that's the sacrifice you need to make to plug into the Jewish tradition in a serious way, you are willing to do it. Because you recognize that the long-term payoff will make you happier, your marriage stronger, your relationship with your children deeper, your community more noble.

2. Your decision was also reasoned, because much of contemporary society probably is giving you the message that you should "get on with life," defined as conventional secular education and the financial rewards that it brings. You, on the other hand are (at least in the eyes of many) "taking a year off." You may not even be able to get college credit for this experience. Over the course of the next few months you are going to get phone calls from friends and relatives asking if you are "having a good time over there," as if the most intense intellectual experience on the planet is like one big vacation. Unless they've lived through a yeshiva experience, they are not going to understand it. And unless they understand it, your friends, your family, and western society in general are just not going to be able to give you the respect your deserve. Nevertheless, you have thought it through and *decided* to come learn, not because of passion or whim, and often despite social pressure. This was a reasoned decision.

And it was a reasoned decision to acquire more reason. We might joke about a yeshiva experience being "brainwashing," but you should know that this has never been the Jewish way. We might challenge you to refine your beliefs and behaviors, but those challenges should only come through discourse and discussion. We encourage a free exchange of ideas. Don't let your teachers get away with anything (although certain second-order questions of faith may be best saved for after class). Teachers will challenge you respectfully, and they expect to be challenged right back, respectfully. Your decision to come here was an adult decision because at the beginning of your adult lives you have a lot of very important choices to make, and you may have sensed that you need to sharpen your Jewish intellect in order to make those decisions responsibly. Which brings me to the third point.

3. Responsibility: You have come here because you realize that your future is in your hands, and you need to develop the intellectual, moral and ethical skills in order to fulfill the awesome responsibilities of being a husband or wife, a father or mother, a human who can create or destroy your world and the world of those around you.

As a young adult, you need to come to terms with the fact that you are an autonomous independent agent of your own actions. You may feel that you "have to" get married someday. That you "have to" go to college. That you "have to" have children. The fact is that as autonomous adults, you don't have to do anything. You may want to, you may choose to. But unless you have a psychological imbalance, you will not act out of compulsion, but rather out of choice. That's what makes your decisions morally valuable, and that's why you can earn divine reward (or, God forbid, the opposite). From this point on your parents may tell you to do something, but as an adult you always have to option of saying "no." The very fact that you have the ability to say "no" means that *you* are responsible. "I was just following orders," or, "but daddy said," just doesn't wash in a world of adults. Chazal say: אין שליח לדבר עבירה, "there is no messenger when it comes to transgression." The messenger is held responsible, not the one who sent him.

Don't get me wrong, I'm not encouraging you to disobey your parents. I just want you to be aware that you are *choosing* to listen to your parents, and that makes *you* responsible for your actions. You should trust your parents, and you should almost always defer to them. But you should also think critically and act out of responsible choice, not habit or compulsion.

The greatness of truly great people is often most apparent when they are able to control their responses to situations in which smaller people would act reflexively. Here in Israel you will have plenty of opportunities to practice not losing your cool in situations where most people would blow their stack. Exercise your most basic human quality—your free will. Only in the most unusual and extreme cases does God take away someone's free will, and then the theologians comment endlessly to explain how such a thing can happen. For most of us, the claim that "I couldn't stop myself" is both theologically sloppy and ethically lazy. So just as you have acted like an adult by deciding to come to Israel this year, I encourage you to continue to make active choices. Don't accept anything I write or that your teachers say just because we say so. You have to *choose* to accept what we teach. Alternatively, don't allow the lessons that confront you to just evaporate; if you reject some particular lesson, at least make certain that this rejection is an active, informed choice.

Elul and Responsibility

It is appropriate that the yeshiva calendar year begins in the Hebrew month of Elul, because these three attributes of adulthood—sacrifice, reason, and responsibility—are the main lessons of Elul and the following month of Tishrei.

Elul is the season for taking responsibility for our own destiny and that of those around us. The forty days from Rosh Chodesh Elul to Yom Kippur commemorate the days that Moshe returned to Mount

Sinai to receive the second set of tablets. Recall that the first tablets were broken after the sin of the golden calf. At Sinai, the Jews had directly participated in God's revelation of the Ten Commandments, one of which was the prohibition of idolatry. Yet only forty days later, they made an idol, danced around it, and offered sacrifices to it. In the aftermath, God threatened to destroy the entire Jewish people and to start over again, creating a new nation out of Moshe and his descendants. The situation looked bleak, and the Rabbis teach that Moshe did the unthinkable: he began to despair.

The Torah in *Shemot* 32 describes Moshe's dialogue with God as follows:

> And Hashem said to Moshe, "I have seen this nation and behold it is a stiff-necked nation. And now, leave Me and I will show My anger among them and consume them, and I will make from you a great nation." And Moshe beseeched Hashem, his God, and said, "Hashem, why are You so angry with this people...."

On God's saying to Moshe, "leave Me," Rashi comments: "We have not yet heard that Moshe had prayed for them, still God said, 'leave Me!' Rather God opened a way and informed Moshe that the matter depends on him, that if he prays for them, God will not destroy them."

In this passage, we see God's great compassion, but we are also left wondering why Moshe did not pray for the people more spontaneously. Why did he have to wait for God's hint that it all depends on him? The Talmud in *Berachot* 32a deals with this issue. It explains that Moshe, during his forty days on Sinai, was on a level of prophetic sensitivity unprecedented in human history. Then with the sin of the golden calf, God abruptly said, "Go down!" This was meant not just physically, that he should descend from the mountaintop, but spiritually as well. Moshe was being told to descend from his elevated spirituality. After all, that prophetic gift had only been given Moshe for the sake of the people. Now that the people were no longer worthy, Moshe's mission was superfluous. The Sages report that immediately, Moshe became weak, lacking even the psychological strength to speak.

In the shadow of *Klal Yisrael's* tremendous transgression and God's devastating response, Moshe felt defeated and powerless. He despaired. The message that God then taught was that there is always time for repentance and prayer. Even when we lose prophecy, this power is always in our hands. Even at the darkest moments, we are responsible for our own destiny. We can remake ourselves.

Newly empowered, Moshe returned to the top of the mountain, leaving the Nation of Israel to reflect on this message for the whole month of Elul.

This year, you begin your year in Israel with this same message: your future is in your hands. It can be glorious or it can be mundane. You may climb to the highest levels of nobility, or you can descend to the pit of selfishness and cruelty. It all depends on what you choose to do with your

ספר שערי תשובה לרבינו יונה שער ב

והנה נחתום הענין הזה במאמר נכבד אשר לחכמי ישראל זכרונם לברכה (אבות פרק א, משנה יד): היה הלל עליו השלום אומר: אם אין אני לי מי לי? וכשאני לעצמי מה אני? ואם לא עכשיו אימתי? ביאור הדבר - אם האדם לא עורר נפשו מה יועילוהו המוסרים, כי אף על פי שנכנסים בלבו ביום שמעו, ישכחם היצר ויעבירם מלבבו, כענין שנאמר (הושע ו, ד): "וחסדכם כענן בקר", ונאמר (משלי י, כ): "כסף נבחר לשון צדיק לב רשעים כמעט"... אכן צריך האדם בשמעו המוסר לעורר נפשו ולשום הדברים אל לבו, ולחשוב בהם תמיד, ועליהם יוסיף לקח, ומלבו יוציא מלין, ויתבודד בחדרי רוחו, וישוב יהפוך יד תוכחתו על נפשו, ולא יסמוך על תוכחת המוכיח לבדו. ותוכחתו לבקרים ולרגעים תהיה, עד אשר תקבל נפשו המוסר, ועד אשר תטהר.

adult responsibilities of autonomy. Will you use it or will you ignore it? Will you focus it towards beneficence or will you squander it on materialism? Your teachers can help point the way, but ultimately you are responsible for 100% of your true education. They can give you a gift, but you can only take it home with you if you choose to pack into your own suitcase.

Appropriate in this season of repentance, this is the message contained in one of the most famous passages of Rabbenu Yonah's *Shaarei Teshuvah* (2:26):

> **Rabbenu Yonah ben Avraham Gerondi** (d. 1263), was born in Catalonia and then moved to southern France (Provence) where he became an important student of Rabbi Shlomo of Montpellier. He subsequently became the rabbi of Toledo, Spain. His commentaries (compiled by his students) on the Rif are an essential part of the talmudic canon, as is his commentary to *Pirkei Avot.*

Hillel, may peace be with him, said, "If I am not for myself, who will be for me? And if I am for myself alone, what am I? And if not now, then when?" (*Avot* 1:14). If one does not awaken himself, how will he be helped by ethical injunctions? For they may enter his heart when he hears them, the evil inclination will cause him to forget them and will remove them from his heart, as it is said, "For you goodness is as a morning cloud" (Hosea 6:4).... When one hears reproof, he must awaken himself, take the words to heart, reflect upon them constantly, and add wisdom to them, and bring forth thoughts from his heart, and commune within the chambers of his spirit, and relay the reproof to his soul, and not rely upon the words of the one who reproves alone. He must confront himself with the proof every morning and every moment, until his soul receives it and is purified.

Learning to Grow

I always find this passage striking, even frightening. As students, we spend much of our time reading and hearing statements that teach and encourage ethical growth. Perhaps you can recall some lecture that you found particularly moving or a book that was unusually inspiring. Rabbenu Yonah shocks us with the revelation that this passive inspiration is not nearly enough. For one or two days, your behavior may change, having been affected by the speech, exhibition, or essay. The ethical message may have truly "entered your heart" on the day that you heard it. Perhaps you even wept. And still, all this can easily evaporate like a morning cloud that promises life-giving rain but ultimately disappoints. Like so many tourists, you can cry real tears at Yad Vashem (the National Holocaust Memorial Museum) in the morning, get back on the bus, and spend the afternoon at the beach.

Never trust that early feeling of passive inspiration, the rain clouds that appear over parched earth first thing in the morning. Instead, take responsibility and make the lesson your own.

Rather than prematurely acting on external inspiration, we are enjoined by Rabbenu Yonah to live patiently with our discomfort, to consider how the ideas we may hear this Elul truly and personally apply to us as individuals, and to find germane applications that are meaningful, practical, and sustainable. Rabbenu Yonah teaches that the listener must "awaken *himself*, take the words to heart, reflect upon them constantly, and add wisdom to them...." No book can do that for you. No parent or teacher can do that for you. You need to transition from passively *being awakened* to actively awakening yourself.

This year, it might be helpful for you to reframe your entire job description. Rabbi Kalonymus Kalman Shapira, the famous Rebbe of Piaseczno and the Warsaw Ghetto, taught that even a young student should see himself as his own main educator. Only in that way will he view his teachers as constructive partners and not as foreign dictators of external impositions. Rabbi Shapira trusted and expected his students to be mature and proactive in their own personal development, even if they were still only children. His advice certainly applies to young men and women.[1]

Elul and Sacrifice

Taking responsibility for your destiny is one aspect of adulthood and one aspect of Elul. This is one virtue which you have already displayed by exercising your autonomy and choosing to spend this year in Israel. I encourage you to continue to take responsibility for your life, and then slowly accept responsibility for the lives of those around you: your family, your community, and your nation.

The second aspect of adulthood, the ability of sacrifice short-term comfort for long-term ideals, is the second major theme of Elul.

The Arizal taught that the name Elul ("אלול") made up of the initial letters of the phrase אני לדודי ודודי לי, "I am to my beloved and my beloved is to me" (Song of Songs 6:3).[2] Elul is a time of joyous reunion with our Divine "beloved." The idea, he says, is that having been focused on caring for our physical needs in the physical world for an entire year, we've become distracted. As we approach Rosh Hashanah, the anniversary of the creation of our human species, we need to reconnect to the reason for our creation in the first place. We were created as complex beings—both physical and spiritual—to act as a bridge, in order to project the light of spiritual greatness into an otherwise morally neutral material world. It is very easy for us to become so distracted by the living of life that we forget about this ultimate purpose of life. We would do well to turn down the volume on our noisy material comforts and desires, to better hear the more subtle music of our spiritual mission for which we were created.

---

1. חובות התלמידים, הקדמה ד"ה "לא די ללמד"
2. ספר פרי עץ חיים שער ראש השנה פרק א'

Learning to Grow

Rabbi Yehudah Aryeh Leib Alter (1847–1905), was born in Warsaw. Both his parents died when he was a child, and he was brought up by his grandfather, the *Chiddushei ha-Rim*, who took him to meet the Kotzker Rebbe. After the death of Rabbi Chanoch Heynech HaKohen Levin of Aleksander he became the Ger Rebbe. His *Sefat Emet* on the *parashah* is one of the most popular and important works of Chasidut.

The *Sefat Emet* writes that this same idea is hinted to in the contrast between the way *Mizmor le-Todah* (a psalm we say every morning) is written and how it is read. It is written ולא אנחנו, "and not we," but it is read, ולו אנחנו, "we are His." There is a change in one letter, and this change does not affect the pronunciation, but it does change the meaning. And what a change it makes! The *Sefat Emet* says that we need to recall that we have not been placed on the earth to care for our own hedonistic needs, but rather to care for God's will. We need to say, "לא אנחנו," we are not here solely for ourselves. Rather "ולו אנחנו," we are here as ambassadors of a Divine mission.

This attitude of self-sacrifice and service creates the relationship of "I am for My beloved." And once we focus on that joyful purpose of life, God responds by granting us a life of blessing. He responds with "my beloved is for Me," a flow of life-affirming blessing which we receive on Rosh Hashanah, the anniversary of our creation.

The customs of Elul reflect this ideal. We wake early—pulling ourselves out of our comfortable beds—to say *Selichot*. We blow the *shofar* to wake us from our intellectual slumber as well. Some people have the custom to fast. We all make an extra effort to study longer, more intensely. And again, you have already expressed this ideal by coming to spend the year in a place considerably less comfortable than your own home, in order to explore your connection to your people and our values—in order to find your individual way in our shared divine mission.

The third and final aspect of adulthood is the idea of using the intellect to make informed decisions about a way of life. That will be the topic of the next chapter.

Chapter 3

Rosh Hashanah

Creation of the World in Thought and in Action

In the second chapter I discussed two of the three defining traits of adulthood: the ability to make sacrifices of short-term comfort for long-term pleasure and the ability to accept responsibility for one's actions and destiny. Now I want to reflect on the third attribute: the ability to choose a way of life based on independent rational thought. This is actually the big message of Rosh Hashanah.

Some time ago, my wife and I were considering doing some renovations to our home. We wanted to build a guest suite, including a new bathroom, some closets, and a new library. We sealed a door that had led to this space from the kitchen, and opened a new door through a wall, so that the suite could be accessed more privately. We then tore down another wall to make the space bigger. The problem was, though, that without the wall, there could be no separate library, so we rebuilt the wall. Now a new problem arose: since the space was smaller than we had intended, there was no room for the beds. There was only one corner of the room where the beds could go; unfortunately, it was precisely the corner in which we had just opened the new door. So we sealed that door as well, and now we needed a door. The best option was to put the door next to the library, and to do so we needed to cut a hole through the wall that we had torn down and then rebuilt.

This process of demolition and construction went on for several weeks. Fortunately, it was all on paper. Had we actually performed each step, our simple renovation would have taken us about nine months and over $100,000, before we ever settled on a decent plan. But since we did it all on paper, the planning cost us about one dollar in writing supplies and several hours of our free time.

This is how all good construction is done: first you fix your eyes on a goal, then you draw up plans, then you talk with engineers and contractors, then you refine the plans. Only at the very end do you start to build. Once the shovel hits the ground, every change and deviation from plan is astronomically expensive. On paper, I can move a wall with an eraser and pencil for free. A huge million-dollar project can be picked up and dropped somewhere else at no cost. But once it is built, you can't move it even an inch without incurring huge costs.

Now, at the beginning of the year, is the time for you to plan what you want to get out of the year. Without having a sense of goal, you simply can't start. In my example, I wanted to build a guestroom. But what if I had no idea what I wanted to build? I'd be nuts to start knocking down walls and building windows hoping that somewhere along the way I'd become "inspired." What do you want to build this year, a year which might be the only year of serious, intense learning in your life? Do you just want to have a good time, do you want to improve your skills, meet you future spouse, become a *tzaddik*? Until you answer that question, you can't begin to move.

The Talmud in *Rosh Hashanah* reports the disagreement between two first-century Tannaim, Rabbi Elieazer and Rabbi Yehoshua. Rabbi Elieazer claimed that the world was created in the Jewish month of Tishrei, while Rabbi Yehoshua claimed that the world was actually created in the month of Nisan. The medieval French commentators known as the Tosafot[3] resolve the conflict by arguing that both opinions are true, that "these and those are both words of the living God." In fact, God thought about making the world in Tishrei but He actually made the world in Nisan.

We need to wonder: does God consider things and then change His mind? Is God fickle or indecisive? Of course not. How then can we understand His Divine reconsideration?

תלמוד בבלי מסכת ראש השנה דף י/ב

תניא רבי אליעזר אומר בתשרי נברא העולם בתשרי נולדו אבות בתשרי מתו אבות בפסח נולד יצחק בראש השנה נפקדה שרה רחל וחנה בראש השנה יצא יוסף מבית האסורים בראש השנה בטלה עבודה מאבותינו במצרים בניסן נגאלו בתשרי עתידין ליגאל רבי יהושע אומר בניסן נברא העולם בניסן נולדו אבות בניסן מתו אבות בפסח נולד יצחק בראש השנה נפקדה שרה רחל וחנה בראש השנה יצא יוסף מבית האסורין בראש השנה בטלה עבודה מאבותינו במצרים בניסן נגאלו בניסן עתידין ליגאל.

תוספות שם

אומרר"תדאלוואלודבריא-להימחיימואיכאלמימר דבתשרי עלה במחשבה לבראות ולא נברא עד ניסן

In fact, God created the world twice. In Nisan He actually created the world, but in Tishrei He thought about creating the world. That means that He created the world in thought, in theory. In Tishrei He set the goal and drew up the plans. Of course, God could have done everything—perfectly—at once. But He broke the process down into steps in order to teach us how to create, and in order to stamp certain seasons of the year with a spiritual influence that we can use in our own self-creation.

God permeated the month of Tishrei with a spiritual influence that makes it easier for us to begin the planning process of self-creation, to create ourselves in our heads. How do we think, what are

3. On *Rosh Hashanah* 27a.

our priorities, values, and goals? It is for this reason that we do not have a "new" year. Literally, we are celebrating "*Rosh Hashanah*," the "Head of the Year." We are aligning our heads.

We know that when God created man, He created us in His likeness; but what, exactly, is the "likeness" of God? Certainly it is not some physical image. Rashi explains, "'In our likeness': to understand and to think."[4] It is this human faculty, the ability to think straight, to plan, and only then to execute that makes us so much better than the beasts of the field. Animals react based on instinct. Our ability to consider makes us not only human; it makes us a bit divine. The more we develop this faculty, the more we will be able to see how all the complexities of life inter-relate.

Philosophers ask, and we also sometimes wonder: are we body or soul; emotion or intellect; are we individuals or members of society; Jews or members of all of humanity? Of course, we are all of these things. The job of the mind is to recognize all the facets of life and find the proper place for all aspects of human existence. Then we can get great pleasure from life, and create harmony out of dissonant internal conflict.

The object and challenge of Rosh Hashanah, therefore, is to get a clear perspective on existence at the start of the creation process. Like a seed planted in autumn, our thoughts are allowed to quietly germinate underground throughout the cold winter months. The roots grow down deeply—all winter there is fantastic growth!— but the plant does not express itself on the surface until the spring. Winter is an amazing time. The earth looks sterile; the leaves have fallen from the trees, and only dead crippled branches remain. Then spring arrives and the earth erupts with life, all of it stemming from the roots that quietly developed under the snow.

Tishrei is a time for planting: firstly, by deciding what we wish to grow, what we wish to become. I encourage you to use the Tishrei

---

4. Rashi on *Bereshit* 1:26.

holidays to get clarity. Study the prayers of Rosh Hashanah and reflect on the words. You will be spending many cold winter months internalizing the principles and goals you choose in Tishrei. Then in Nisan, the "month of spring," the doors of the yeshiva will open and you will have an opportunity to express out in the world that which you now plant.

The Hasidic master Rabbi Zadok HaKohen taught that this lesson is symbolized by the very names of the months. In Hebrew, the first letter of the name "Tishrei" is the last letter of the Hebrew alphabet. The second letter is the penultimate letter of the alphabet. The third letter is the third to last letter of the alphabet. This symbolizes the order construction in the planning stages. For example: if I want to build a building, I first need to know what the final use will be—office space, residential apartment, airport. Then I think about what materials I will need; then I find

ספר מחשבות חרוץ פרק יא ד"ה ואברהם
ואז הוא הרת עולם זמן המחשבה וההריון כמו שכתוב תוס' בר"ה, (כ"ז ע"ח) בשם ר"ת דהמחשבה היה בתשרי והמעשה בניסן, וכן לידת יצחק בניסן בפסח, וע"כ בניסן היה יציאת הדבור מהגלות דמצרים שנאמר כי גרים הייתם וגו', שהיה שם בסוד נפש הגר עד מתן תורה שזכו להיות כנסי' שלימה מיוחדת להש"י, ובניסן נתגלו אותיות הדבור עד שנפתחה הפה להסיח ולספר ביציאת מצרים כל הלילה ולשיר שירת הים, וזהו חודש האביב דאתוון כסדרן כי סדר האותיות הם ממטה למעלה תחלה א' ואח"כ ב' למעלה ממנו... וזהו בניסן דאז היה בריאת עולם בפועל שההארה בו מצד השגת התחתונים, וע"כ אז התחלת בנין כנסת ישראל לאומה שלימה והחודש הזה לכם דייקא ראש חדשים, ולמלכי ישראל מניסן מנינן שאז התחלת מלוכת ישראל והתגלות כנסיותם, והולכים ומתעלים בסיון להשיג אותיות הכתיבה בקבלת התורה שבכתב, ואח"כ בתשרי אותיות המחשבה שאז הוא בריאת עולם במחשבה וע"כ סדרן למפרע, שזהו הסדר שמצד השם יתברך מעילא לתתא כפי סדר השתלשלותן מתחלת המחשבה עד סוף המעשה שהוא על סדר תשר"ק...

a source for the materials; then I can estimate cost; then I can think about financing. In planning, I think about the end first, and then I work my way backwards until I get to where I am currently standing. This is the explanation of the phrase: the last in action is the first in thought (סוף מעשה במחשבה תחילה). In Tishrei, therefore, where we emphasize the planning, the last letter

> **Rabbi Zadok HaKohen Rabinowitz of Lublin** (1823-1900) was born into a Lithuanian rabbinic family and then became a follower of the Chasidic Rebbe, Rabbi Mordechai Yosef Leiner of Izbica. As a young man he gained widespread acclaim as a brilliant talmudist. Rabbi Zadok was a prolific writer in all areas of Judaism: *halachah*, Chasidut, Kabbalah, and ethics. Since his works are notoriously difficult, his commentaries to the Torah, פרי צדיק, might be a good place to get a taste of his Torah.

comes first, then the second to last and so on. In contrast, when we actually build, we first arrange the financing, then we contact the supplier of steel, then we buy the material and so on until the building is completed. In actually building, we put first things first. Therefore, the spring—when God actually created the world—is called *Aviv*. Again, in Hebrew, the first letter is the first letter of the alphabet, and the second letter is the second letter of the alphabet.

As we start to gain intellectual clarity, Rabbi Zadok continues to explain, we feel a need to pronounce our most profound insights vocally. In Tishrei, however, these feelings are still too raw and unformed for us to articulate them clearly. Instead, our longings for greater self-awareness, our desires for self-perfection, our yearnings to witness God's revelation of Himself in this world can only break free in a primordial utterance of joy and awe. This is the *shofar* blast. The long *tekiah* represents our joyful belief in a world that will ultimately be filled with clarity and unity. This is the big goal, the end of history, and is therefore represented by the last letter in the alphabet, the תו. The short blasts represent our trembling, standing in judgment. When confronted with the greatness of God on the day of His coronation, we sense our own imperfection. Nevertheless, we hope that this imperfection will not be our end, but will just be a passing stage on the way to our self-actualization. These short blasts, the *shevarim* and *teruah*, are therefore represented by the second-to-last and third-to-last letters respectively. Together, they spell the name of the month Tishrei.

All this is true in Tishrei, when our ideals are still fresh and unformed, and can therefore only be articulated as a primal sound. As we allow these ideas to develop over the cold winter, they differentiate and grow into forms we can express with greater eloquence. The metaphor I used above was one of planting a seed. Rabbi Zadok notes an analogous metaphor used by the Rabbis: conception, impregnation. You will note that in the prayers for Rosh Hashanah we refer to the day as, "היום הרת עולם," which means that this is the day that the universe was *conceived*. Just as a baby begins its life as a single-celled, undifferentiated embryo, so our reflections in Tishrei contain the potential for complex life, but are still too unformed to come out into the world in the form of majestic behavior. We cannot even express these ideals in the form of comprehensible words; only as a primitive blare. But just as the embryo develops, hidden away from the eyes of the world, into a complex being capable of independent life, so our feelings develop into clear principles for a moral life. And just as the mother finally gives birth, expressing her creation out into the world, so in the spring we can finally express ourselves clearly and articulately.

This is why the Jewish festival of the spring is called *Pesach*, which is understood to be a composite of the words *peh sach*, literally, "the mouth that speaks." In Tishrei we can only trumpet feelings on the *shofar*, and during the winter we will allow those feelings to germinate. Finally, in Nisan, on the night of the Seder, we will be able to articulate our principles and beliefs clearly and eloquently. Therefore the mitzvah of the night is one of speech, and whoever speaks at great length is considered praiseworthy.

Tefillin as Symbol for Aligning Head

Judaism is quite a practical religion. We believe that action is more essential than study[5]; nevertheless, we cannot act properly until our goals are focused, and until we have developed the conviction necessary to act, and sometimes to sacrifice, on their behalf. Rosh Hashanah is the time of the year for the clarification of these goals, and over the course of a winter of long and hard study, those goals should become transformed into driving convictions.

This holds true every year, for every individual. This is all the more true for you, this year, as you study in yeshiva or seminary. In many ways, this year is the Rosh Hashanah of your life. It is the beginning of your adulthood, in which you can set the goals and develop the convictions necessary to carry you successfully through marriage, parenthood, professional development, and communal action.

My *rebbe*, Rabbi Beryl Gershenfeld, pointed out that according to the Kabbalah, the letters of the word *"Tishrei"* also hint to the three words: תפילין, שי״ן, רא״ש. If Tishrei is the month in which we re-calibrate our heads, we should know that God, in His kindness, gave us a precision calibrating instrument that we can wear every day. The *tefillin* sit above our heads, representing the most sublime of goals, so lofty that they are beyond complete human comprehension. As lofty as they are, however, the letter *shin*, embossed on each side of the *tefillin*, look and act like the roots of a plant, drawing the light down from the *tefillin* into our consciousness, our *rosh*.[6]

---

5. See *Avot* 1:17.
6. Note that שי״ן רא״ש שי״ן = שורש.

Learning to Grow

Only Jewish men are obligated to wear *tefillin*; nevertheless, the message of the *tefillin* is as relevant for women as it is for men. If we understand that message, and draw it down into our consciousness, we will have come a long way to understanding our ultimate goals.

I get mail every day. Much of it goes straight into the trash. I pay the bills and file them away until tax season. There are other letters sent to me by my grandmother that I save and look at from time to time. Love letters recreate emotions of connection, and we cherish them in ways we do not cherish bills from the electric company.

Our *tefillin* is a love letter from God to the Jewish people, and we bind it to our head and to our heart, to remind us of that love, how it was consummated, and to remind us not to leave God's love for us unrequited. By reflecting on the four passages contained in the *tefillin*, we can get a better sense of God's love for us, and that can motivate us to recognize Him as king in Tishrei and beyond.[7]

The first passage in the *tefillin* (*Shemot* 13:1-10) describes how God cared for us and took us out of the bondage of Egypt. If you love someone, you care for their needs. God saw us suffering and redeemed us from slavery. This kind of love, however, could be quite limited. After all, I might see a suffering animal and relieve its pain, even if I have never seen it before and expect never to see it again. If helping the beast comes at no cost to me, why shouldn't I help it, even if I have no strong love for it?

The second passage in the *tefillin*, therefore, describes the cost God was willing to endure in order to help us. *Shemot* 13:11-16 recalls not just how the Jews were saved, but how the Egyptians— creatures of God, created in His image—were sacrificed so that we could go free. This is love to a greater degree, but it still does not show an intimate connection between God and the Jews. The Egyptians,

---

7. The following is based on Maharal, *Gevurot Hashem* 39, as explained by Rabbi Gershenfeld.

of course, were wicked people. Pharaoh brutalized us, and bathed in the blood of our children, who were no less created in God's image. A judge might punish the criminal; that does not mean that he takes the victim into his own home.

The third passage of the *tefillin*, the *Shema*, therefore, emphasizes that God identifies Himself with us. He is not just "God," but is "*our* God." As in marriage, we take his name, and are commanded to love Him back. Once again, however, we could question the appropriateness of this analogy. After all, many couples are formally married, but are separated, leading parallel lives that never truly connect.

The fourth and final passage ("And it shall be if you listen to my commandments" – *Devarim* 11:13-21) therefore, shows that God continues to watch over us, giving us reward and (when necessary) corrective punishment. We are not just "married" to the divine; we live in His house with Him. He cares for our daily needs and watches over us like a cherished treasure.

When we reflect on the ultimate degree to which God watches over us and cares for us, we should be inspired to love Him back, to proclaim Him king over the entire universe and (this is more difficult) over ourselves, to the exclusion of all other ephemeral forces that seem to govern our lives. And as we do so, we will surely see His hand guiding us as He guided our ancestors.

These are some of the concepts that should help us recalibrate our ideas and ideals at our "Head of the Year." And just as we wear the *tefillin* on both our head and our arm, so will the reflections of Rosh Hashanah illuminate our minds and empower our actions during this year of growth.

Chapter 4

Truth: Objective or Subjective

Finding the Right Path, Finding Your Own Path

When I was just starting to teach, I met a fantastically dynamic couple who had organized a group of college students to come to Israel for a few weeks. It was summer break in the United States, and for many of these young men and women, this would be the most intense Jewish experience of their lives. Unfortunately, or perhaps fortunately, several of these groups descended upon one of the hosting institutions at the same time, overwhelming the teaching faculty and leaving the organizers desperate to complete their program. Someone mentioned my name, and although I had never formally taught before, I soon received a telephone call, asking if I was available to give a series of classes on Jewish philosophy. Being an older student, I was eager to see what life was like on the other side of the desk, and I agreed immediately.

They would soon come to regret their offer.

At the time, I had been reflecting on a paradox that exists within Judaism. On the one hand, God created one Torah that expresses His unified and perfect will. One the other hand, our tradition is filled with a multitude of arguments and opinions on every subject, from the most practical behavior to the most esoteric matters of theology. If Torah is The-Absolute-God-Given-Truth, I wondered how we are expected to relate to the vigorous debate that is our heritage.

My conclusion was that Truth—at least the way we perceive it and act upon it—is in fact relative and unique to each individual. We each have our own Truth, our own legitimate perspective, and so long as we remain faithful to our own Truths, the Absolute Truth of the Torah is interesting only on the theoretical level.

When I expressed this to my class, the organizers were somewhat taken aback. They had not invested months of work recruiting students, raising funds, and scheduling their program only to have these students learn that the Absolute Truth of the Torah is only theoretically interesting. If these college students needed only to be faithful to some inner voice, they could just as well have stayed on campus. After all, hadn't they all grown up on this same sort of vapid relativism? Wasn't this the common conclusion of all their secular philosophy classes?

Well, yes and no. Let me explain myself.

I remember that my first year in yeshiva was a difficult one for me. I had arrived in Jerusalem with an Ivy League college education, and lots of idealism and motivation, but with very little knowledge of Torah. My Hebrew skills were very poor, and my opinions informed more by Western popular culture than by the Jewish tradition I realized was sacred. In short, I knew that I had a lot to learn.

But the problem was more complex than that. I knew that I was a good person, that I had made sacrifices to be in yeshiva in the first place and I was willing to make more along the way if necessary. I had a perspective on life that I knew was largely correct, even if it was in need of much subtle refinement. This put me on the defensive. I was willing to change and grow, but not too much and not too fast, if only because I didn't want to abandon an identity that was both legitimate and uniquely mine. And although I had been religious for only a short while, I had already heard statements made by clearly misguided rabbis that made me cautious.

For example, months earlier I had attended a class in the United States at a location that shall remain nameless. I have no recollection of the class's main subject; I guess I blocked it all out. All I remember is that at some point the teacher, a rabbi from a distinguished rabbinic family, suggested that all homosexuals should be put on an island together to infect each other with AIDS and die.

Now, I didn't know a lot, but I knew that this was wrong, and I refused to believe that Judaism could really condone an attitude so noxious. To this day I feel guilty about not walking out in protest. I have since mentioned this story to other Torah scholars who agreed that this teacher expressed a shocking lack of compassion that has no place in the tradition of our Patriarchs. In any case, I had been placed on alert. I had always considered myself a critical thinker. Suddenly I was a skeptic as well.

When I finally arrived in yeshiva I was assigned to an advanced first year seminar. My Talmud *rebbe*, Rabbi Shaul Miller, zt"l, was such a well-known talmudist that visiting scholars would often remark, "you can't appreciate who you have teaching you." And in fact, I didn't.

Although I found his Talmud class stimulating, I couldn't relate to his attitude at all. Rabbi Miller was clearly a *ba'al yirah*, a man whose perception of God in the world and in his life was so acute that he was brimming with awe. Unfortunately, I found his perception of the divine to be a bit oppressive. He didn't seem to be relaxed and happy, but rather uptight and afraid. When he would lead the prayers on holidays, I was left unmoved by his *Hallel*—the psalms of joyous praise—that sounded more like an elegy than an uplifting song of joy. Sometimes he positively wept in agony over the sorrow of an imperfect planet.

Happy holiday, indeed.

It seemed that he was most cheerful when discovering a new prohibition or stringency (a "*chumra*"), like when he suggested that my *tefillin*—which I had checked only several months earlier—might not be kosher for some technical reason that still escapes me.

So here I was, expected to accept as God-given truth instruction from a man to whom I could not relate, and to whom I didn't want to relate. I was happy and felt good about myself and the decisions I had made. I wanted to continue to enjoy the *Hallel*. Once I was told that my *tefillin* were kosher, I didn't want to have to spend the rest of my life wondering if perhaps they were not.

Here I was confronted by an attitude that I considered oppressive, and yet I couldn't walk away, because I had come to yeshiva to discover what God wanted from me. And here I was being told—or so I felt—that God wanted me to emulate a man who was not enjoying life, and who would be only too willing to give back his soul to his Creator at the earliest opportunity. I began to hate Rabbi Miller, which felt really distasteful—downright sinful.

One day, we were studying the laws of caring for the sick on the Sabbath, and there was one law that I found particularly challenging. We were taught that you can, and must, violate Shabbat to save a life. For what it's worth, that made sense to me: life is sacred. We were also taught that you may not violate Shabbat if there is no danger to life. This also made sense to me: Shabbat is also sacred. What I found difficult was the law that one may not violate a Torah prohibition in order to save a limb. [8]

Now I have never been particularly enthusiastic about amputation, and I was disturbed by the following thought: if I were to have a limb cut off on Shabbat, my friends could happily carry me to the hospital

---

8. Later I would learn that this law is mostly of academic interest since, practically, we would almost always violate Shabbat to save a limb

through a public domain, but they would have to leave my severed part behind on the pavement. I was willing to accept this law; but I can't say that I liked it.

Rabbi Miller, however, thought that this was terrific. He seemed particularly animated that afternoon, reflecting the attitude of Job: God has given and God has taken away; may the name of God be blessed.

I reacted by matching his apparent insensitivity with my own. I made some sharp and critical comment—something like, "Sure, I'll leave *your* arm behind." As you can imagine, this outburst justifiably offended my teacher, and put a chill over the rest of the class. Later that day, Rabbi Miller called me into his study. He told me that I had offended him, and that as my *rebbe* he was not allowed to forgive me until I considered what I had said and apologized sincerely.

"That's it," I thought. "Now I've done it: I've gone and offended a rabbi. I'm going to burn in hell."

As soon as I left Rabbi Miller, I stepped into the office of Rabbi Gershenfeld, and asked him for an emergency meeting in order to help get some clarity on this offense in particular and on my relationship with Rabbi Miller in general. That night, in Rabbi Gershenfeld's home, I expressed my dilemma: I didn't like Rabbi Miller's attitude, I felt he was unhappy and uptight. I hated him.

Rabbi Gershenfeld thought for quite a while and then he said something for which I will be forever grateful.

"You're right," he said.

Rabbi Miller, he told me, had always been a big *ba'al yirah*. Then, he had suffered a benign brain tumor, which was something of a misnomer since it had almost killed him. In fact, the tumor did take his life several years later. The year before I arrived, he had been unable to teach, and had become ever more conscious of the frailty of man and of the ephemeral nature of life. Miraculously, he had recovered and was able to return to the classroom. But always acutely aware of the presence of his Creator, Rabbi Miller had become even more focused on the reality of death. He was struggling against disease, and so when he led the *Hallel* he not only thanked God for life, he was also begging for more. His suffering left him appearing... yes, uptight and a bit unhappy.

Rabbi Gershenfeld affirmed the legitimacy of my perspective on life, and showed me a wonderful Gemara about the need for tolerance of others. He advised me to learn from Rabbi Miller as much as I could, given that he was perhaps the strongest talmudist in the yeshiva. But that didn't mean that I needed to emulate him. I could find other role models. In the meantime I should consider myself privileged to be able to study under such an accomplished scholar.

I thanked Rabbi Gershenfeld for his advice, as I would come to do many times in the future, and returned to Rabbi Miller to offer a heartfelt apology. Rabbi Miller accepted my words immediately, almost dismissively, as if to say that this was all a formality, best quickly put behind us so that we can get on to the real project of learning Torah. Freed by Rabbi Gershenfeld's affirmation of my own attitude, I felt liberated. I no longer felt like I was expected to remake myself in the image of Rabbi Miller.

After I apologized, Rabbi Miller asked me to reflect on the emotions that led to my offensive remark. We spoke for a while, and then he showed me a passage in the kabbalistic writings of Rabbi Chaim Vital, the closest disciple of the Arizal, that brilliantly explained the psychology of anger. Written in black and white was a penetrating analysis of the emotions that had passed through me the day before. Rabbi Miller shared it with me happily, caringly, without a hint of personal insult or rancor. He revealed nothing but joyful enthusiasm, because he was teaching Torah and nothing else mattered. In fact, he seemed almost glad to have been offended, because the experience was such a great teaching aid.

Perhaps offending a rabbi should be made part of every yeshiva curriculum.

From that moment on, I learned a tremendous amount from Rabbi Miller. I can't say that I have become like him as a person, or that I have ever really wanted to. But from that moment I certainly did aspire to achieve his love and knowledge of Torah. And yes, his *yirat shamayim*—his sense of awe before the Creator. Above all, I learned to admire his perspective on the Torah, on truth, even though his perspective was very different from mine.

The question before us then is really the topic of this chapter: how can there be so many different legitimate approaches to the Torah? After all, God is one, His Torah is one, and He gave it through His greatest prophet. An understanding of this paradox will give us a theoretical platform from which we can then examine other issues that are both pertinent and practical: How can you distinguish between legitimate perspectives and illegitimate perspectives; what do you do when you encounter a teacher who just doesn't speak your language?

The Midrash relates a dramatic and cryptic story about the angels' reservations concerning the creation of man:

> Rabbi Simon said: At the time God came to create Adam, the heavenly hosts formed factions and groups, some saying

בראשית רבה פרשה ח:

א"ר סימון בשעה שבא הקב"ה לבראת את אדם הראשון, נעשו מלאכי השרת כיתים כיתים, וחבורות חבורות, מהם אומרים אל יברא, ומהם אומרים יברא, הה"ד (תהלים פה) חסד ואמת נפגשו צדק ושלום נשקו, חסד אומר יברא שהוא גומל חסדים, ואמת אומר אל יברא שכולו שקרים, צדק אומר יברא שהוא עושה צדקות, שלום אומר אל יברא דכוליה קטטה, מה עשה הקב"ה? נטל אמת והשליכו לארץ הה"ד (דניאל ח) ותשלך אמת ארצה, אמרו מלאכי השרת לפני הקב"ה רבון העולמים מה אתה מבזה תכסיס אלטיכסייה שלך, תעלה אמת מן הארץ, הדא הוא דכתיב (תהלים פה) אמת מארץ תצמח.

66

not to create him and some saying to create him. As is written, "Kindness and truth met, charity and peace kissed" (Psalm 85). Kindness said man should be created, because he does acts of kindness; and truth said man should not be created because he is entirely of falsehood. Charity said man should be created because he does acts of charity. Peace said man should not be created because he is filled with strife. What did God do? He took truth and threw him to the earth, as is written, "and He cast down the truth to the earth" (Daniel 8).

The heavenly hosts said before God, "Master of the Universe, how are You disgracing Your seal?!"[9] He replied, "Raise truth from the earth!"[10] So is it written, "Truth will sprout from the earth" (Psalm 85) (*Bereishit Rabbah* 8:5).

> *Bereishit Rabbah* is the first volume of a relatively late collection of rabbinic commentary on the non-legal parts of Tanach, called *midrash aggada*. The earliest midrashim date from the time of the Mishnah, which was codified in the second-third century CE. Midrash is a specific form of rabbinic exegesis: *midrash aggada* (like *Midrash Rabbah*) often relates additional stories and ethical lessons, while *midrash halachah* (like the *Mechilta*) gives legal rulings.

Why did God punish truth? Presumably truth had made a reasonable claim. Clearly it wasn't lying; after all, it is the truth. And why would the Omniscient One consult with this disorderly committee of virtues in the first place?

Evidently, Rabbi Simon taught that so long as certain virtues remained obvious and necessary, we people could not have been created with the fundamental human trait of ethical autonomy founded on free will. Simply stated: for man to be man, he must

9. Based on Rashi.
10. According to the Maharal of Prague this was God's response.

be full of falsehood. Were we not capable of rationalizations and self-deceptions we would never—could never!—steal, trespass, or transgress. We would be like the angels; not human in the way God desired us to be. God wanted us to be subject to temptations, if only so that we could transcend them.

Were moral truth to be not only eternal and absolute but also an inescapably obvious beacon in the sky, we would have no ethical wiggle room and therefore no free will.

Let me explain this statement with an analogy from a basic law of nature: gravity. Gravity is absolutely obvious in our lives. We rely on it without a second thought. We may play with it (sky-diving, bungee-jumping, hang gliding) but never do we consider truly ignoring it. Were moral truth to be similarly obvious in our lives, we would only dream of sin in the way some of us dream of flying, as a remote fantasy.

Truth, therefore, was speaking the truth. So long as it remained an obvious beacon in heaven, we creatures of falsehood could not be created. God responded not by punishing truth, but by temporarily suspending its obvious revelation. This temporary suspension of truth is similar to exile, and the Midrash highlights this analogy by citing a verse from the book of Daniel that deals with exile. In order to create humanity, God exiled truth from heaven. He threw it down to the ground.

Maharal associated this divine exiling of truth with the giving of the Torah. The giving of the Torah was more than just a commanding of obedience to a fixed code of law. In many ways, it was the handing over of the keys to the Torah; it was the giving of ownership. We were never intended to remain passive recipients or mindless slaves. Rather, having received the keys, we have the responsibility to transmit the Torah, and the authority to interpret the Torah, along with the obligation to act upon the Torah as we understand it. By giving us ownership over the Torah, God graced us with the most powerful tool for confronting truth and for bringing it into our lives; He gave us the most powerful tool for transcending the falsehood on which our free will was predicated.

Despite this very powerful potential for good, the angels considered the giving of God's pristine Torah to be disgraceful. Ideally, we should live our lives in congruence with that Torah which we have received. But once it was given to us together with the power to make value judgments, we could just as easily ignore it, misinterpret it, resent it, or outright reject it. We might develop immoral rationalizations to justify base behavior, and then in an ultimate act of shameful dishonesty give this counterfeit morality the divine seal of approval, "Torah True!" Just like the work of a master counterfeiter undermines the authority of the government mint, so the angels were concerned that human involvement in the process of Torah interpretation and legislation would undermine God's precious seal.

This is, by the way, the deeper meaning behind another famous Midrash, in which the angels fought with Moshe when he came to receive the Torah. They were never concerned with our being commanded the 613 commandments; instead, they were protesting the authority of interpretation being passed to our very slippery, all too human hands.

God was willing to take the risk. True, the giving of the Torah threatened its integrity, but God willed that we should accept the responsibility to preserve the Torah to the best of our ability and to act upon it. Through our study and performance of the Torah we elevate ourselves, we cleanse ourselves of that falsehood that originally allowed us to be fallible. We become a bit more angelic. The Torah helps us subordinate our baser drives to our higher ideals. We develop more self-control and express our essential spirituality. We elevate the world and we elevate the Torah that had descended into it. Effectively, we "raise truth from the earth," by raising the earth itself. By demonstrating God's extreme unity—by showing that He and His will hold true in even the coarsest, most unlikely of places— we contribute to the fulfillment of the very purpose of the creation.

The revelation of Divine unity through this process is analogous to the similar revelation of Divine unity through the cycle of exile and redemption. Again, Rabbi Simon highlighted this analogy by referring to a verse from Daniel that deals with exile. In the realm of morality as in the realm of history, God hides His face and allows confusion and chaos to rule. This demonstrates that there is no possible alternative to Divine law, both for individuals and for societies. The very darkness of exile creates a contrast that—together with the subsequent revelation of absolute truth and the redemption of Israel—throws into relief God's ultimate kindness, power, and wisdom. Rabbi Simon compressed this idea into an agricultural metaphor: Like the earth that hides a seed and then causes it to sprout with new life, the giving of the Torah not only hid the absolute truth, but it also provided an important medium so that someday, the necessity of those truths would become apparent to all.

Into what "earth" was the Torah planted? Into each of us. We humans are called *Adam* – אדם – from the word for "earth," *adamah* – אדמה. Like the earth, we are full of potential; we have truth planted inside of us. We have to accept those truths, allow them to germinate, nurture them, and help them to grow. But this "planting" also implies that so long as the one absolute truth has not been redeemed, we can only access it through the very personal and individual perspectives that we each have. This concept is hardly foreign. For example, our souls all stem from one spiritual source, yet each of us is an autonomous individual. Similarly, the Torah derives from one unified source, but it is revealed to each of us differently.

Truth: Objective or Subjective

You may have heard of the concept that there are seventy different perspectives on the Torah. Rabbi Moshe Chaim Luzzatto takes this concept even further and asserts that just as there were 600,000 souls present for the giving of the Torah, so there are 600,000 perspectives on the Torah. He compares these perspectives to sparks or to the many shades and colors that dance inside a flame. And just as a fire must be stoked to produce illuminating flames, and just as flint must be struck to produce sparks, so the Torah must be studied with profound reflection for its lights to shine.

So is there one absolute Truth? Yes, but it is hidden and inaccessible. The best that we can do is to discover and express our individual legitimate and subjective truths. We discover that individual truth by confronting the Torah with passion and focus, together with intellectual humility and selfless objectivity. And here is the irony: if you try to achieve objective absolute truth, you will succeed in encountering a personal truth that is both subjective and legitimate.

Beware: If you have an agenda, if you try to impose any bias whatsoever—be it liberal or conservative, feminist or chauvinist, capitalist or socialist—on the sacred texts that you study this year, you will achieve only counterfeit truth. As my friend Rabbi Eli Pielet points out, the Rabbis already warned us that wine stored in golden vessels is likely to spoil as the ostentatious vessel overwhelms the more subtle contents.[11] If you wish to be a vessel to express a valuable truth, you

> **Rabbi Moshe Chaim Luzzatto** ("Ramchal" 1707–1746) was one of the greatest kabbalists of the eighteenth century. He authored many classic works, including *The Way of God*, *The Knowing Heart*, and *The Path of the Just*. The latter is perhaps the greatest work of ethical instruction since the close of *Pirkei Avot*. *Derech Etz ha-Chaim* is his ethical introduction to his mature treatise on Kabbalah, *Klach (138) Pitchei Chochmah*.

---

11. מהר"ל, נתיב התורה פרק ב

also need to cultivate humility.

And if you do struggle hard to empty yourself of all prejudice and bias, if you try to understand the objective absolute Torah as it is, then you will reveal your own unique perspective in every letter. You will allow your unique soul to express itself honestly and creatively. This does

> **ספר דרך עץ חיים - לרמח"ל**
>
> והנה בהיות השלהבת מתלהטת, כבר אמרתי שיש בה כמה גוונים מרוקמים, וכן נמצאים כמה עניינים גדולים נכללים בשלהבת של האור הזה. אמנם עוד עניין אחר נמצא, כי יש כמה פנים לתורה, וכבר קבלו הקדמונים, שלכל שורש מנשמות ישראל יש כולם בתורה, עד שיש ששים ריבוא פירושים לכל התורה מחולקים לששים ריבוא נפשות של ישראל. וזה נקרא שהתורה מתפוצצת לכמה ניצוצות, כי בתחילה מתלהטת, ואז נראים בה כל האורות הראויים לעניין ההוא, ואותם האורות עצמם מאירים בששים ריבוא דרכים בששים ריבוא של ישראל. וזה סוד (ירמיה כג כט): "וכפטיש יפוצץ סלע". הרי לך, שאף על פי שהתורה היא בלי תכלית, ואפילו כל אות ממנה היא כן, אך צריך ללבותה, ואז תתלהב:

not mean that you will necessarily create new and different legal rulings. (Although sometimes you might, and you have the right to try to convince the generation's scholars to accept your view.) Nevertheless, you will start to develop your own understanding of commandments, the spirit behind the law, and the more refined behavior that this spirit suggests.

Because absolute truth is absolutely hidden, you will notice that we rabbis and teachers don't always speak with one voice. We each have our own perspectives that stem—at least ideally—from many souls struggling for many years to understand the Torah as it is. Even in one institution, expect teachers to emphasize different aspects of the Torah, to the point where one teacher may even contradict another. From my perspective, this is a sign of a healthy institution.

As a student, you have the obligation to create a living dialogue with a teacher who speaks your language. When you pluck the E string on a guitar, all the other E strings in the room will begin to resonate in sympathy. When your soul begins to resonate in sympathy with your teacher, you have found someone who is especially qualified to help you develop your unique perspective, even if he (or she) is not the greatest scholar in the institution. Cultivate that relationship.

This does not mean that you can't learn from your other teachers as well. You can and must learn from everyone. But it is legitimate that from some teachers you will learn information that is essential for a Torah life—as I ultimately learned from Rabbi Miller, zt"l—while from one individual you will discover the very the essence of that life.

I want to conclude this chapter with an important lesson from Maharal that illustrates and

ספר גור אריה על בראשית כה:כז
אהלו של שם ואהלו של עבר. כאן לא קשה איך הניח שם ולמד במדרשו של עבר, דהא אמרינן לעיל (אות כט) גבי "למדרשו של שם" (רש"י פסוק כב) שלא להניח הגדול ולשאול הקטן, הכא שאני, דלמוד התורה יכול ללמוד מן הקטן כמו מן הגדול, ולעולם לא ילמוד אדם אלא (מאי) [ממי] שלבו חפץ, ואפילו אם הוא קטן, דלאו מכל אדם זוכה ללמוד. ודווקא לגבי שאילה אין לשאול הקטן במקום גדול, ולפיכך לעיל "למדרשו של שם" דוקא, וכאן שם ועבר:

refines this last point. The Torah refers to Yaakov as a "dweller of tents." Rashi seems puzzled by the use of the plural "tents," since most of us have only one home. The Torah should have simply referred to Yaakov as a "tent-dweller" (יושב האוהל, perhaps). Rashi, based on a midrash, concludes that Yaakov actually sat in two distinct tents. He studied from both the senior monotheist of the generation, Shem the son of Noah, and from Ever, Shem's righteous grandson.

Maharal finds Yaakov's behavior in need of explanation. After all, Shem was Ever's grandfather. He was older and wiser than Ever. Why would Yaakov sometimes turn away from the elder Shem to sit and study with the younger Ever? Maharal's conclusion is very relevant to us: one can learn Torah from someone smaller or someone greater; the important thing is to learn from someone that you like ("from one whom his heart desires"). If the Torah of even a smaller scholar resonates in your heart, learn from him, because no one can really learn from everyone or just anyone.

Maharal continues that if you have a question in some matter of practical *halachah*, you should find the greatest scholar available. But

> **Yehudah Loew ben Bezalel** ("Maharal," d. 1609) was a leading rabbi in Prague and the surrounding area. Although he was also a master of the legal portions of the Torah, he is most famous for his commentary of the non-legal (aggadic) portions of Talmud, his super-commentary on Rashi's biblical commentary, and his philosophical works. He is known for expressing kabbalistic ideas in non-mystical language.

in subjects that are more theoretical, do as Yaakov did. Cultivate a relationship with a teacher who speaks your language.

Chapter 5

Working on Character

עבודה מוסרית

When God created the first human being He pronounced, "Let us make man."[12] The Midrash asks the obvious question, "to whom was God speaking?" and then gives a variety of explanations. Some explain that God was speaking to the heavenly hosts, emphasizing our angelic potential; others say that God was speaking to the earth that contributed the raw material of our bodies while God contributed the spiritual soul. But according to a third opinion, God consulted with the souls of the righteous themselves. According to this opinion, following our initial creation, God invited us humans to be partners in our own continuing self-creation, just as we are partners in the creation of the world.

> Rabbi Yehoshua of Sachnin in the name of Rabbi Shmuel said, He consulted with the souls of the righteous. As is written, "These were the potters [literally, 'formers' יוצרים], and those that lived among plantations and hedges; there they lived with the king, occupied in the king's work" (1 Chronicles 4).

---

12. Genesis 1:26.

... "they lived with the king, occupied in the king's work": The souls of the righteous live with the King of kings, the Holy One blessed be He. Those with whom the Holy One blessed be

בראשית רבה פרשה ח:ז

רבי יהושע דסכנין בשם רבי שמואל אמר בנפשותן של צדיקים נמלך הה"ד (דברי הימים א ד) המה היוצרים ויושבי נטעים וגדרה עם המלך במלאכתו ישבו שמה, המה היוצרים, על שם וייצר ה' א-להים את האדם עפר מן האדמה, יושבי נטעים, על שם ויטע ה' א-להים גן בעדן מקדם, וגדרה, על שם (ירמיה ה) אשר שמתי חול גבול לים, עם המלך במלאכתו ישבו, עם המלך מלך מלכי המלכים הקב"ה ישבו נפשות של צדיקים שבהן נמלך המלך הקדוש ב"ה ובָרָא את העולם.

He consulted and created the world (*Bereishit Rabbah* 8:7).

This self-creation certainly means in matters of the flesh as well as matters of the spirit. We are expected to care for our bodies, our personal health. We are expected to care for society and for the ecological health of the planet—to cultivate and guard the garden. But we are even more responsible for our spiritual self-creation. After all, God consulted with the souls of the *righteous* in particular, and that term is a spiritual and moral one.

In previous chapters we have discussed the cognitive aspects of self-creation: accepting responsibility for ourselves as adults, and setting idealistic goals in our heads. Now at the beginning of the long winter term, the time has come for us to get down to the difficult work of righteous self-creators, first on a moral plane, by refining character.

But where to begin? We all have flaws. In fact, God created us flawed deliberately, so that we should be able to participate in— and take credit for—our own self-creation. Clearly, the first step is to recognize this sobering fact. In a world in which we all seek justification and unconditional affirmation, in a world in which a self-help book titled *I'm OK – You're OK* is a bestseller (over 15 million copies in print), we have to be humble, and brave, and admit, "I'm *not* OK; you're *not* OK… but *that's* OK!"

The problem is, once the dam of self-deception comes down, the deluge can be overwhelming. We can easily state, like Isaiah, "From the sole of the foot even unto the head there is no soundness in it; but wounds, and bruises, and festering sores…." So what should we work on first: kindness, patience, temperance, self-control, contentedness, humility, modesty, bravery, alacrity, careful speech…? And what does "working on yourself" mean, practically, anyway?

Rule 1: Pick One

It is all too easy to squirm out of these legitimate questions by repeating some tired truism like, "Well, it all depends on your particular personality and circumstances…." But such an evasion would be both unfair and unnecessary, because there are some useful rules that can offer direction. Before I try to state these rules I want to make explicit the premise that underlies the first question: character traits should be worked on one at a time. Only by focusing attention on one

Rabbi Shlomo Wolbe (1914–2005) was born into a German Jewish family and became religious while studying at the University of Berlin. Eventually learning at the Mir Yeshiva, he became close to the *mashgiach*, Rabbi Yeruchom Levovitz, and his approach to musar. After WWII he helped found a yeshiva in Be'er Yaakov, Israel, where he was the *mashgiach* for over 30 years. In 1981 he moved to Jerusalem, where he founded a *beit ha-musar* in the format developed by Rabbi Yisrael Salanter. He continued teaching at several Jerusalem yeshivas and was simply known as "the Mashgiach." His most famous work is the two-volume *Alei Shur.*

attribute can a person properly reflect on his or her current state, analyze successes and failures, and prepare strategies to deal with future challenges. Rabbi Shlomo Wolbe suggested that small groups of friends should meet regularly to discuss one attribute over the course of three to six months.[13] This means that over the course of your year in Israel you may be able to work on two to three topics, at most.

You may encounter classical Jewish systems of self-evaluation that do focus attention on a broad spectrum of attributes at once. The seminal work *Cheshbon ha-Nefesh* works this way, and its system was widely used in the great *musar* yeshivas. This also seems to be the approach of what may be the most popular and influential work of this genre, the *Mesillat Yesharim* of Rabbi Moshe Chaim Luzzatto. Back in the good old days, people were refined enough that, with effort, they could trace any failure in behavior back to some root vice.

Unfortunately, in our generation such a broad focus doesn't work very well. Compared to previous generations we tend to be coarser, so when we slip up not just one red flag goes up, but half a dozen. Were we to focus on all of our failings at once we would most likely succumb to despair. We also don't know ourselves very well, so a broad focus could easily lead to confusion.

Imagine for example that at the end of the day you reflected on some small failure—let's say a roommate asked for help with the dishes and you found some convenient reason to excuse yourself. Now try to find the root of the failure. Did you succumb to laziness? Perhaps sloppiness? Lack of altruism, or kindness, or empathy? Arrogance? There could be a whole swarm of vices at work here, making an accurate diagnosis very difficult. And without an accurate diagnosis there is just no way to make a strategy going forward.

Instead, my teachers have recommended that we pick just one attribute at a time and work on that alone. Assume that you had chosen to work on sloppiness. When your roommate asked for help

13. *Alei Shur* II, pp. 190-191.

with the dishes and you wiggled out of it you may have failed in many ways, but you *certainly* failed in your declared short-term goal. Now you can evaluate what went wrong, and devise a game plan to deal with similar situations in the future.

There is another advantage to picking one attribute and working on that full time. When someone develops excellence in one area, he or she can apply it with more or less efficiency almost anywhere. If, on the other hand, a person is just mediocre in everything, every action will be performed blandly, at best. Let me illustrate with an analogy.

Around the home I tend to be "Mr. Fix It." I've got my tool box and my tools and from time to time I go around the house hammering and drilling. Several years ago my young children witnessed all this and, like any good kids, wanted to emulate their father. When they received some money for Chanukah, they went to the local general store and bought a set of plastic toy tools: a plastic hammer, a plastic screwdriver, etc. Now everyone knows what you can do with plastic tools: nothing. It's better, I told them, to take the toys back to the store and use the money instead to buy one real tool. Naturally, they bought a hammer, which was quite a good choice. Because you know what you can do with a good hammer? Obviously, you can hammer nails very well. You can also remove nails very well. But hammers are not only good for nails. If you are stuck with a bunch of screws, and you don't have a screwdriver, you can also hammer screws. This is not the most elegant solution, but it works. A saw if best for cutting wood, but if you don't have one you know what you can use? That's right: a hammer.

Character attributes are very similar. They are not so much the actions that you do as much as they are the attitudes that inform every action. That being the case, you can apply any given attribute almost anywhere. Sometimes it will be a perfect fit; sometimes it just gets you through the situation having done adequate good and no harm.

Take, for example, the attribute of giving respect. Clearly, this is a top-drawer attitude in many situations: dealing with parents and teachers, eulogizing the dead… being sentenced by a judge (try to avoid that application). In other situations, you might expect different attitudes to be more dominant. For example, at a young child's birthday party, you would probably want to draw more on the attitude of joy. But if you happen to be working on showing respect, and you arrive at a birthday party focused on your project, you will get through it with flying colors. You will complement the parents on the cake, and the clown on the magic tricks, and the other parents on the behavior of their children, and the maid on the cleanliness. Most of all, you will treat the young guest of honor in a way that most children would find unusually flattering—respect. So in attributes as well, it is better to have one really good tool than a whole set of plastic tools.

Rule 2: Pick Something Easy

Alright then, rule number one is to pick one attribute and work on that for a couple of months. But what should you pick? This is a question that you need to answer for yourself, preferably with the help of someone you trust and respect. Still, one helpful rule should make your choice simpler.

Pick something easy. This advice is tested and true for a number of reasons.

First, you are inexperienced at self-improvement. If you pick something too difficult, you will probably fail in this effort and may even despair of the entire project. It is tempting to say, "I am so arrogant; I've just got to work on humility." Resist that temptation. Start with something easy first. You will gain practice in the exercise and motivating confidence in your relatively easy successes.

Second, as we just saw, it is better to have one good tool than to have a bunch of plastic ones. Therefore, your first goal should be to acquire one good tool. If you work on an attribute that you already find natural, you can easily move from "good" to "excellent." After all, if a music instructor had a student who was naturally good at the flute she wouldn't advise, "Hey, you are already good on the flute, so you had better work on the piano." Rather, she

Rabbi Eliyahu Eliezer Dessler (1892–1953) was a founder of the Gateshead Yeshiva and *mashgiach ruchani* of Bnei Brak's Ponevezh Yeshiva. His father, Rabbi Reuven, was a close student of the Alter of Kelm, and at the age of 14, Rabbi Dessler was one of the youngest students to learn in Kelm. Many of his writings have been collected in the five-volume *Michtav me-Eliyahu* and translated into English under the title as *Strive for Truth!*

would first encourage him become a world-class flautist. Similarly, if you are already a kind person, develop that natural kindness until you are world-class. That attribute will serve you well no matter where you might find yourself.

Most significantly, that which comes easily is probably a reflection of your soul's root and indicates the unique contribution that you can make to the world. Rabbi Eliyahu Dessler taught, in the tradition of the Rabbi Yisrael Salanter's *musar* movement, that a person must begin his divine service by discovering his most essential attribute, developing it to its perfection according to the ways of the Torah, and by being faithful to it.[14]

---

14. *Michtav Me-Eliyahu* II, pg. 161.

81

Based on a Mishnah in *Avot*, Rabbi Dessler taught that everyone tends to identify with one of the three most basic attributes: kindness, self-restraint, or truth. Just like the three patriarchs Avraham, Yitzchak, and Yaakov first perfected themselves in these corresponding three traits, so each of us should find the trait that resonates most strongly in him or her, and perfect that.

Later, after we have achieved excellence in our dominant trait, we must each round out our characters by working on the other complementary attributes. That stage might seem more difficult since we must often work against our natural inclinations. A classic example of this difficulty is Avraham's overcoming his dominant kindness with self-restraint so that he could sacrifice his son. On the other hand, having already honed a more basic attribute, we will be working from a position of relative strength having both practiced the art of self-development and having acquired some level of ethical excellence.

Reducing basic self-improvement to one of the three primary attributes, Rabbi Dessler's approach makes our choice of a starting project much simpler. If you have some other strong virtue that you really want to hone, you need not feel constrained by Rabbi Dessler's recommendation. But if you have no idea where to begin, you may find his advice very helpful.

Focus and Balance

This approach encourages focusing a lot of concentration on achieving excellence in one dominant attribute, and you might rightly understand it as being a bit unbalanced. I therefore believe that an important caveat is in order. I am not endorsing such a narrow focus in performance of commandments or in what might be termed "lifestyle." The law is the law; the commandments are the commandments. I do not believe that one should focus attention on achieving "excellence" in any one commandment or set of commandments until he or she has acquired a basic care in all of them. Until you know and fulfill your most basic duties in all the commandments, the adoption of extra stringencies in some of them is unhelpful at best and perhaps self-deluding. So long as you are weak in your legal commitment in any aspect of Jewish law—be it ritual, personal, commercial, or communal—your first and only goal should be to buttress that commitment across the board.[15] Similarly, the acquisition of a dominant, excellent character trait need not—and probably should not—translate into an unbalanced lifestyle. As humans, we have both spiritual and physical needs that we must never deny. The goal of our Torah is to help us sanctify all aspects of our existence, and we can only do that if we participate in all normal human activities and care for all normal human needs: study and prayer; community and family; economic activity and physical exercise. By definition, this requires striking some balance. Naturally, some people will find their equilibrium in one place and other people with find their equilibrium in another. The point of equilibrium will also shift at different times in a person's life. Your balance this year will be very different from your balance in the first year of medical school. But no one may ever ignore any basic category altogether.

Character traits are different, because as I noted above, they are not the actions that we do, as much as they are the attitudes and sensitivities with which we invest every action. Whether your focus is kindness, or joy, or awe, or humility, you need to pray, eat, and hold down an honest job. Of course, the actions themselves will be colored by the attitude that informs them. That's the way you make

---

15. Note that in the classical system of Rabbi Moshe Chaim Luzzatto's *Mesillat Yesharim*, the trait of *perishut* (separation)—in which a person accepts upon himself extra-legal stringencies—follows the trait of *nekiut* (cleanliness). In cleanliness a person acquires a practical commitment to all the details of the full spectrum of Jewish law. At that point he is referred to as "righteous," a *tzaddik*. Separation is the first step towards the higher level of saintliness, *hasidut*.

your personal mark on the commandments, the reason why the heavenly hosts will distinguish your blessing on an apple from that of your friend. So focus and excellence in one trait does not imply and should not encourage lack of balance in behavior. If fact, the real glory is when you are able to apply that one great trait in diverse circumstances: kindness, for example, with a roommate, and in class, and at a wedding, and at a funeral, and alone with God in prayer.

Rule 3: Be Extreme, Take It Easy

Not only should you pick something easy to work on, you should take it easy while you work on it. This principle is both essential and a bit complex so allow me to elaborate.

Knowing—intellectually—the definition and importance of any given trait is one matter, and making that intellectual discovery was part of what we discussed in the chapter on Rosh Hashanah. Our job now is to take that knowledge and to integrate it into what Rabbi Gershenfeld has termed our "spontaneous emotional response system." Our tradition teaches several methods for translating ideals into character (and character into action), and we will deal with several of them in chapter 12, but the most basic method is behavioral. We become kind by behaving kindly; we become organized by behaving organized. The whole system of commandments trains us to be virtuous in this way, and is one reason why God gave us so many different commandments to perform[16]:

> בראשית רבה פרשה מד
> רב אמר לא נתנו המצות אלא
> לצרף בהן את הבריות. וכי מה
> איכפת ליה להקב"ה למי ששוחט
> מן הצואר, או מי ששוחט מן
> העורף, הוי לא נתנו המצות אלא
> לצרף בהם את הבריות:

---

16. See Maimonides, "Eight Chapters," chapter 4.

Rav said, the commandments were only given in order to refine the creations. Is God affected if one slaughters and animal from the throat[17] or if one slaughters an animal from behind?! Rather the commandments were only given in order to refine the creations (*Bereishit Rabbah* 44).

Sometimes, however, the performance of commandments is not enough, and we have to adopt deliberate behaviors that match the trait that we need to enhance. At first they feel artificial, and you think everyone around you perceives that you are acting strangely. Then they become second nature.

I remember when I was a child I spoke with a very strong lisp. Whenever someone would point out to me that I should say "sss" and not "thhh" I would try it, but the correct pronunciation just sounded weird, wrong. So I continued to talk in my own special way, which to me sounded perfect. When I was eight years old, I decided to trust all the adults and to do it their way. For a couple of weeks I felt like I was talking ridiculously, but I persevered. After a while, the correct pronunciation became natural and sounded normal to me, and the lisp sounded strange.

Working on character is not so different. You have to behave with a virtue that feels artificial for quite a while until it becomes natural. ("What? Not gossip?! What am I going to talk about?! I'm going to sound strange!") Unfortunately, the correction of bad habits is considerably more complicated and stressful than the correction of a lisp. In part, the difficulty arises from the need not just to adopt virtuous behavior, but to adopt deliberately *exaggerated* behavior. This will feel weird to you and perhaps look weird to others for one good reason: It is weird.

---

17. According to the laws of ritual slaughter.

The Rambam probably best detailed this method and explained the psychological mechanics behind it. His famous formulation is worth citing at length:

And know that these virtues and vices of character will be acquired and assimilated into the soul by repeating the actions that [normally] stem from that trait many times, over an extended period, until we have become accustomed to them. If the actions are good, we will have acquired a virtue; and if the actions are bad, we will have acquired a vice.... And if this person's soul has already become ill,

שמונה פרקים לרמב"ם פרק ד

ודע, כי אלו המעלות והפחיתויות אשר
למידות, אמנם ייקנו ויתישבו בנפש, בחזרה על
הפעולות ההוות מזו המידה פעמים רבות בזמן
ארוך, והתרגלנו אליהן. ואם יהיו הפעולות
ההן טובות - יהיה הנקנה לנו מעלה, ואם יהיו
רעות - יהיה הנקנה לנו פחיתו... ויהיה האיש
הזה כבר חלתה נפשו - צריך שינהג ברפואתו
כדרך רפואת הגופות בשווה. וכמו שהגוף,
כאשר יצא משיווי, נראה אל איזה צד נטה
ויצא, ונעמוד כנגדו בהפכו, עד שישוב אל
השיווי; וכשישתווה, נסלק ידינו מאותו ההפך,
ונשוב לעשות לו מה שישאירהו על שיווי -
כן נעשה במידות בשווה. משל זה: אם נראה
אדם שנקנתה לו תכונה בנפשו, יקמץ בעבורה
עם עצמו, וזוהי פחיתות מפחיתויות הנפש,
והמעשה אשר יעשהו מפעולות הרע, כמו
שבארנו בזה הפרק. הנה כאשר נרצה לרפא זה
החולי, לא נצווהו בעין יפה, שזה כמי שירפא
מי שגבר עליו החום בדבר השווה, וזה לא
יבריאהו מחוליו. ואמנם ראוי להניעו לעשות
פעולת הבזבוז פעם אחר פעם, ותיכפל עליו
פעולת הבזבוז כמה פעמים, עד שתסור מנפשו
התכונה המחייבת הקמצנות. וכמעט שתיקנה
לו תכונת הבזבוז, או יהיה קרוב אליה; ואז
נסלק ממנו פעולות הבזבוז, ונצווהו להתמיד על
פעולות העין היפה, ויקבלן על עצמו לעולם,
ולא יותיר ולא יחסר.

he must act therapeutically, exactly as one would heal the body. When the body has lost its equilibrium, we will see to which side it has turned; we counter this imbalance with the opposite until equilibrium is reestablished. We then stop acting in this opposite way and continue behaving in a balanced way. So too with character. For example: if we see a person that is overly acquisitive (and this is a vice of character and the acts that he does are bad as we have explained in this chapter), and we wish to heal this disease, we will not command him to act generously. This would be like treating a fever with a moderate [temperature]. Rather it would be appropriate to command him to squander his property time and again, and he should repeat this action of squandering until the trait that has brought him to acquisitiveness has been removed from his soul—until he has almost acquired the trait of wastefulness, or close to it. Then we will stop him from squandering his property and we will command him to act consistently with generosity, and so should he then behave constantly—neither too much nor too little (Maimonides, *Shemonah Perakim*, Chapter 4).

According to the Rambam, our traits should be balanced and not too extreme in either direction, with the result that our behavior will be moderate as well.[18] One should eat not too much, nor too little. One should be willing to take reasonable risks, give a reasonable amount of charity, etc. The Golden Mean is the virtuous path of moderation and vice is a deviation from that mean. The Rambam famously prescribed that we should counter a vice—an immoderate extremism by definition—by temporarily adopting its opposing extreme.

So much for the theory. In practice this advice needs to be qualified carefully. As Rabbi Shlomo Wolbe pointed out,[19] the sudden adoption of extreme behavior can be psychologically traumatic for anyone. This is especially so for one who is already overbalanced in the other

---

18. The exeptions are arrogance and anger, which should be completely avoided.
19. *Alei Shur* II p. 190.

Rabbi Elijah ben Solomon Zalman Kramer (1720–1797) is known as the Vilna Gaon ("the Master of Vilna") or by the acronym "Gra." He was one of the most influential rabbis of the modern period, being a brilliant and prolific talmudist, halachist, and kabbalist. He was also the foremost leader of the mitnagdic reaction against the excesses of the early Chasidic movement. Through his student Rabbi Chaim of Volozhin, the Gra was one of the founders of the modern yeshiva system. He sent students to settle the Land of Israel, so many of the customs in Jerusalem today are *minhag ha-Gra*.

direction. You have a lot to accomplish this year both in your personal development and in your studies. You don't want to burn too much psychological energy on exercises that are simply too difficult. What's more, the shock to the system could easily lead to despair or rebellion.

When I was a student in yeshiva I had the opportunity to study *Mishlei* (Proverbs) with the commentary of the Vilna Gaon. In this work, the Gaon emphasized repeatedly the need for a person to refine his character. In his commentary to *Mishlei* 4:16, he defined the purpose of life as follows: "and if he doesn't strengthen himself, for what does he live?" Again, in his comments to *Mishlei* 4:26, the Gaon taught that just as a merchant moves the weight of his scale bit by bit until the scale balances, so one who is working on character must accustom himself bit by bit. Puzzled, I asked one of my teachers, an elderly, sensitive scholar, "Doesn't the advice of the Gaon contradict the advice of the Rambam. The Rambam said that we should go to the extreme; the Gaon said that we should go slowly."

Working on Character

My kind teacher looked at me with a quizzical expression that seemed to say, "Child, have you never actually worked on your character yourself? Do you have so little practical experience in these matters that you could possibly entertain such a question? Do you only know books, but not yourself?" (OK, so maybe I'm reading into his facial expression too much—but that's what it felt like.)

In fact, what he actually responded was both elegant and obvious. "You must go to the extreme... but, slowly."

I was reminded of summer camp when I was ten years old. One of the counselors of the waterfront staff was making himself a pair of water-skis in the woodworking shop. For a ten-year-old, any twenty-year-old counselor appears heroic, but this guy was so cool he was more like a demi-god. I still remember his method. He took two planks and put the tips of each of them in a large curved vice, and then put the whole apparatus into a tub of water. Every day he would take the boards, tighten the vice a little more, and put the boards back into the tub. Slowly they would warp into the desired shape, but the curve was wildly exaggerated. No one would want water-skis with tips so radically warped. Still, every day he would turn the screws just a bit, and put the boards back into the tub. After about a month the vice was tight and the tips curved up crazily. When he removed the vice the tips leveled out considerably, but much of the curve held. The skis had warped perfectly.

Wood is organic, and like all organic things it changes slowly. Had my counselor turned the screws all the way on the first day the board would have snapped. Had he not taken them to an extreme, the adjustment would not have held. He therefore warped the boards to the extreme, but slowly. We humans are also organic. We also need to move slowly otherwise we risk snapping. Similarly, since we may have internalized bad habits over the course of many years, we need to overbalance for a while just to be normal.

So when you pick a project, find little exercises that will continually challenge you, but that will never break you. There should be a constant sense of psychic resistance, a little tug, but never real strain. Certainly not pain.

Let me give you a practical example. My first year in yeshiva I had the good fortune to study Rabbi Moshe Chaim Luzzatto's *Mesillat Yesharim* with Rabbi Beryl Gershenfeld. At one point we were discussing the level of growth termed *perishut*, "separation." In this level we attempt to break our addiction to physical pleasure though ascetic exercises. Judaism teaches that we must not deny our physical side; we can and even should use the pleasures of the physical world for spiritual good. Nevertheless, just like you can't use your car properly if you are a speed demon, and you can't use alcohol properly if you are an alcoholic, so you can't use the physical world optimally if you are addicted to physical pleasure. Deliberate acts of "separation" can be very important habit-breaking exercises at some point in your spiritual development.

Once again, that's the theory. What—I asked Rabbi Gershenfeld— might be a legitimate application for a student like myself? After some discussion we came up with the following. Every day at 4:00 p.m. the yeshiva took a quick break for coffee and tea, and I always had a cup of tea with two teaspoons of sugar. We concluded that for some time, as an exercise, I would have only one teaspoon of sugar. These are empty calories anyway, pure physical pleasure. The tea would still be sweet. The sacrifice would be small. But there would be a slight psychic tug, a little challenge that would begin the process. When it became too easy, it might be time to give up the first spoon of sugar as well.

This might sound ridiculously trivial. "This is Jewish ethics?" you might ask. How could I take pride in such a petty exercise? Here, ironically, is another advantage of small actions: they are so small that they cannot lead to hubris. If anything, the fact that even they are often challenging can be quite humbling.

Now that the winter term has begun, you have time to choose a project and to become an active participant in your own self-creation. Take some time to introspect. Think about your strengths and weaknesses; locate your potential greatness. Once you have done that, get some advice from someone you respect. Together you can pick one trait that speaks to you and find some appropriate exercises. As you try to become an expert, you may have to be a little extreme for a while. Keep in mind that such extremism is not a Jewish ideal, but it is a very necessary means. And make certain to move to that extreme deliberately and slowly.

Chapter 6

Kindness in the Little Things

Being a Good Roommate and Guest

The month before I got married, Rabbi Gershenfeld donated several hours of his very precious time to discuss with me some of the secrets of a good marriage. One passage in the Rambam made a particular impression, not only because of the classic concepts but also because of the spin my Rebbe put on it: "And so did the Sages command that a husband should honor his wife more than himself and love her as himself…" (*Hilchot Ishut*, ch. 15).

"You have to honor your wife like a queen. Your wife is a queen," he told me. "And you know what this means? This means that you must never leave your dirty socks on the floor. You wouldn't leave your dirty socks on the floor in front of a queen; you must never leave your dirty socks on the floor in front of your wife."

I couldn't believe my ears. Here in the Rambam was printed one of the must idealistic visions for marital bliss. What a lofty ideal: love your wife like yourself; honor her more than you honor yourself. And Rabbi Gershenfeld reduced it to dirty socks!

And of course, that's what made this such a fantastic and memorable teaching. The Rambam's vision was truly lofty, and my Rebbe, a master educator, realized that just such ethereal ideals are the most in danger of gently floating out the window and out of sight. The solution is to anchor them to the ground, quickly and firmly, by some mundane and practical application. In this case, Rabbi Gershenfeld never intended the sock application to be exclusive. You don't fulfill the command of the Sages by just picking up socks; but if you do leave your socks on the floor, then you haven't even begun, and all your lofty idealism isn't worth much.

Maintaining these two perspectives is one of the greatest challenges to a creative life. We need to get the big picture for inspiration and direction. Sometimes we need to back away from the trees in order to see the whole towering, magnificent forest. But if we want to build the forest, we can only do it one seed at a time. Sometimes I'll go to an art museum and I'll find myself moving back and forth before one painting for a quarter of an hour. First I'll look at the painting, then I'll move in and look at the brush strokes, then I'll move back again and see how all the dabs of paint blend harmoniously and seamlessly into one another, then I'll come close again to study how one detail was executed. Back and forth.

Where is the greatness of the painting: in the overall vision, or in the individual brush strokes? Clearly, in both. Real art is a product of inspiration expressed through a collection of small, mundane dabs of paint.

In 1914, Mrs. Claude Bennington of London sat for a portrait painted by one of the greatest American painters, John Singer Sargent. This is how she described the master's painting method: "He would dash on some lines with the charcoal, rub out with the French roll, occasionally retreat to the far end of the studio and then almost run at the portrait."

Sargent would check the match of the painting to the original model by frequently distancing himself from them both. He would consider both, and then take all his creative energy and "dash" at the canvas, sometimes to execute only a single stroke, while the vision was still fresh in his mind's eye.

Now imagine standing at the back of the studio as Sargent began his work:

A dab of blue… A smear of red.

"Bravo!" we all shout. "Brilliant! Masterful!"

Um, well, probably not. So far, the "painting" is just a mess. Is that Mrs. Claude Bennington's strong, noble chin emerging from the canvas… or is it four dogs playing poker? Hard to tell. But that's the nature of art. While it's happening it just doesn't look so artful.

To create a work of art, a great painter needs to oscillate constantly between a broad inspiring perspective, and a particular disciplined and seemingly mundane brush stroke. To create a life that is full of ethical beauty, we need to do the same thing: we need to oscillate between a broad inspiring vision of human majesty, and particular actions that, when viewed out of context, might seem mundane and uninteresting.

A Deeper Look at Ethical Greatness

Anyone who is at all aware of the human greatness inside of him or her will look at our troubled world and will feel driven to make a difference. God created us all in His image, and one explanation of this identity is that we have each been made a creator of worlds, like God. Therefore, when we look at the condition of our people in particular and of humanity in general, and are inspired to act, we are naturally expressing the most fundamental aspect of ourselves, our hidden divinity.

When we look at the historical leaders of our people, men like Moshe and Avraham, we recognize that these people not only changed our nation, but they changed the world. How did they do it? What inner strengths made them great ethical leaders; what external actions gave life to their inner visions?

Kindness in the Little Things

The Midrash describes God's testing young David and Moshe, to see if they would be worthy leaders. Their striking example deserves to be quoted at length:

"God will test the righteous" (Psalms 11) — How does He test him: through shepherding sheep. He examined David with sheep and found him a beautiful shepherd, as is written, "and He took him from the sheep pens" (Psalms 78).... He held back the older ones before the younger ones, and took out the younger ones to graze so that they could eat the soft grass. Afterwards he took out the elders so that they could eat the medium grass, then he took out the mature ones who

מדרש רבה שמות פרשה ב פסקה ב
(שם) ה' צדיק יבחן ובמה הוא בוחנו במרעה צאן בדק לדוד ומצאו רועה יפה שנא' (תהלים עח) ויקחהו ממכלאות צאן מהו ממכלאות צאן כמו (בראשית ח) ויכלא הגשם היה מונע הגדולים מפני הקטנים והיה מוציא הקטנים לרעות כדי שירעו עשב הרך ואחר כך מוציא הזקנים כדי שירעו עשב הבינונית ואח"כ מוציא הבחורים שיהיו אוכלין עשב הקשה אמר הקב"ה מי שהוא יודע לרעות הצאן איש לפי כחו יבא וירעה בעמי הה"ד (תהלים עח) מאחר עלות הביאו לרעות ביעקב עמו ואף משה לא בחנו הקב"ה אלא בצאן אמרו רבותינו כשהיה מרע"ה רועה צאנו של יתרו במדבר ברח ממנו גדי ורץ אחריו עד שהגיע לחסות כיון שהגיע לחסות נזדמנה לו בריכה של מים ועמד הגדי לשתות כיון שהגיע משה אצלו אמר אני לא הייתי יודע שרץ היית מפני צמא עיף אתה הרכיבו על כתיפו והיה מהלך אמר הקב"ה יש לך רחמים לנהוג צאנו של בשר ודם כך חייך אתה תרעה צאני ישראל הוי ומשה היה רועה

would eat the tough grass. The Holy One, Blessed be He, said, "One who knows to shepherd sheep each according to his strength will come and shepherd My nation...."

Moshe too was tested only with sheep. Our Rabbis said, when Moshe shepherded the sheep of Yitro in the desert, a kid escaped from him and he ran after him until he came to a protected area. When he arrived in the protected area, he chanced upon a pool of water. The kid stopped to drink. When Moshe caught up to him he said, "I did not know that you were running because you were thirsty; you must be tired." He placed him on his shoulder and began walking. The Holy One, Blessed be He, said, "You have mercy to lead the sheep of flesh and blood; so, by your life, you will shepherd my sheep, Israel" (*Shemot Rabbah* 2:2).

This famous and beautiful Midrash has been studied and taught for over one thousand years, and one master after another, each in his own way, has drawn from it profound life lessons. One of the greatest teachers of the twentieth century was Rabbi Nosson Zvi Finkel, affectionately referred to as the Elder of Slabodka, or simply the "Alter." The Alter learned from this midrash[20] that human greatness stems not from boldly dramatic actions, but from consistent, small kindnesses. This is why the Torah pays such attention to our historical leaders' care for animals. Teaching in the direct tradition of the Alter, Rabbi Shlomo Wolbe lectured that just as the loftiest mountains are composed of invisible atoms, so ethical greatness is simply a composite of good actions, each one of which is so small it can be easily overlooked.

If we were to witness Moshe that day in the desert, we might have responded, "Isn't that nice how he took care of that lamb? He must be quite a sweet man and a dedicated shepherd." We would probably perceive the act as simple kindness: more compassionate than usual perhaps, but not so far out of the ordinary. I am certain that in similar circumstances many of us would have acted the same way. Have none of us ever shown kindness to a pet? Of course we have. Why then

---

20. See his work *Or ha-Tzafun* 2:1.

was Moshe's life so different from ours, so perfect?

This midrash teaches that Moshe did not live such a noble life by punctuating it with a few dramatic actions, just as Sargent did not paint masterworks by punctuating them with a few magnificent strokes. God did not choose Moshe *because* he left the luxury of Pharaoh's palace to stand beside his people, or even because he risked his own life when he killed a taskmaster to save

Rabbi Nosson Tzvi Finkel (1849–1927) is known as the Alter ("Elder") of Slabodka. He was a student of the Alter of Kelm. His yeshiva, Knesses Yisroel, was the ultimate *musar* yeshiva, fostering spiritual growth through both Talmud study, and a direct focus on character building. He moved his yeshiva to Hebron (it later moved to Jerusalem, where it is known as the Hebron Yeshiva, or by its original name, Knesses Yisroel). He was a master educator and his students included the following rabbis: Eliezer Yehuda Finkel (Mir); Yitzchok Hutner (Chaim Berlin); Yaakov Kamenetsky (Torah Vodaas); Aaron Kotler (Lakewood); Dovid Leibowitz (Chofetz Chaim); Yaakov Yitzchok Ruderman (Ner Yisroel); Yechezkel Sarna (Hebron Yeshiva), Yechiel Yaakov Weinberg (Hildesheimer Rabbinical Seminary).

an oppressed Jew. Rather, it seems that Moshe's life was so noble because it was a continuous series of little kindnesses, each one almost insignificant by itself.

Just as in a painting: If we look at the picture only from up close we see the technique, but we miss the great vision in the "petty" brush strokes; if we look only from afar we see great periods of development and change, but we never know how to learn from them, how to emulate them. Only if we zoom in and out do we see both the great vision and the deliberate method. Similarly, Tanach zooms out and tells us about Moshe's mission; the rabbis zoom in and teach us about his method.

Similarly, perhaps the greatest leader in Tanach is David. He so personified the character of leadership that his is the eternal Jewish monarchy. When someone's personality is so infused with a certain attribute, that attribute expresses itself in all that the person does, in every relationship he has. When you are King David, the attributes of bravery and responsibility do not lay dormant, waiting passively until unleashed by some dramatic confrontation. When you are King David, the attribute of altruistic leadership does not lay dormant waiting for the next crisis. Instead, these attributes inform every encounter and every relationship. They direct the shepherding of sheep in the pasture, just as they direct the deployment of forces on the battlefield.

In the examples of Moshe and David, we see an interesting relationship between Tanach (the written scripture) and the Midrash (the corresponding interpretation in the oral tradition). The function of the written law is often to reveal the big picture. It is, after all, written, revealed, and therefore it communicates truths that are more publicized. In that big, revealed picture, we see the dramatic inflection points in the lives of our great leaders and teachers. We see the wars, and the plagues, and the self-sacrifice. In contrast, the Rabbis of the Midrash tend to examine on the same biblical lives from a more hidden—and more practical—perspective: how did these leaders slowly achieve their great status; how did they eat breakfast on the day before the war, or the plague, or the great self-sacrifice? The Torah is written from these two perspectives because for us to develop, to learn from Moshe and David, we need both. Just as we draw on inspiration from the high drama of the written Tanach, so too we need to learn to act with the small consistent kindnesses revealed by the Oral Law.

The *Chesed* of Avraham

This principle, that we need overarching inspiration together with small consistent action, holds true for any virtue that we might hope to acquire. In this chapter, I wish to continue emphasizing the importance of this principle for acquiring the virtue of kindness. To that end, I would like to turn to the patriarch Avraham, since the tradition often cites him as the very personification of this virtue of kindness.

Avraham dedicated his life to kindness—what is often termed *chesed*, and translated as "grace"—and anyone familiar with the book of *Bereishit* could probably think of several good examples of his kindness with little effort. I have probably asked my classes the following question over a dozen times: "If you were the author of the Midrash and you wanted to cite a typical example of Avraham's *chesed*, what story would you choose?"

- The time 99-year-old Avraham scanned the horizon outside his desert tent, looking for travelers to host, in the midst of a heat wave, and only three days after his circumcision?
- The fact that Avraham continued to tolerate his money-grubbing nephew Lot, although his noxious presence interfered with Avraham's ability to receive prophecy?
- The time that Avraham stood in prayer and negotiated with God for the benefit of Sodom?

The Midrash passes over all these obvious examples and instead notes that Avraham buried his wife Sarah:

And afterwards Avraham buried — This is what is written, "One who pursues righteousness and kindness will find life, righteousness and honor" (Proverbs 21). *One who pursues righteousness* — This is Avraham.... *And kindness* — That he gave kindness to Sarah.... The Holy One, Blessed be He, said to him, "My craft is giving kindness: you have grasped My craft; come and wear My raiment...." *And Avraham was old of many days...* (*Bereishit Rabbah* 58:9).

מדרש רבה בראשית פרשה נח פסקה ט:
ואחרי כן קבר אברהם הה"ד (משלי כא)
רודף צדקה וחסד ימצא חיים צדקה וכבוד
רודף צדקה זה אברהם שנאמר ושמרו
דרך ה' לעשות צדקה וחסד שגמל חסד
לשרה ימצא חיים ושני חיי אברהם מאת
שנה ושבעים שנה וחמשה שנים צדקה
וכבוד אמר רבי שמואל בר יצחק אמר לו
הקב"ה אני אומנותי גומל חסדים תפסת
אומנותי בוא ולבוש לבושי "ואברהם זקן
בא בימים..."

At first glance, this Midrash seems strange. Any widower would bury his wife! Praising Avraham for this most basic courtesy is like praising Einstein for being able to multiply, like praising Babe Ruth for being able to walk around the bases. Perhaps the Midrash intended to highlight the *quality* of Avraham's kindness—the way he cared for Sarah, or the fact that he bought a special burial cave for her; but I don't see any clue in the Midrash itself to indicate that this was the emphasis. Instead, it seems to me that the Midrash lauded the burial itself, and that is puzzling.

We must conclude that the Midrash chose the example of Sarah's burial not because it was the most *dramatic* example of Avraham's kindness—for that, it could have cited the other examples I mentioned above—but because it was the most *typical*. Unfortunately, on the death of a loved one, too many of us pay not just our "final respects," but also our only respects. In the case of Avraham, his burial of Sarah was truly a final kindness in a lifelong series of little kindnesses, each of which addressed a genuine need. Presumably, Avraham demonstrated the same greatness in the way he spoke with Sarah, in the way cared for her clothing and living arrangements. In citing Sarah's burial, the Rabbis pointed out that despite the remarkable stories of Avraham's altruism found in the book of Genesis, the real greatness of Avraham stemmed from the consistency with which he performed small kindnesses. Like the burial of Sarah, these little acts of kindness hardly seem heroic on their own. When taken out of context, each one would hardly have been worth mentioning; but like small dabs of paint, when taken together they form a magnificent picture.

Here too we see the relationship between the focus of the written law and that of the oral law. The written law emphasizes Avraham's striking achievements; the oral law stresses the more mundane work required to develop the character that is able to accomplish those achievements.

In the case of kindness, that mundane common denominator seems to be a genuine concern with basic legitimate needs: lambs who need soft grass; a kid who needs water; a wife who needs a burial. Part of the artistry of the ethical master is his ability to identify those needs from the point of view of the needy. It is all too easy to give someone what *you* would have liked to receive. It is much more difficult to identify the basic and legitimate concern of the other.

One story from the life of Rabbi Akiva teaches this idea quite beautifully. The Talmud relates that once a student of R. Akiva fell ill. R. Akiva visited the student, and did something so special that the student later recovered and exclaimed, "Rabbi, you have given me life!" Let me ask you to guess what R. Akiva did, but while considering this, please recall a bit about R. Akiva as a person. He was

the teacher of both Rabbi Meir, to whom we credit most laws in the
Mishnah that were taught without any specific attribution, and Rabbi
Shimon bar Yochai, the period's greatest mystic. As their teacher, we
can only imagine that Rabbi Akiva had access to the most profound
knowledge of the legal and mystical traditions together. How then,
would someone like that save his ill student?

Did R. Akiva channel all his religious devotion and pray for a
speedy recovery?

Presumably he did, but that is not reported, nor did the student
thank him for that.

Did R. Akiva use his mystical knowledge to write a therapeutic
amulet or to fashion some other charm?

Again, the Talmud is silent on the matter.

Did R. Akiva learn Torah with the student, in the spirit of the
verse, "For they are life to those that find them, and healing to all
their flesh" (Proverbs 4:22)?

If he did, we have been told nothing about that either. Let's read
how R. Akiva saved his student's life according to the Talmud:

He said to them, wasn't thus the
case of the student of R. Akiva
who fell ill and the Sages did
not enter to visit him. And R.
Akiva went in to visit him. And
because he swept and mopped
the floor in front of him [the
ill student], he lived. He said
to him, "Rabbi, you have given
me life!" R. Akiva went out and
taught, "Whoever does not
visit the sick, is like one who
spills blood"... (BT *Nedarim* 40a).

תלמוד בבלי מסכת נדרים דף מ/א
אמר להו לא כך היה מעשה בתלמיד
אחד מתלמידי רבי עקיבא שחלה
לא נכנסו חכמים לבקרו ונכנס רבי
עקיבא לבקרו ובשביל שכיבדו
וריבצו לפניו חיה אמר לו רבי
החייתני יצא רבי עקיבא ודרש כל
מי שאין מבקר חולים כאילו שופך
דמים ...

The commentaries[21] teach that R. Akiva saw that the floor was filthy and moldy, and simply harmful to the health of the student. He ordered that they clean up, sweep, and mop the floor. This done, the air became refreshed and the student recovered. R. Akiva's action was shockingly simple, but that is the nature of true kindness—the sort of kindness for which the Patriarchs, Moshe, David, and R. Akiva were praised. Such kindness consists of small, mundane actions that are within the reach of anyone and everyone at any moment. The only difficulties lie in getting outside of one's own concerns in order to see the genuine concern of the other, and in maintaining consistency day in and day out.

R. Akiva, precisely because of his greatness, might have glided effortlessly into a role that is the caricature of a great sage. He might have overlooked the filth, recited his psalms and benedictions, said his "comforting" words of Torah and exited. But had he played that ostensibly "religious" role, he would have completely overlooked that which was critically important to his sick student. A truly religious man, R. Akiva was genuinely concerned with the needs of his student, and he responded accordingly, even if his perspective had to become somewhat janitorial.

The Other's Need

When R. Akiva focused on the filthy floor in his sick student's room, he did not do so because he had some compulsion for cleanliness. This was just the focus that R. Akiva had to adopt in that particular situation and was a particular application of a more general attitude towards other people. That general perspective, that ethical artistry, consists of a regular and compassionate focus on the genuine needs of others. Ethical greatness is no more than focusing on the normal, mundane needs of whomever you encounter: young lambs that prefer soft grass; sheep that

21. See *Shittah Mekubbetzet.*

desire water; a wife that needs a burial; an ill student who needs the floor swept. There is very little here that is obviously heroic. But that doesn't mean that the acquisition of such an extroverted perspective is easy.

For years, scientists believed that the sun revolves around the earth. Then we learned that the earth revolves around the sun. Unfortunately, most of us feel inside that all that exists revolves around each of us. Emotionally, the universe is neither geocentric nor heliocentric, but profoundly egocentric. Too often we visit the sick, and bury the dead, and feed the hungry... and all the time we are thinking: how does this make me look, how will this affect my permanent record? Even when we succeed in acting truly altruistically, we often define our friends' needs based on our own desires. As my father once formulated the problem: we might bring chocolates and flowers to a depressed friend, knowing that such a gesture would cheer *us* up; unfortunately, the depressed friend is both allergic and diabetic.

So, to break out of the gravity of our own inflated egos, to get outside of ourselves and see what someone else truly needs, is actually quite an achievement. But it is also an achievement that the Torah expects of us. Many of our commandments stand on this foundational perspective, and the more we labor to fulfill these commandments, the more we assimilate this perspective into our own beings. Charity, for example, is both a universally accepted virtue, and a specific Jewish commandment. Not surprisingly, the Torah formulates the commandment with an emphasis on this outward-looking perspective.

ספר דברים פרק טו

(ז) כי יהיה בך אביון מאחד אחיך באחד שעריך בארצך אשר ה' א-להיך נתן לך לא תאמץ את לבבך ולא תקפץ את ידך מאחיך האביון: (ח) כי פתח תפתח את ידך לו והעבט תעביטנו די מחסרו אשר יחסר לו:

רש"י שם

אשר יחסר לו - אפילו סוס לרכוב עליו ועבד לרוץ לפניו:

Kindness in the Little Things

> If there be among you a needy man, one of your brothers, within any of your gates, in your land which Hashem your God gives to you, you shall not harden your heart, nor shut your hand from your needy brother. But you shall surely open your hand to him, and shall surely lend him sufficient for his need in that which he lacks (*Devarim* 15: 7-8).

Rashi commented on this last clause, "in that which he lacks," finding it seemingly redundant; the verse could have ended, "and shall surely lend him sufficient for his need." (In fact, some gentile translations leave out the "extra" clause altogether!) But of course the Torah is never redundant. Rashi, based on a Midrash, explained that the final phrase comes to add an element of subjectivity to the wants of the poor man. When we give charity, we need not make the poor man rich, but we must care for whatever lack causes him subjective pain. We must give him that which *he* needs based on his previous lifestyle and expectations.

A very wealthy person who loses everything might be crushed not just by hunger, but by the need to walk on foot. We are commanded to care for such a person's wants from his perspective, and not just those necessities that would comfort us. In the words of Rashi from the tradition of Hillel the Elder: we should provide this person with "even a horse on which to ride and a servant to run before him." Naturally, in a world of scarce resources, we need to make sure that everyone is fed and clothed before we take care of one person's relative luxuries. Nevertheless, in a perfect world, we would provide for such luxuries as well, because in the eyes of the riches-to-rags pauper, they are not luxuries at all. The Talmud[22] even relates a story of the great sage Hillel running before the horse of such a man, playing the role of a steward in the spirit of this verse.

---

22. *Ketubot* 67b.

We might imagine that charity would be based on standard objective criteria: 2,000 calories a day, two pairs of trousers, two sets of shirts and underwear, one pair of shoes. But the commandment of charity was not given only in order to help the poor. After all, God can help the poor all by Himself. The commandment of charity was also given in a manner that helps the *commanded* develop his own character. In the case of charity, we are commanded to break out of our subjective standards, and even out of formal objective standards. The Torah commands us instead to view the person across from us as he views himself. Having cultivated that perspective we can then care for the little genuine needs, and often highly subjective needs, of everyone whom we encounter.

The Danger of Art Appreciation

Many people appreciate art. You can imagine going to some gallery on the opening night of a new exhibition. Everyone is milling around, holding glasses of champagne, and speaking in weighty tones about the symbolism in this work or the technique in that. Everyone is so absorbed by art around them that you can almost forget that none of them have ever *produced* anything themselves. They love art. They understand art. But the difference between an art critic and an artist is whether one is then willing to do the little uninspiring brush strokes in order to create a painting. The art critic spends so much time talking about art that he never really creates anything of beauty himself. True, you need to appreciate a finished work in order to become motivated, but ultimately you need to roll up your sleeves and get working.

Many of us are taking our first steps towards ethical artistry. And the first step is becoming inspired with the greatness of the Patriarchs and the Matriarchs. After that initial inspiration, we then need to guard ourselves from the dangers of becoming "Torah critics."

I remember when I was first becoming observant and was so impressed with the idealism I found in the Orthodox community.

Kindness in the Little Things

Then I met a young woman who told me that as much as I felt inspired, she felt disenchanted. She told me that the people she knew were apathetic when it came to acting with *chesed*, with genuine kindness.

I responded, "How can you say that? Every other speech, in synagogue or at the Shabbat table is about *chesed*!"

To which she replied, "Oh, sure—they *talk* about it."

One of the dangers of being an art critic is that you can fool yourself into believing that *your* life has something to do with art. Similarly, one of the dangers of becoming sensitive to the greatness of the Torah is that we can trick ourselves in to believing that we are living up to the example of the Patriarchs just by learning about them. This is not Torah; this is "Torah Criticism."

Certainly we need to learn. Each of us needs to ask: am I spending enough time back away from the picture, so that I can find inspiration and perspective, so that my actions will be deliberate and guided towards creating a cohesive work of beauty?

But afterwards, we need to ask just as critically: do I take all of that inspired creative energy and then use it to lunge at the canvas— to daub a seemingly insignificant drop of extroverted kindness on the life of another person?

You can tell that you are off balance if at the Shabbat table you are so involved in the discussion about Avraham's *chesed* that you leave the hosts to clear away all the dishes by themselves while you continue to talk to the other guests.

I've actually seen this happen.

In fact, Shabbat in general is a great time to test this balance. As a guest, you are naturally in the position of a passive "taker." Try to overcome this by finding little genuine needs in your host's lives. Try to transform yourself into a giver. This transformation is much more difficult than just bringing a box of chocolates that your hosts probably don't need and could have bought themselves. This transformation will require you to demonstrate real empathy. After all, you are unmarried, you don't have little children, nor do you regularly host guests yourself. Naturally, you have very little idea of what stresses are acting on your hosts. As an aspiring ethical artist, you have to step back from the canvas and ask yourself: what little things do my hosts genuinely need, perhaps even more than that box of chocolate.

You can't cheat either. You can't just literally lift examples from Tanach and hope to apply them here. Your hosts most likely don't need soft grass, water, or a burial.

Instead, you will need to reflect and consider, to find an equivalent desire in the life of the person across from you. By finding some genuine little need you can adopt, both in quality and in kind, the greatness of Avraham, David, and Moshe. Permit me to make a few recommendations, some of which might be more appropriate for young men and others more appropriate for women:

- Don't ask if you can help do the dishes. Many hosts would be too embarrassed to accept. Just start doing them. You needn't worry: unless your hosts are very well off and have a couple of maids in the kitchen, no one will be offended. The alternative is that the host will do the dishes while you sit down to converse about the kindness of the Patriarchs. And that would be simply ridiculous. (This example applies to both men and women.)
- Entertain or otherwise distract the kids. Dirty dishes cause much less stress than hyperactive kids do. Read them a book, ask to see their toys, take them for a walk. They might be shy or reticent. Keep trying; they will come around. I've heard many exchanges where a guest says, "Can I read you a book," and the kid replies, "No," and the guest feels like he has fulfilled his obligation. He hasn't. That's just the beginning of a little dance in which you get to know the child and the child gets to know you.

- Get the kids out of the house so that the parents can have a nap. Most young parents have far more stressed lives than you do and can use some rest. If you feel like you need to rest yourself, nap on Friday afternoon, or go to bed early Wednesday night. There is no reason why you can't prepare for your *chesed* twenty-four hours in advance by taking a nap or (dare I suggest it?) going to bed on time.

- Don't ask if you can help prepare for Shabbat when you arrive half an hour before candle lighting time. The food is probably cooked by then. Instead, ask when you are invited if you can come Friday morning to help prepare. Of course, an hour before Shabbat might be a great time to help set the table or to make a salad.

- Make sure to bring a *dvar Torah*.

- Remember some of the people you went to for Shabbat this year on the week *before* Passover, when everyone could use some help cleaning. I'm sure they would love to see you again.

SCENE: Late Friday Night

Wrong

STUDENT/GUEST: So, when do you have lunch tomorrow?

HOST: We say Kiddush about 11:00. Looking forward to seeing you then.

STUDENT: Great, see you after services! Good Shabbat.

Right

STUDENT/GUEST: So, when do you have lunch tomorrow?

HOST: We say Kiddush about 11:00. Looking forward to seeing you then.

STUDENT: Great, see you after services! I'll come by at about 10:40 to help set the table. Please leave that for me. Good Shabbat!

Please note that none of these examples are any more or any less dramatic than the actions of the Avraham, David, and Moshe we saw above. They really are not. Don't think that the virtue of these great people is beyond your grasp, because my simple suggestions are just the kinds of things that they did. What made those people so great is that they did these actions with such consistency. That's the challenge for you as well. To take this year and make it an art studio by becoming inspired and then by doing the drab work of little genuine kindnesses consistently.

By making your bed for the sake of your roommate, by making sure not to leave dirty dishes in the sink, you are really participating in acts of *chesed* that are biblical in their proportions. The trick is making them a regular part of your lives. That is ethical artistry.

Postscript: The General Rule of the Torah

In several places, the Rabbis of the Midrash discuss the commandment they consider to be an overarching, all-encapsulating, general principle. All the commandments are holy, but one somehow summarizes all the rest, and if you can grab onto it, you've grabbed onto them all.

The problem is that the Rabbis disagree on which commandment is that general rule, that *klal gadol*. A relatively obscure Midash (brought by the Maharal) recounts a three-way argument, which is ultimately resolved in favor of one opinion.

Ben Zoma says, "We have found a more encompassing verse, and that is 'Hear O Israel.'" Ben Nanas says, "We have found a more encompassing verse and that is, 'You shall love your neighbor as yourself.'" Shimon Ben Pazzi says, "we have found a more encompassing verse and that is, 'and you shall offer the one sheep in the morning' etc." Rabbi Ploni rose and proclaimed, "the law is like Ben Pazi, as is written, 'like everything that I have shown you, the design of the tabernacle,' etc."

ספר נתיבות עולם ב - נתיב אהבת ריע - פרק א
ותמצא בחבור עין יעקב בהקדמת הכותב שמצא בחבור מדרש אחד וז"ל, בן זומא אומר מצינו פסוק כולל יותר והוא שמע ישראל וגו'. בן ננס אומר מצינו פסוק כולל יותר והוא ואהבת לרעך כמוך. שמעון בן פזי אומר מצינו פסוק כולל יותר והוא את הכבש האחד תעשה בבקר וגו'. עמד ר' פלוני על רגליו ואמר הלכה כבן פזי דכתיב ככל אשר אני מראה אותך את תבנית המשכן וגו'.

The first opinion mentioned emphasizes the theological: the unity of God and the unique relationship that Israel has with Him. According to Ben Zoma, one who is aware of God's presence in everything, how all existence stems from Him and returns to Him, will meditate on his Creator, love Him and cling to Him, "with all your heart, and with all of your soul, and with all of your might." He will never stray from the proper path because he is acutely aware that there is no other path.

This is a profoundly moving and religious ideal, but Ben Nanas thinks that it still falls short. Instead of the theological, Ben Nanas emphasizes the ethical dimension of the Torah, summarized in one of Judaism's greatest gifts to the world, "you shall love your neighbor as yourself." Why settle for meditating *on* God and His infinite kindnesses towards the world, when instead you can act *like* God by performing acts of kindness yourself, based on His divine model. After all, the verse concludes, "love your neighbor as yourself, *I am God.*" A mystical experience may be rich and fulfilling, but it can also be paralyzing as you sense your individuality dissolve into God's infinite oneness. God Himself, however, is far from paralyzed. Ben Nanas suggests that you can actually be closer to God by being as much like Him as is humanly possible: active and giving. As the

Rabbis teach, you can actually "cling" to Him by feeding the hungry, clothing the naked, and healing the infirm.[23]

As lofty as this ideal seems, Ben Pazzi believed that this too falls short, but it is hard to understand how the verse that he cites is more all-encompassing. If fact, it sounds downright prosaic: "you shall offer one sheep in the morning, and the second sheep in the afternoon." We have gone from meditating on God, and then acting like God to... sacrificing two sheep? The point is, of course, that the verse about the sheep commands not just any sacrifice; this verse is a quotation from the portion of the daily offering, the *korban tamid*, which literally translates as the "continual offering." This was a relatively modest sacrifice, considering that it was brought on behalf of the entire nation: one sheep in the morning and another in the afternoon. Nevertheless, this sacrifice had a remarkably powerful effect on the world. Like the acts of kindness we've been discussing in this chapter, its influence was not a function of size, but of consistency. It was offered *every* morning and *every* afternoon, and therefore serves as a model for religious artistry.

Ben Pazzi might agree that Ben Zoma's ideal, symbolized by the *Shema*, is great. But this great ideal can only be realized through deliberate and consistent attention. After all, anyone can have a mystical high from time to time; only when it permeates one's existence can it truly be called "religious."

Similarly, each of us can act kindly on occasion, when the spirit moves us. In a shining moment we might even love our neighbor as ourselves. But any individual will be *identified* as "kind" only if he or she makes this attribute a consistent (if modest) part of the daily routine.

The Midrash seems to conclude that Ben Pazzi was the most correct. The Torah rarely calls on us to perform dramatically heroic

---

23. See, for example BT *Shabbat* 133b and Rashi on *Devarim* 13:5.

acts, but it does expect us to modify our behavior, slowly and deliberately, and by doing so to change our own identities. We can be art critics and ethics critics, or we can be ethical artists. It all depends on the small sacrifices that we are willing to offer every morning and afternoon.

Chapter 7

Seder

Order as the Moral Starter Set

Chapter 5 discussed picking one moral attribute and working on that, and that alone, for a significant amount of time. I suggested choosing something that comes easily, something that is closest to your individual, essential greatness.

If you've actually tried this, you may have discovered another problem that makes progress difficult, if not impossible: few of us know how to "work" on anything.

As it turns out, there is one character trait that is the requisite catalyst for the successful development of all the other traits, and unless you find that it comes naturally you might well choose to work on that first. This trait is called "*seder*," which loosely translates as "order" or "organization." Unfortunately, this translation makes me think exclusively of daily planners and those little plastic pencil holders that sit atop overly neat desks. *Seder* relates to the inner life as much as it does to desktop management, and it is effectively the "starter set" that anyone involved in personal development needs to acquire in order to get down to work.

Some people in business school refer to this concept as "time-management," but in reality it is "self-management." After all, you cannot master the clock; it is going to keep on ticking no matter what you do. But you can master yourself and use your valuable time more efficiently.

What's great about this trait is how useful it is in every aspect of life. No matter what profession you choose to enter, no matter where you live, in peace-time or in war-time, if you are an organized person you will be able to navigate any situation more constructively, efficiently, and creatively. You can be in business, law, health-sciences, or education, and if you master this topic you will act better, and with greater calm, and you will climb to the top of your profession. You can be a parent, a spouse, a child, a brother or just a good friend, and if you pay attention to just a few of the ideas in this chapter, your relationships will become deeper and more meaningful.

Organization as Motivation

In anything you ever do, be it in college, yeshiva, or business, you will need three ingredients in order to be successful: opportunity, ability, and motivation.

Today, most of us have extraordinarily wide opportunity. Western countries generally, and the United States in particular, are the most free and affluent countries in history. You can choose your profession and life-style, your city and neighborhood. Many U.S. presidents have come from the most humble roots, as have many of the world's wealthiest individuals listed in the Forbes 500. So the age of serfdom is over; the walls of the ghetto have fallen. Today, you may travel as you wish, study as you wish, and work as you wish. And yes, worship as you wish. This gives you an awesome opportunity, and an awesome responsibility.

On the other hand, we do not all have equal ability. Not everyone can be successful in everything; but everyone can be exceptional in something. God made us with diverse talents because we can better honor Him with diverse service—within the structure of the law, of course. As you study Torah and refine your character, you will slowly divorce yourself of your biases and fantasies. Then you will be better able to evaluate where you should invest your time and effort. Rabbenu Bachya, in his classic *Duties of the Heart* (eleventh-century Spain), clearly states that each individual should choose his profession based on his natural inclinations and in light of his intellectual and physical abilities.[24] Different people will be inspired to pursue different occupations; each person must realistically decide how to channel that inspiration towards practical action.

Real work begins when you actually develop your innate talents, overcome personal handicaps, set goals, and achieve them. True, you cannot be successful in everything. True, you can be exceptional in something. Nevertheless, you may end up being generally mediocre, or worse. The controlling factor that will distinguish an exceptional life from a mediocre one is motivation, will, a burning desire to succeed.

What is the secret of true motivation? First, as we discussed in chapter 2, you must think like an adult and take responsibility for your own lives. Not your parents, not your teachers—nobody but you is ultimately responsible for what you choose to do.

Second, you need to evaluate what is really meaningful to you, to be inspired. This question—what do you *want* to become, what you want to do with your year of study, with your life—is something your teachers can help you explore. But ultimately, these are questions that, as a young adult, only you can answer.

Lastly, once you are motivated toward a goal, that fiery will— that burning YES—must become expressed essentially in structure, organization, self-management.

Rabbi Shlomo Wolbe[25] pointed out that this first lesson of adulthood is expressed in the first blessing you may have recited as a

24. "Gate of Trust in God," chapter 3.
25. *Alei Shur* II pg. 319.

Jewish adult. In our tradition, an adolescent reaches majority on the evening of the twelfth birthday for a girl, the thirteenth birthday for a boy. The first blessing of the evening prayers is *ha-ma'ariv aravim*, in which we celebrate the wonderful order revealed in the created world. The blessing itself teaches from where this order derives: " and orders the stars in their constellations in the firmament according to His will."

Order in the universe derives from, and is evidence of, the will of God. From the smallest atom to the largest galaxy, the universe is structured with rigor and wisdom. Just as we can infer the existence of the designer from the existence of design, so we can infer the greatness of the designer from the greatness of the design. Structure evidences will, and true will must find expression in structure. The converse is also true: chaos indicates a lack of purpose and will.

This year and for the rest of your life, you must apply this most basic lesson whenever you take on a meaningful project. Any endeavor that you determine to be of value must be shown respect by setting aside a fixed time and place in which you can focus on it exclusively. Rabbi Reuven Leuchter, a teacher of mine and a close student of Rabbi Wolbe, once defined this attitude of *seder* for me as "doing things *lechatchilah*"—meaning properly from start to finish, without cutting corners, without distractions. He explained to me that only by acting with *seder* do we demonstrate respect for the activity, and only then will it have a positive impact on us and on our environment. Without *seder*, even potentially great actions fall in value to the level of damage control, at best.

For example, I can think of no more important project than a parent cultivating a relationship with his or her children. When you have children you shouldn't just bumble into your relationships with them. Instead, you must set aside special times for each child for study, conversation and play. If you plan an afternoon at the zoo, you demonstrate that you are motivated and care by picking your kids up on time, staying until the end, and focusing your attention on them throughout. If you are on your cell phone with your stockbroker the whole time, then your children will perceive that while your body is in the zoo, you are hardly with them at all. You may have taken off from work to be with them, spent money on entrance fees and ice cream, and still the message that they perceive could be: daddy doesn't really want to be with me. Given all the effort of the outing, the marginal cost of going to the zoo with *seder* is quite small—picking them up five minutes earlier, turning off the cell phone, enjoying the elephants with a childlike spirit—but therein lies all the fun and all the profit.

A few years ago I read a book about a famous climbing expedition up Mount Everest. Summiting Everest is an incredibly dangerous undertaking that requires tremendous planning under the best of circumstances. In this book, the bulk of the narrative was actually about the *preparation* that preceded the actual climb: training before the trip, setting up base camp, acclimating to high altitude, learning how to use equipment. All that structure, that preparation, shows that these people were serious about climbing Everest.

Someone who shows up at base camp with only a canteen, a compass, and a set of snow shoes is making a fool of himself. He is not demonstrating discipline; he doesn't really want to make it to the top.

A structured, deliberate approach to any mission distinguishes real productive work from amateurish amusement. In the 1990s, the U.S. Department of Labor commissioned a study that researched why so many recipients of welfare have difficulty mainstreaming into productive jobs. One remarkable conclusion of the research was that many unemployed people simply never internalized the most basic attitude towards work: you need to show up, on time, every day. Even if all you do is flip burgers, you won't be successful if you only come to work when it strikes your fancy. Developing character, skills, and a healthy respect for the tradition is even harder than flipping burgers. You simply won't see real success if you only focus on them intermittently.

When I was in college I had good grades and liked my classes and began to entertain the idea of going into academia professionally, so I dropped by the office of one of my professors to ask him about the academic life.

"Well," he began, "I wake up at 5:00 a.m. and go for a five-mile run. Then I come home and make myself breakfast. In the morning I read a book, and then I make myself lunch. After lunch I do some writing until dinnertime, and then after dinner I read a novel."

A serious yeshiva *bachur* might not consider such a schedule exceptionally intense, but I had not yet been exposed to the beautiful rigor of yeshiva, so I found myself struck dumb. All that I could pronounce was a vapid "wow," although I tried to say it with significance. The expression on my face clearly exposed my unspoken alarm: "where exactly does TV fit in to all this?"

The professor smiled at me patronizingly, "Do you want to be an intellectual, or a dilettante?"

Sheepishly, I thanked him. Then I went back to my dorm room and looked up the word "dilettante."

It means "amateur," and I realized that like most students, I was still only an amateur intellectual. To be a real academic means reading books and writing papers. Every day. In fact, to be real at any endeavor you have to dedicate significant time on a regular basis.

This is certainly true of *avodat Hashem*—literally "the *work* of God"—as well. Dabbling in Torah study, prayer, or ethical development is not *avodah* at all, and you can't expect real progress to stem from such dilettantism.

Nor can you really expect to enjoy the experience. At best, it is damage control. If you want to experience something properly—be it a concert or ball game, or a lecture or prayer service—you get there on time, you stay until the end, and you focus while you are there. Otherwise you aren't fully there, and you can't expect to find the moment enriching.

I know that many times when I pray hurriedly and carelessly for twenty minutes, afterwards I'll feel like I carried a heavy burden for an hour. Damage control. At other times I'll pray for an hour: I'll arrive on time, and recite every passage in step with the congregation, skipping nothing. At the end I'll feel uplifted, and the hour passed quickly as if it were only twenty minutes. By acting with *seder*, deliberately and carefully, a day that might have begun in chaos and confusion instead began in harmony and light. Now I say to myself, "You are going to pray today anyway, you may as well enjoy it."

A Deeper Look at Seder

Rava said: every day is more cursed than the previous one, as is written, "in the morning you shall say, 'if only it were evening!' and in the evening you shall say, 'if only it were

תלמוד בבלי מסכת סוטה דף מט/א
אמר רבא בכל יום ויום מרובה קללתו משל חבירו
שנאמר בבקר תאמר מי יתן ערב ובערב תאמר
מי יתן בקר הי בקר אילימא בקר דלמחר מי ידע
מאי הוי אלא דחליף ואלא עלמא אמאי קא מקיים
אקדושה דסידרא ואיהא שמיה רבא דאגדתא שנא'
ארץ עפתה כמו אופל צלמות ולא סדרים הא יש
סדרים תופיע מאופל.

morning!'" To which morning does this refer? If you say the next morning—who knows what it will be like? Rather, it must be referring to the previous morning. If this is the case, what sustains the world? The *Kiddusha de-Sidra* and the *Yehei Shmeih Rabba* of *aggadata*, as is written, "A land of gloom, as darkness

itself; and of the shadow of death, without any order." Behold,
if there is order, it emerges from the darkness! (BT *Sotah* 49a).

A world without order is chaotic and disorienting, and such is our
world since the destruction of the Temple and the disruption of its
divine service. When we had the Temple, all of the universe could
somehow be perceived as being organized around this locus. The
Temple was both the vehicle for our connecting the creation back to
its source, and consequently the conduit through which sustaining
blessing flowed into the world.

Since the destruction of the Temple, the forces of entropy have
slowly detached the creation from its metaphysical moorings. Chaos
reigns, and with it comes the spiritual disorientation and psychological
angst that lead so many of us to search for meaning, for organizing
first principles, in so many distant and often bizarre places.

The Talmud asks: in such a prolonged spiritual blackout, what
can possibly sustain the world? The Talmud answers that two small
rituals sustain the entire world. One is the *Kiddusha de-Sidra*. This
is a brief passage recited towards the end of the morning prayers
every day. It contains a few verses from the prophets about the angels
praising God, together with the translation into Aramaic, which was
the language commonly spoken at the time this ritual was instituted.
Effectively, it provides a short opportunity for the entire community
of worshippers to be involved in regular daily study. It describes the
angels, standing fixed in their heavenly stations, and invites us—
actually enables us—to imitate them. The passage is brief; generally
it is recited in less than a couple of minutes. But like the angels, it
is fixed, unchanging, and involves the entire community—not the
heavenly hosts, but the projection of them on Earth.

This short passage is the *Kiddushah de-Sidra*, literally, "the
sanctification of order." This structured, regular moment of Torah

study and divine service resolves the chaos and illuminates the darkness.

The second passage that sustains the world is the *Yehei Shemeih Rabba de-aggadata*, which is a similar ritual and performs a similar function. Traditionally on Shabbat afternoon the local rabbi would give a sermon on some non-legal subject, which is generally referred to as "aggadah," or homiletics. These speeches included stories and lessons from the Bible, and would attract the broadest spectrum of the community, scholars and common people alike. The effect of the entire community coming together for study regularly, even if only once a week, was such a powerful sanctification of heaven that a special prayer of sanctification ("*Kaddish*") was instituted to conclude the event. This prayer is called the *Kaddish de-Aggadata* or the *Kaddish de-Rabbanan*, because of its special blessing: "for Israel, and for the Rabbis, and for their disciples and for all the disciples of their disciples, and for everyone who is involved in Torah, whether in this land or in each and every place...."

At such a gathering, the moment when the entire community answers as one, "may the great Name be blessed forever and forever," shines another ray of light into the chaos of exile. It serves as a universal flash of clarity, disperses the disillusionment and disorientation, and provides a conceptual framework to sustain the world for another week.

This is the power of *seder* in the life of the community: it sustains the world. You as an individual have the ability to harness that power on a personal level, to bring light into your own life, by having an ordered framework that brings organization to chaos.

Order in Crisis

Rabbi Wolbe points out that someone who has cultivated the attribute of *seder* can create calm and order even in times of great confusion and crisis. Of course, at a time of crisis, no one is expected to cling dogmatically to his regular schedule. But someone who appreciates the power of *seder* will attempt to create islands of calm in the chaos. He will adapt and organize based on the skills he has learned in his *seder*; he will act proactively in light of the situation, rather than just react reflexively and intemperately.

I remember a happy crisis in my life: my wedding day. I call it a crisis only because one's wedding day is by nature very unlike a normal day. It is frenetic, filled with friends and relatives, hopes and anxieties. Many people find their wedding day to be a time in which they are so swept along in the stream of events that they are only able to reflect on the day in retrospect. They certainly feel joy, but to some degree they also feel out of control.

When I got married, I had been studying in a Jerusalem yeshiva and living in the dorm. I had read Rabbi Wolbe's chapter on *seder* and took his advice to heart. Knowing that my wedding day would be something of a circus, I decided to limit the chaos as much as possible. For example, many people in Israel like to pray at the Kotel on their wedding day, but I decided that I would be able to concentrate best by staying in the yeshiva. I had my seat; I knew the pace. And by staying put I had one of the most focused and memorable services of my life.

I knew that I could not possibly have a full morning of learning. I don't learn well when fasting anyway, and like many grooms I was spending my wedding day fasting. Clearly I was going to be distracted. So I had decided days earlier to use that morning for last-minute errands like arranging for a bridal bouquet and buying the gold wedding band. Still, I couldn't imagine spending the most important day of my life without any Torah. A couple of friends volunteered to learn some light topics with me after *Shacharit* and *Mincha*. I gave myself only half an hour each time, but that was enough to inform the day with the spirit of Torah.

Learning to Grow

My wedding was going to be in a hotel, and my parents were staying there. The natural choice was to pack my suit and take a cab to the hotel for a shower. But I knew that as soon as I arrived the circus would begin. I decided instead to take a short nap in the afternoon, and to shower and change in the crusty dormitory where I had been living for the past year. After all, I knew where the soap was, where the shoe polish was; I had a favorite necktie (in retrospect it was a bad choice, but I felt comfortable). In my mind this was almost like any Shabbat eve, only the bride was different.

I give this as an example of a blessed crisis, but the attitude is just as relevant for tragic crises as well: a child in the hospital; a war; a wrongful arrest. The attribute of *seder* can create familiar islands of calm, can bring a new organizing structure to all the chaotic stimuli that otherwise might undermine a reflective and proactive approach to life.

Seder in Yeshiva and Seminary

Seder can help you maintain your equilibrium in a time of crisis, but real growth happens when the routine tasks of a constructive life are approached with *seder*. Whether you are pursuing a college degree, starting a business, or cultivating relationships in your family, an attitude of *seder* will help you identify those activities most worthy of respectful attention, and will help you actively manage and truly enjoy the project at hand.

This year, you are fortunate to be in a laboratory of *seder*, where you are expected to use this attribute for the highest of purposes: becoming a better person by connecting to God through His revealed will. It is not by accident that the traditional yeshiva schedule is divided into "*sedarim*": morning *seder*, afternoon *seder*, night *seder*, *musar seder*. The great Rosh Yeshiva of Volozhin, the Netziv, often used to refer to the Rabbis' statement in the Talmud Yerushalmi, describing a yeshiva as "a house of *seder*."[26] Just by following the schedule you will learn how ordered discipline will help you achieve your most important goals, and how good it feels to be involved in the process without cutting corners.

Naftali Tzvi Yehuda Berlin, (the "Netziv" 1816–1893), indirectly succeeded his father-in-law, Rabbi Yitzchok of Volozhin, as the Rosh Yeshiva of the Volozhin Yeshiva. In addition to his deep analysis, he emphasized the importance of fidelity to early sources, such as the Geonim, Rif, and, Bahag. He gave a weekly lecture on the week's Torah reading, forming the basis of his *Ha-Emek Davar*. He viewed *Bereshit* as informing the ethical basis of a just society, a necessary prerequisite for the Torah that would be revealed in *Shemot*.

The more you actively consider being orderly in all that you do, the more these activities become part of *avodah*, work, divine service. This is most obvious and explicit in your studying and praying, your working on character by making a personal accounting and writing in your journal. By showing up on time, staying until the end, and focusing while you are there, you demonstrate respect and allow that activity to impact on you in the most powerful way.

But *seder* is also relevant to the way you eat lunch: not so little that you are hungry but not so much that you are drowsy all afternoon, the way you sit with self-respect and the way you clear the lunch table.

Seder is relevant in the way you go to sleep at the right time. Perhaps the greatest and most difficult act of self-discipline for an

---

26. JT *Sukkah*, chapter 1, cited in Rabbi Baruch ha-Levi Epstein, *My Uncle the Netziv*, pg. 169.

eighteen-year-old is sticking to a reasonable bed time. If you are not getting enough sleep, your prayers will feel hollow and your studies will lack enthusiasm and vitality. Getting eight hours of sleep every night is a project in character development worthy of the *musar* masters.

Seder is relevant in the way you schedule regular exercise and recreation. By taking these basic human needs into account in a regular way, you show that you are interested in your physical body participating fully in your spiritual growth. Recreation is not what you do to escape the study hall or the class room; it is a regular way you guarantee the vigor of your Divine service.

So *seder* relates less to what you do, and more to the way you approach anything that is truly worth doing. If it is worth doing, it is worth doing well. By showing up on time, staying until the end, and focusing while you are there, you demonstrate that you are not just a dilettante. In almost every activity you can bring light to your life. And if that activity is valuable enough, it can bring redemption to the world as well.

Chapter 8

Authenticity

Avraham and His Servant Eliezer

I imagine that your teachers have been discussing the patriarchs and matriarchs at some length, especially as we read through the portions of the Torah that deal with their lives and accomplishments. In chapter 6 we also touched on Avraham's kindness that was extraordinary mostly in its consistency. For some contrast, I would like to turn to a central, but little-understood and enigmatic figure in Avraham's life: Eliezer, his faithful servant.

Eliezer's life was strange and tragic, and we should reflect on it in order to understand both his greatness and an ominously powerful human ability we all share: the ability to deceive each other, and to deceive ourselves.

But enough introductions. Who was Eliezer?

The elder servant of Avraham was his servant Elieazer. And from where was he his servant? After Avraham walked out of the furnace in Ur Kasdim, all the leaders of the generation came to give him presents. And Nimrod took his servant Eliezer, and gave him to Avraham as a slave for life. When Eliezer acted with kindness towards Yitzchak, Avraham gave him his liberty. And the Holy One, Blessed be He, awarded him his payment in this world, and made him a king, and he is Og, the king of Bashan (*Pirkei de-Rabbi Eliezer* 16).

פרקי דרבי אליעזר (היגר) - "חורב" פרק טז
זקן עבדו של אברהם והיה עבדו אליעזר, ומהיכן היה עבדו אלא שכיון שיצא מאור כשדים באו כל גדולי הדור ליתן לו מתנות ולקח נמרוד עבדו אליעזר ונתנו לו עבד עולם, וכשגמל חסד ליצחק הוציאו לחירות ונתן לו הב"ה שכרו בעולם הזה וקיימו למלך והוא עוג מלך הבשן:

According to the Midrash, Eliezer was also known as Og the wicked king of Bashan. Og, as you may know from *Bemidbar* 21, led his people in battle against the Jews as they came to enter the land. According to the Talmud, he was a giant who personally tried to throw an entire mountain on the Jews.

But how can this be true?

How could sweet Eliezer, the faithful servant with all those cute (but thirsty) camels, the self-effacing servant who searched for Rivka despite his hope that Yitzchak would marry his own daughter,[27] the humble servant who prayed at the well, the patient servant who successfully negotiated with vile Lavan and Betuel, the trusted servant who safely brought Rivka back for Yitzchak unharmed... how could he be Og, the enemy of Jews, the monster who tried to crush Moshe and the Jews, who tried to bury them alive?

People are complex, and although we sometimes read Tanach as some cartoon-like melodrama, the characters of the biblical personalities were actually complex and ambiguous. This striking midrash is trying to provide a window into the darkly complex soul of this great and tragic man and it deserves study for what it teaches about Eliezer, and for what it reveals about each of us.

27. See Rashi to *Bereshit* 24:39.

Authenticity

First, some questions:

- If Eliezer was intended to be a slave for life, why did Avraham set him free at all, and why on this particular occasion? After all, Eliezer had shown remarkable courage and dedication before, most famously at the war against the four kings, in which—according to one opinion—he and Avraham alone defeated this great army.

- Why did God decide to give Eliezer all his reward in this world? What, in general, leads God to apportion reward in one world as opposed to the other; and how might this rule be relevant in the case of Eliezer?

- Why would saintly Eliezer mutate into the evil Og? Are there any indications of this dark side of his personality anywhere in the text?

- Who was he anyway? Where did he come from, and how did he end up as the servant of Nimrod?

Let's start with the background. Og/Eliezer was such a giant because he was from an earlier—literally antediluvian—time. He was one of the few survivors of the flood, but he survived in a highly unusual way.

"And there remained only Noach" (*Bereshit* 7:23) aside from Og the king of Bashan who sat on a plank underneath the gutter of the ark. And he swore to Noach and his sons that he would be their slave for life. What did Noach do? He

פרקי דרבי אליעזר פרק כג
וישאר אך נח וחוץ מעוג מלך הבשן
שישב על עץ אחד תחת סילונית של
תיבה ונשבע לנח ולבניו שיהיה להם
עבד עולם מה עשה נח נקב חור אחד
בתיבה והיה מושיט לו מזונו בכל יום
ויום ונשאר גם הוא שנ' רק עוג מלך
הבשן נשאר מיתר הרפאים:

129

drilled a hole in the ark and passed him his food every day, and he too remained. As is written, "Only Og king of Bashan remained from among the giants" (*Devarim* 3:11) (*Pirkei de-Rabbi Eliezer* 23).

Og promised Noach that he would serve him and his children forever, if only they would feed him and allow him to cling to the outside of the ark. One of the only survivors of the age of the giants, Og was huge and powerful, clearly the strongest servant in the era post-deluge. It should come as no surprise then that he would be taken by Nimrod, the king of the populated world, as his personal servant. It should also come as no surprise that he could—as the faithful Eliezer—beat the armies of the four kings almost single-handedly.

But why would Og be saved only outside of the ark? Presumably, he deserved to be saved, and was one of only a handful of people who merited that distinction. He must have risen above the corruption of his generation. Why, then, the bizarre treatment? What does the image of the desperate, wet giant, clinging to the outside of the ark represent?

To help answer this question I would like to turn to a fundamental teaching of Rabbenu Bachya Ibn Pakuda in his *Duties of the Heart*. Rabbenu Bachya wrote that every commandment that we perform has two basic components: the action we

> We know very little about **Rabbenu Bachya ibn Pakuda**, the author of the *Chovot ha-Levavot* (*Duties of the Heart*). He lived in Spain, probably in the second half of the 11th century, and he was a *dayan*. His book is one of the most beloved ethical treatises our people has ever produced, and was one of the first works of Jewish thought written in Arabic to be translated into Hebrew.

perform with the limbs of our bodies, and the feeling and intention with which we infuse those actions. For example, a wealthy man may give charity with a silver coin in his hand, and a compassionate smile on his face. His legs may run to the door to greet the pauper. These are all physical actions done with the physical body. And although they generally indicate enthusiasm and authenticity, no one can ever know what is actually in the heart of the benefactor. He may be trying to assuage a guilty conscience; he may be concerned with establishing a saintly reputation. In short Rabbenu Bachya distinguishes between the "duties of the body" and the "duties of the heart," and although this division did not originate with him, his elucidation remains both classic and seminal. Given the title of his book, you can probably guess which he felt needed greater emphasis, at least in his generation.

Rabbenu Bachya used this division to explain divine reward and punishment. The duties of body are performed by the body, and therefore earn the performer of the commandment corporeal reward, which he enjoys in this world. The duties of the heart, on the other hand, are not really a matter of the heart at all. They belong to the realm of the spirit, and are always hidden and pure.[28] They, and only they, earn the performer of the commandments a spiritual reward in a world that is hidden and pure. This formulation is both simple and elegant, and can help us understand the fate of poor Og. If he deserved all of his reward in this world, this indicates that his actions—as great, courageous and self-effacing as they appeared to be—were all somehow divorced of intention, spirit, and heart. He was righteous on the outside, but pathetically hollow on the inside.

This understanding of Og may also explain the symbolism of his being saved on the outside of the ark: his external actions might have seemed noble, but his inner intentions were murky; lacking an inside, he deserved to be saved only on the outside.

Eliezer's problem was one with which we are all acquainted. Very often we act in a certain way because of social pressures, or because

---

28. *Duties of the Heart* 4:4.

we coldly and intellectually understand the importance of a certain behavior, while our heart is not in it. We know, and we act, but we lack authenticity and the warm embracing fullness of life that this authenticity provides. For example, a young woman might know that she should dress with a certain modest dignity, and she may actually dress that way, but all the while she feels an inner struggle, desiring to let loose. A young man may understand that much "popular culture" is a waste of time (at best), and he may even commit to abstaining from its more coarse elements during his year in yeshiva, and yet he continues to feel its pull. They both know what is right, but neither *feel* that it is good. The result is that even as they behave with excellence, they feel little joy in their achievements, and that is a shame.

It is also unsustainable. Social pressure and intellectual muscle can only go so far. Ultimately, if your heart wants something, you will likely break down and go for it. Alternatively, if your heart is not into even the greatest of projects, you will end up cutting corners, waking late, and otherwise slipping into mediocrity or worse. Poor Eliezer knew the good and did the good, but was dangerously unstable because he didn't have the motivating safety net of a rich inner life.

Like so many well-meaning but unstable people, when he was in a good environment he behaved well, but when he was in a bad environment he was at risk. For example, when the four powerful kings captured the city of Sodom together with Avraham's nephew Lot, Eliezer (as Og) ran to tell Avraham the bad news. The midrash, quoted by Rashi, points out that his motivation was entirely reprehensible. Knowing that Avraham could not tolerate injustice, Eliezer reported that Lot had been taken prisoner, hoping that Avraham would rashly attempt a rescue and be killed. But his motivation was not merely homicidal; ultimately he was motivated by an adulterous lust for Sarah. He hoped that with Avraham's early demise he could then take the widowed Sarah as his own. This is what Eliezer was thinking in Sodom, clearly under the influence of that corrupt society, and that is what carried him back from the battle.

Strangely, no sooner than he returned, Eliezer fell under the positive influence of Avraham, pivoted on his heel, and fought alongside his master until the four kings were defeated. In fact,

> בראשית יד,יג
> ויבא הפליט, ויגד לאברם העברי...
>
> בראשית רבה (וילנא) פרשה מב
> ויבא הפליט, ריש לקיש בשם בר קפרא הוא עוג
> הוא פליט... הוא לא נתכוון לשם שמים אלא אמר
> אברהם זה קונינן הוא ועכשיו אני אומר לו נשבה
> בן אחיך והוא יוצא למלחמה ונהרג ואני נוטל את
> שרי אשתו, א"ל הקב"ה חייך שכר פסיעותיך
> אתה נוטל שאת מאריך ימים בעולם ועל שחשבת
> להרוג את הצדיק חייך שאתה רואה אלף אלפים
> ורבי רבבות מבני בניו, ואין סופו של אותו האיש
> ליפול אלא בידן שנאמר (דברים ג) ויאמר ה' אלי
> אל תירא אותו כי בידך וגו':

according to one opinion, giant Eliezer and righteous Avraham fought the battle all by themselves. Lacking a stable inner life, Eliezer was something of a chameleon, taking on the color of his environment. When in Sodom he was driven by thoughts of passion and intrigue. Next to Avraham he fought bravely for justice.

Externally, Eliezer appeared to act heroically from start to finish, and to such a degree that generations later Moshe worried that this meritorious behavior would empower him (as Og) against the Jews. Even a great prophet like Moshe was unable to penetrate the inner ambiguity of his actions and intentions, until God had to reveal to him that he need not fear—what appeared to be a mitzvah was actually a homicidal ruse!

Earlier I asked why Avraham did not reward Eliezer with his freedom after this act of military heroism. Now it is clear that his behavior at this point was deserving of very little applause. The report of Lot's capture was motivated by selfish passion; the battle and victory were supported only by the holy environment of Avraham's saintly presence.

These qualifications can be contrasted with Eliezer's successes searching for, finding, and returning with Rivka. Eliezer remained true and faithful even while away from Avraham's direct influence, and despite the fact that he—hoping that Yitzchak would marry his own daughter—had good reason to fail. Eliezer saw the hand of God guiding him and aiding him. He communicated this to Rivka's family so convincingly that they too admitted that a divine plan was unfolding before them. Away from the saintly environment of Avraham's home, faced with the wicked Lavan and Betuel, Eliezer's faith was put to the test, and this time he passed.

Avraham had no illusions about his unstable servant. He knew that Eliezer might fail terribly. According to one midrash, Avraham even expressed concern to Yitzchak that Rivka might have been molested by the servant on the way home. When it became clear that Eliezer had succeeded even in a hostile environment, Avraham rewarded Eliezer with his freedom. He had remained loyal and stable; he must have developed a heart, an authentic inner life.

This may have resolved the reason that brought Eliezer to be a servant in the first place. Remember him clinging to the outside of the Ark, begging for life, committing himself to indentured servitude for life. This promise was not arbitrary. Indeed, it was an act of recognition that, lacking an emotional love for ethical excellence, he needed to find stability. He therefore committed to serve those better than himself, to fix himself in a nurturing environment. As a giant, he had much to offer. As someone ethically weak, he had much to gain.

Finding himself in Avraham's house, he slowly internalized the ideals of his master. Finally, Avraham sent him out on a solo mission to bring back Rivka. He left the protective bubble of Avraham's camp, but carried with himself Avraham's ideals. He prayed as Avraham would, spoke as Avraham would, and completed the mission to Avraham's satisfaction. No longer needing to be indentured to Avraham, Eliezer was given his diploma. He graduated and left as a free man. Presumably, his heart was whole and even if he should stumble, he would not fall.

Or would he?

Avraham didn't see any blemish in Eliezer's performance, and I am not aware of any statement of the Rabbis that clearly explains why Eliezer then deserved to receive all his reward in this world alone. But God knew that he was still lacking and unstable. Ultimately he became an enemy of Avraham's descendants and tried, quite literally, to crush them all. What was the tragic flaw that remained in his character, so small that presumably even Avraham couldn't see it, but large enough to corrupt him completely? I don't know, but clearly, he was not yet ready for total independence.

Just as poor Eliezer was split, so are we all split to some degree. We all do acts of kindness—and give charity, and learn well and pray on time—with mixed motivations. By itself this is not terrible. Indeed, as Rav taught in the Talmud, we should behave well even for selfish reasons, since those very actions will help habituate us in virtuous behavior: לעולם יעסוק אדם בתורה ובמצות אף על פי שלא לשמה, שמתוך שלא לשמה—בא לשמה.[29] But we must understand how precarious and hollow our spiritual lives remain so long as we have not realized true authenticity.

This year, you have left the nurturing environment of your home, and have entered a nurturing environment of a different kind. Good environments introduce us to noble values and provide us with emotional warmth. They show us the way, and make us feel safe as we learn new attitudes, skills, and sensitivities. But if you rely on your

---

29. BT *Pesachim* 50b.

environment too much, it can stunt your growth. Ultimately, you can't sing with your father's voice, or cling to God with your Rosh Yeshiva's faith. You have to find your own faith and your own voice. Eliezer teaches us how vulnerable we all are until we do so. Having learned from his checkered example, you should now begin the quiet work of developing your own rich inner life. As you do so you will achieve stability and joy, reward in this world and the next.

Chapter 9

Peaks and Valleys

Dealing with Mood Swings

Anyone who has spent any time in a place of growth and change will be personally, perhaps excruciatingly, familiar with the topic of this chapter. You might have experienced a couple of enthusiastic weeks during which you learn with laser-sharp focus, pray with a full heart, and relate to your friends with genuine affection. And then suddenly the well dries up. You find no flavor in your studies; your prayers seem rote as the words plop from your limp mouth; your roommate smells bad.

My friend Rabbi Menachem Deutch once told me a comforting story about one of his students and the student's father. Rabbi Deutch teaches in a very advanced yeshiva in Jerusalem and this particular student had come from France to study there after high school. His parents were not religious, but they had sent the boy to yeshiva anyway, fulfilling a promise they had made to an aged kabbalist years before.

It seems that for several years after their marriage, the parents had tried, without success, to have children. The father, a very intelligent and successful cardiologist, was well connected within the medical community in Paris, and they went from doctor to doctor, trying one treatment after another, only to be repeatedly disappointed. At some point the father turned to his wife in desperation with one final proposal. "Look," he said, "neither of us are religious, but we are both Jewish. Maybe a rabbi can help us." Their incredulous friends and family members understood the pain of these otherwise rational people, and responded to their inquiries with sympathetic encouragement. Ultimately they found themselves seated in the humble study of a white-bearded mystic and poured out their troubles before him.

After they had finished, the kabbalist declared with complete confidence, "I can promise that you will have a son in one year. But you must promise to send him to Jewish schools, and when the time comes you must send him to a yeshiva in Jerusalem." The couple had little idea of what yeshiva was, but they were desperate. They agreed immediately, and one year later the wife gave birth to a son.

Just as the rabbi kept his promise, so did the happy parents. They sent the boy to Jewish schools in Paris, and when he turned eighteen they sent him to my friend's yeshiva in Jerusalem. Naturally, they were a bit doting, and they soon came to visit the boy and to meet his teachers.

"How is our son doing?" asked the French heart doctor.

My friend hesitated. "Well, I have good news and bad news," he began. "On the one hand, your son is obviously very bright. On his good days, there is no student who can compete with him." Rabbi Deutch attributed the student's natural intelligence to the genes he had obviously inherited from his very sharp father, to the doctor's obvious delight. But quickly, the father's expression shifted to one of concern.

"So what's the bad news?" he insisted.

"Like I said, on his good days your son is a wonderful student. But I have to admit to you that he has his ups and downs."

With this, the father's expression of concern completely dissolved into one of relief, even satisfaction.

"I don't understand," Rabbi Deutch continued. "Naturally you'd be happy about your boy being quite gifted; but why are you so happy about him having ups and downs?"

"Rabbi," the doctor explained, "I may not be a Torah scholar, I may not even be religious, but I am a heart doctor. And one thing I know is that up and down is good," with this he pulsed his figure up and down, like the graph of an E.K.G., and then he winked. "Flat is bad."

Living things, organic, growing things all go through cycles consisting of periods of accelerated development, followed by periods of relative dormancy. These cycles are recorded in the rings of a tree trunk, in layers of fossils, in the ridges of a snail's shell. Anything dynamic, moving, and energetic will have times of performance and time of inactivity. And the more dynamic and energetic the object, the more down time it will need.

Take for example, different modes of transportation. If you were to tell me that you want a vehicle that will never break down, will never spend a day in the shop, do you know what I would recommend? A tricycle. I have seven children—three sets of twins and a single somewhere in between—and when the oldest twins were two years old, we bought them tricycles. They rode them, abused them, grew out of them and passed them down to their younger brothers who abused them some more.

OK, finally they broke. But until then, they spent not one day in the garage. The brake pads never needed to be changed, because they had no brake pads, or spark plugs. They didn't even have a chain to be lubricated. So they were very dependable, with no down time. But they weren't very high-performance either. They didn't have many lows, but their highs were pretty flat as well.

Learning to Grow

If you are looking for something more high-performance, you might consider a good 21-speed bicycle. This will take you 20 miles per hour easily, at least downhill, if you are in decent shape. You can ride up hills and over trails, and if you are a bit handy with basic tools, your bike will need never be taken to a professional mechanic. But it will have down time. You'll need to adjust the gears and oil the chain. You'll get a flat tire and need to stop and fix it. The brake pads will need replacing from time to time. But again, if you are handy, your bike will never be down for more than an hour.

Nevertheless, if you are interested in something more high-performance, something that moves at more than 20 MPH, you should look at a car. For a few thousand dollars you can get a simple vehicle that can travel, legally, down the highway. But of course, the more high-performance the car is, the more downtime you must expect. Simpler cars may need only a few hours in the shop every year, but a European sports car, being much more high-performance, will require proportionally more attention. Some cars, if you give them the wrong gas or oil, if you look at them the wrong way, will need to sit for a week in the garage until special parts are ordered from Italy.

The Boeing F-15 Eagle is a tactical fighter designed to out-fly any other plane in the sky. In order to gain and maintain air superiority, the F-15 can climb to 30,000 feet in about 60 seconds. It can turn tight, and catch up to enemy aircraft at Mach 2.5. In 1983 an Israeli pilot even landed his F-15 safely after a midair collision left him with only one wing.

The F-15 Eagle is clearly a high-performance vehicle.

But have you ever seen what happens when an F-15 lands? About twenty men in white jumpsuits surround the aircraft from all sides, take it apart, clean each component, and put it back together again. It flies high and it flies fast, but like all high-performance vehicles, it needs a proportionally great deal of downtime.

140

Guess what: you who have come to yeshiva or seminary are not tricycles, and you are not bicycles. You are F-15 Eagles. This year you will have moments of spiritual joy at the highest altitudes. This year, you can expect growth spurts at Mach 2. But like all organic beings, your growth will not be in a straight line; you will have ups and downs. And because you are so high-performance, your downs may be proportionately greater.

This is a fact of life that you need to recognize. What's more, this recognition cannot remain in the form of passive acquiescence. You need to study the dynamics of mood swings, in order to manage them, in order to sustain the peaks and to make the valleys a little shallower.

First of all, I think the dynamics of mood swings need study because they can produce a lot of confusion among good serious students. Everything was going great, and then suddenly, the well dries up, we lose enthusiasm and pleasure in our studies, and we start to have doubts about our self-worth. We may even question whether we were really made for learning in the first place. If only to ease a bit of psychological pain, this discussion is important reassurance.

Secondly, we need to understand that if our fall is not properly managed, it can have a disastrous effect on our continued growth and on our general behavior as religious Jews.

Rabbi Chaim Shmuelevitz on the Dangers of Mood Swings

The Mir Rosh Yeshiva Rabbi Chaim Shmuelevitz taught that although mood swings are natural, they are also dangerous and need to be understood and managed.[30]

The experiences of his own life were dramatically filled with extreme highs and lows. When Rabbi Shmuelevitz was only seventeen,

---

30. *Sichot Musar* 5731, chapter 13.

he lost both of his parents within a very short time. This extreme low was soon followed by a similarly extreme high, when at the tender age of eighteen, he was invited by the world famous Rabbi Shimon Shkop to give a lecture in the Grodno Yeshiva. At age 31, Rabbi Shmuelevitz was appointed as a Rosh Yeshiva of the prestigious Mir Yeshiva. Then, with the outbreak of World War II, he was forced into exile with the yeshiva, fleeing from Mir to Vilna, then to Keidan, to Kobe, Japan, and then finally to Shanghai, China, where he stayed for over five years.

Rabbi Chaim Shmuelevitz

So Rabbi Shmuelevitz had good cause to be moody, yet he was always known for his equanimity. I was told by the son of one of the Shanghai exiles that at one point the Mir Yeshiva was at sea for days and days. Looking out at the unchanging blue horizon, disoriented and scared, a student finally blurted out, "Where are we?!"

Rabbi Shmuelevitz looked up from his volume of Talmud and responded nonchalantly, "*Ketubot* 13b." At home or at sea, Rabbi Shmuelevitz always kept an even keel.

In an essay on our topic, Rabbi Shmuelevitz taught that being on a low level is certainly not a good thing, but still worse is a fall *to* a low level from a higher one. To have prayed well, and learned well, to have experienced the pleasures of intellectual and spiritual challenge in the study hall, and then to have it all evaporate—that can be very disorienting and traumatic. Unless we understand and manage the fall, we might give up. We might say: hey I tried it and it just doesn't work for me. We might claim that God has given us a "sign" that He just doesn't want us in the *beit midrash*. We might feel rejected by the Torah, by God Himself.

According to Rabbi Shmuelevitz, precisely this kind of fall drove the Jews in the wilderness to worship the Golden Calf, despite the fact that just over a month earlier they had experienced the direct revelation at Sinai. This was an unusual and tragic crash, since usually the descent into idolatry is slow and incremental. The Talmud states that one who breaks his dishes when angry is guilty of idolatry.[31] After all, today his *yetzer hara* said to do this destructively irrational act, and he obeyed; tomorrow, it may say to do a slightly more outrageous act, and he may well obey once again; ultimately, it will tell him to worship idols, and having been slowly trained to follow his urges, he will.

Like all of us, this person is confronted relentlessly by his inner passions. Of course, he should learn to stand his ground against them, to remain true—relentlessly—to his ideals and convictions. In fact, one of the benefits of the system of *mitzvot* is that it continually keeps our powers of self-restraint well exercised. But the person who allows his anger to dictate irrational behavior is slowly doing the opposite: he is slowly training himself to be a slave of his passions. Unfortunately, he will find it increasingly difficult to resist, until even the irrational urge to perform idolatry will be met with only surrender.

This is how a descent into idolatry usually develops. But in the case of the Jews in the wilderness, the process was far faster and dramatic. As the verse says, סרו מהר מן הדרך, "they have turned quickly from the path!" (*Shemot* 32:8). And not surprisingly, the cause of this tragic crash was the sort of depression that we are discussing.

When the Jews left Egypt, they were floating on a cloud, almost literally. They had been witness to signs and wonders, and all for their benefit. They dined on manna bread. They had been elevated

---

31. BT *Shabbat* 105b.

by God until they could hear Him speak to them from a miraculous fire. Finally, His greatest and most humble prophet had been charged with the privilege of climbing the holy mountain in order to receive the divine law.

Then suddenly, believing that Moshe has died and that they were abandoned, leaderless in the desert, they were overwhelmed by darkness and disorientation, fear and trembling. They were tempted to make for themselves an alternative "leadership" in the form of a golden

תלמוד בבלי מסכת שבת דף פט/א

[ואמר] רבי יהושע בן לוי מאי דכתיב וירא העם כי בושש משה אל תקרי בושש אלא באו שש בשעה שעלה משה למרום אמר להן לישראל לסוף ארבעים יום בתחלת שש אני בא לסוף ארבעים יום בא שטן ועירבב את העולם אמר להן משה רבכם היכן הוא אמרו לו עלה למרום אמר להן באו שש ולא השגיחו עליו מת ולא השגיחו עליו הראה להן דמות מטתו והיינו דקאמרי ליה לאהרן כי זה משה האיש וגו':

רש"י שם

כשעלה משה - להר, אמר להם לסוף ארבעים יום אני בא בתוך שש שעות, הם סבורים שאותו יום שעלה בו מן המנין הוה, והוא אמר להם ארבעים יום שלימים, יום ולילו עמו, ויום עלייתו אין לילו עמו, שהרי בשבעה בסיון עלה, נמצא יום ארבעים בשבעה עשר בתמוז היה, בששה עשר בא שטן ועירבב את העולם, והראה דמות חשך ואפילה, דמות ענן וערפל וערבוביא, לומר ודאי מת משה, שהרי באו כבר שש ולא בא, ואי אפשר לומר שלא טעו אלא ביום המעונן בין קודם חצות לאחר חצות שהרי לא ירד משה עד יום המחרת, שנאמר וישכימו ממחרת וגו':

calf. The logic behind this move is beyond the scope of this chapter, but we should recognize the important lesson: in a state of spiritual confusion, our self-destructive inner demons—often personified as the *yetzer hara*—can suggest all sorts of "solutions." And in our terrifying disorientation, we might embrace all kinds of counter-productive idols.

Rabbi Shmuelevitz gives several examples of this in Tanach, and we need to understand that this is a real danger for us as well. Ups and downs are natural, and we need to keep ourselves from being thrown by them into behavior that is panic-driven and harmful.

The general idea, that ungoverned mood swings can be dangerously traumatic is beautifully expressed by the following statement in the Talmud:

Rabbi took the scroll of *Kinot* (the book of Lamentations) and was reading from it. When he got the verse, "He threw from the Heavens down to Earth," he dropped it. He said, "From a high roof to a deep pit!" (*Chagigah* 5b).

תלמוד בבלי מסכת חגיגה דף ה/ב
רבי הוה נקיט ספר קינות וקא קרי בגויה כי
מטא להאי פסוקא השליך משמים ארץ נפל
מן ידיה אמר מאיגרא רם לבירא עמיקתא:

מהרש"א חידושי אגדות שם
נפל מן ידיה אמר מאיגרא כו'. נראה דשלא
בכוונה נפל הספר מידיה ואפשר שהיה
עומד במקום גבוה בעלייה ונפל משם לארץ
ולמקום עמוק יותר וע"י זה נזכר בדרשת
המקרא השליך משמים ארץ

Maharsha comments on this passage that when Rabbi dropped the scroll, he recalled the interpretation that by being sent into exile in Babylon, the Jews were doubly downcast: they had left the Promised Land, and they went to a place of utter vulgarity. Rabbi Shmuelevitz continues that it makes no difference to a scroll whether it rests on a high place or a low place. The thing that can tear and destroy it is the impact of the fall.

He learns from this a lesson to help us appreciate the power of our own emotions: not only is being low dangerous, but the impact of the fall is often the most traumatic. It can be so disorienting that it is very easy to lose the virtues that one acquired. After all, a person tossed up and down on a wavy sea will grab onto anything, hoping that it is a life-jacket; we need to learn not to panic, because if we do, we might just grab onto the anchor and sink straight to the bottom.

This is most obvious with someone who loses a spouse, or a job. They can easily turn to drugs or alcohol for "support." Of course, that just begins a vicious cycle that is very hard to escape.

For the spiritually sensitive, even more modest setbacks can be traumatic and disruptive. If you have been learning well, praying well, and you suddenly hit a wall, unable to focus during *minyan* or in class, or with a study partner... well, that could easily discourage anyone, and drive him or her from the *beit midrash*. And this is particularly true since you have been growing and were inspired— you tasted the sweetness of the fruit and now it has been taken from you! The contrast makes the "valley" that much more painful.

Mood swings are both inevitable, especially in high-performance and sensitive people like yeshiva and seminary students. And they are dangerous. So we need to learn how to fall with grace and how to get back up again.

How Do We Deal?

When we realize that we have hit a wall, that we have been learning great, but somehow the well has dried up and we are feeling total lack of motivation and joy in our studies, what do we do?

First of all, we need to make a careful evaluation of why we are down.

There might be some profound spiritual explanation. This might be some kind of test, or the moment of dark before the dawn and we will explore those possibilities shortly. But my training is a bit more prosaic. Before going deeper, we need to rule out the obvious causes: are you getting enough sleep, enough recreation? Are you physically exhausted or intellectually drained?

The *Chazon Ish*:
Respect Your Natural Limits

Rabbi Avrohom Yeshaya Karelitz (1878–1953), known as the *Chazon Ish*, was one of the most important rabbis of the twentieth century. His scholarship and creativity were rivaled, perhaps, only by his piety and modesty. Having no official position, his influence over the development of religious life in Israel was huge and continues to resonate. Many view him as the twentieth century's personification of a life devoted to Torah, in all its purity, and without compromise.

The *Chazon Ish*

The *Chazon Ish* once received a letter from a student who was complaining of the sort of emotional low we've been describing. He wrote back:

> Your letter reached me. Know my dear friend that there is no sin, and no blame; it is only a law of nature that one becomes exhausted. And it is not right to

החזון איש, קובץ אגרות. אגרת לה
מכתבך הגיעני, דע לך יקירי שאין כאן לא
חטא ולא אשמה, רק מחקי הטבע להתעיף,
ואין ראוי לזלזל בחקי הטבע כי מה שאנו
קורין טבע המכוון בזה רצון היותר מתמיד
של המהוה כל הויות ית', ולכן חובתך
להפסיק לימודך לגמרי על משך שתי
שבועות ותרבה בכלכלה ומזון מבריא
ולהוסיף על השינה והטיול ועוד מעניני
הבטלה, ואולי נכון שתבוא הנה לימים
אחדים ול... עד שתחליף כח.
ואשריך שעמלת בתורה ותשת כחך
עליה וטובה אחת בצער ממאה שלא בצער
ולימוד במיסירה גמורה יום אחד שקול
כנגד מאה ימים, נא להודיעני תכף אם הנך
ממלא עצתי למען תנוח דעתי.

147

treat the laws of nature lightly, because what we call "nature" really means the most consistent will of the One who brings all beings into being, may He be blessed. Therefore, you must interrupt your studies completely for two weeks, and have a lot of good healthy food. Get extra sleep and take walks and other forms of recreation. Perhaps you should come here for a few days and[32] ... until you recharge.

Be happy that you labored in Torah and you've exhausted yourself on it. One portion with pain is greater than a hundred without pain. Study with total dedication for one day is equivalent to a hundred days. Please let me know right away if you're accepting my advice so that I can be at peace (*Collected Letters*, 35).

Clearly, we can learn from the *Chazon Ish* that if you have been learning well, with enthusiasm and energy, you can expect to have some down times that might extend for days or longer. Just like a muscle needs time to recover after being exercised, so the mind needs rest and recreation to stay alert and at peak performance. The Ramchal expressed a similar sentiment in his work on pedagogy:

... For example, a stroll can be a preparation of divine

ספר דרך חכמה לרמח"ל
דרך משל כבר יוכל להיות הטיול
הכנה לעבודה, אם יצטרך לאדם
כדי להרחיב את דעתו שיהיה
מוכן להשכיל, אך אם הטיול
במהותו לא יהיה מן המותרים,
או בכמותו יהיה יותר מדאי,
או יהיה בחברת בלתי מהוגנים
וכיוצא בזה, הרי הוא מכלל
הפעולות אשר לא תעשנה. והנה
כמשפט הפעולות כך משפט
העיונים בלי הפרש כלל, כי כיון
שתכלית כל עניני מציאות האדם
בעולם הוא תכלית אחד, צריך
גם כן שכל עניניו ילכו מהלך
השגתו ותהיה מגמתם הצלחתו.

---

32. The ellipsis here is in the original.

148

service, if a person needs this to broaden his mind in order to think clearly. Nevertheless, if the stroll is unnecessary, or is too long, or is with bad company and the like, then it is the type of action that should not be done… (*Sefer Derech Chochmah*).

Similarly, the Rambam wrote about the benefits of taking walks and seeing beautiful sights as a way of combating "black bile," the medieval medical term for depression. [33]

This is why many yeshivas and seminaries are so generous in scheduling time for recreation. You can expect breaks at the beginning and end of the term, and in the middle. Some institutions give one afternoon a week off. And of course, there is Shabbat and most, if not all, of Friday. Make sure to fill these opportunities with well thought-out recreation that will help you recharge your batteries.

In general, for recreation to be effective, it should be planned, rather than just "bumming around," which could be more frustrating than satisfying. Also, unless you plan quality recreation in advance, you run the danger of trying to grabbing a bit here and a bit there: so instead of a solid rejuvenating experience, you just eat into the time that you should be studying without real benefit.

Lastly, sleep. The Rambam wrote that a person should sleep about eight hours each night. [34] Contemporary sleep scientists tell us pretty much the same thing: the average adult needs about eight hours of sleep in each 24-hour period. [35]

That means that you might need nine hours of sleep, or can get by on only seven. Very few individuals can consistently perform well on only six hours of sleep, night after night, without needing to binge on sleep at some point. If you are feeling down and lacking motivation, honestly assess how much sleep you've been getting. If it is less than

---

33. See the *Eight Chapters*, chapter 5.
34. *Hilchot De'ot* 4:4.
35. See William Dement, *The Promise of Sleep* (New York: 1999).

eight hours (and it probably is, especially if this is your first extended time away from home), the solution to your problem is obvious, if not easy to implement. I once asked Rabbi Shlomo Wolbe, the master teacher, what is the secret to getting up on time. With the patience of a saint he explained to me that it was by going to bed on time.

Giving Birth: Push into the Pain

Let's say you assess your sleep habits and you are, in fact, getting eight hours a night. You evaluate your lifestyle and realize that you should be just fine: you recently had a break, and a restful Shabbat; you are getting enough exercise and healthy food. But despite all this, your motivation is down and you suddenly want to rent a car and drive down to Eilat. What's going on?

Very often, classic Torah sources personify our all-too-human self-destructive tendencies as "the *yetzer hara*," allowing us to identify negative patterns of thought, without identifying ourselves with those thoughts. The Sages taught that we are quietly and continually challenged by unhealthy irrationality, self-doubt, and willingness to compromise greatness for an easy way out. That's an unending part of the human condition. But an overwhelming attack of the *yetzer hara* is sometimes a sign that you are on the verge of accomplishing something great. Each one of us has some special task in life, some special quality that we are intended to sanctify. And it is in that area that each of us is most seriously tested. The closer we come to success, the more "threatened" the *yetzer hara* feels, and it starts throwing up roadblocks. We need to read these attacks as uncomfortable but useful road signs, in order to direct us towards more work in this area that has such great potential. And like a new sword that is heated until it glows and is then plunged into cold water, such final tests of resolve temper our spirit and strengthen us for future challenges.

The Midrash teaches that when Avraham and Yitzchak were on their way to offer Yitzchak as a sacrifice, the Satan was thrown into a panic. This would be an ultimate achievement for them, the final of Avraham's ten tests, and the Satan could not let them go uncontested. The Midrash says that he appeared before Avraham as an old man and appealed to him not to kill his son—after all, such an old man could never hope to have another son. Avraham ignored him, so the Satan appeared beside Yitzchak as a young man and appealed to his feelings of loyalty to his mother. "How many fasts did your mother fast before you were born, and this old man has lost his mind, and wants to slaughter you!" When Yitzchak reported this to his father, Avraham replied, "Pay no attention to him; he only wants to exhaust you." Finally the Satan turned himself into a river to physically block the way. Avraham continued until the water reached his neck. When

מדרש תנחומא (ורשא) פרשת וירא סימן כב
קדמו השטן בדרך ונדמה לו כדמות זקן א"ל לאן אתה הולך, א"ל להתפלל א"ל ומי שהולך להתפלל למה מה אש ומאכלת בידו ועצים על כתפו, א"ל שמא בשהא יום או יומים ונשחט ונאפה ונאכל, א"ל זקן לא שם הייתי כשאמר לך הקדוש ברוך הוא קח את בנך וזקן כמותך ילך ויאבד בן שנתן לו למאה... הלך מעליו ונדמה לבחור ועמד על ימינו של יצחק א"ל לאן אתה הולך, א"ל ללמוד תורה, א"ל בחייך או במיתתך, א"ל וכי יש אדם שילמוד אחר מיתה, א"ל עלוב בר עלובה כמה תעניות נתענית אמך עד שלא נולדת והזקן הוא השתטה והוא הולך לשחטך, אמר אעפ"כ לא אעבור על דעת יוצרי ועל צווי אבי, חזר ואמר לאביו אבי ראה מה אומר לי זה, א"ל אל תשגיח עליו שאינו בא אלא ליעף לנו... כיון שהגיע עד חצי הנהר הגיע המים עד צוארו באותה שעה תלה אברהם עיניו לשמים אמר לפניו רבש"ע בחרתני הודרתני וגלית לי ואמרת לי אני יחיד ואתה יחיד על ידך יודע שמי בעולמי והעלה יצחק בנך לפני לעולה ולא עכבתי והריני עוסק בצוויך ועכשיו באו מים עד נפש אם אני או יצחק בני טובע מי יקיים מאמרך על מי יתייחד שמך, א"ל הקדוש ברוך הוא חייך שעל ידך יתיחד שמי בעולם, מיד גער הקדוש ברוך הוא את המעין ויבש הנהר ועמדו ביבשה...

151

he had done all that was humanly possible, Avraham turned to God and said, "Master of the universe, you have chosen me, and glorified me, and revealed yourself to me. And you said to me 'I am One and you are one, and through you my Name is known on my Earth—and raise Yitzchak your son up as an *olah,*' and I did not demur. Behold I am involved in your command, and water has reached my nostrils: if Yitzchak my son or I drown, who will fulfill your word, on whom will your name be unified?" At this, God scolded the spring, drying up the river, and they found themselves on dry land.

Avraham and Yitzchak were both true knights of faith. If they had any doubts, or if they were confronted with impediments to their spiritual growth, we can't attribute this to such mundane factors as sleep deprivation or a need for more physical exercise. Their obstacles must have been a final and necessary test of their ultimate resolve, like Everest's "Hillary Step," a last rock face to scale before reaching the summit.

We are not as great as our *Avot,* but neither are our challenges as great as theirs were. Usually we *can* attribute our obstacles to something natural and objective; but sometimes we also are confronted with an irrational blockage, a discouraging inner voice of doubt or an emotional river that can't be easily forded. If so, then when we are feeling down for no objective reason, then like Avraham and Yitzchak, we need to push through.

In this respect, spiritual growth is a lot like muscle growth. In weightlifting the slogan "no pain, no gain" means that the last repetition—the ultimate painful push—causes the muscle fibers to tear miscroscopically, triggering new muscle growth. Sometimes we need to muscle through days of low motivation, poor concentration, and distracting doubt. It may be painful, but the growth it triggers can be spectacular.

Rabbi Chaim of Volozhin:
Bribe Yourself to Maintain Consistency

Yeshiva Etz Chaim was founded in 1803 by Rabbi Chaim Ickovitz (1749-1821), better known as Rabbi Chaim of Volozhin.

If you say "Volozhin" to any Torah scholar, he will know what you are talking about without a second thought—the Volozhin Yeshiva; it is, after all, considered the "Mother of the Yeshivas," given the impact its students and faculty had on the development of new centers of intense Torah study in nineteenth- and early twentieth-century Eastern Europe. Even today, many diverse institutions can trace their roots and influences back to Rabbi Chaim of Volozhin and his yeshiva: Yeshivat Rabbenu Yitzchak Elchanan (Yeshiva University's RIETS); Yeshiva Rabbi Chaim Berlin in Brooklyn (named after the son of the Netziv, the Rosh Yeshiva of Volozhin); and the great yeshivas that the developed from Rabbi Yisrael Salanter's *musar* movement such as the Chevron Yeshiva in Jerusalem, the Mir Yeshiva, the Telz Yeshiva, and Beth Medrash Govoha in Lakewood (Rabbi Yisrael Salanter's *rebbe*, Rabbi Yosef Zundel of Salant, was a disciple of Rabbi Chaim of Volozhin).

Rabbi Chaim of Volozhin was arguably the Vilna Gaon's closest student, and he created an institution that would teach in the spirit of his great master: total absorption in Torah, in all its varied aspects. As a master educator, Rabbi Chaim of Volozhin must have had a lot of experience with his students' ups and downs, and his advice, written in his commentary to *Pirkei Avot*, is worth quoting at length.

The main thing for a person to get close to Hashem and to be purified, is that he should see that all of his actions for Hashem be fixed (קבועים), not passed over. So should be one's time for Torah study—like half a day in the study hall—must not be interrupted for anything, even if he has a great business, and similarly for prayer.... And even though one who is always active can't always act with the purest of intentions (לשמה), still he should not drop his

רוח חיים על אבות ב:א

... כי העיקר בבוא האדם להתקרב אל ה' ולטהר גבר יראה כי כל מעשיו לה' יהיו קבועים לא יעברו הן זמנו לתורה כמועד חצי יום ילמוד בבהמ"ד לא ישוב מפני כל אף אם יהיה לו עסק גדול וכן לעבודה... ואם כי העוסק תמיד לא יעשה תמיד לשמה, מ"מ לא יניח עסקו בשביל זה כי הוא פיתוי היצר לאמר לא תעשה לפני כל והוי הצנע לכת ועבוד מאהבה ומפתהו לטוב יותר מיה"ט. וכוונתו כי זה בודאי לא יעשה האדם תמיד ויתבטל לגמרי, אבל אם ילמוד תמיד יגבר היצ"ט עד כי יבוא כ"פ ללמוד לשמה. ועכ"ז ירוויח גם כן מה שלמד שלא לשמה. וגם הוא מבוא גדול לבוא לשמה מאם לא ילמוד כלל... והנה האדם הוא תמיד עולה ויורד ובעת ירידתו נדמה לו כי כל מה שעושה עכשיו מן התורה ומן העבודה אינו כלל בלב שלם ואין מצליח לו והיה רוצה לנוח ולהתגרות בשינה עד יעבור אותו הזמן וישוב לזריזותו. וזה ידוע הרבה להולך בדרך התורה. אבל באמת אינו כן כי האדם בנקל יוכל לעלות למדריגתו אם הוא עוסק אפי' ע"י התרשלות משלא יעסוק כלל כי יתרחק מן התורה ויותר יקשה לו להזדרז עוד...

activities because of this. That would be a seductive trick of the evil inclination, saying, "Don't show off, be more modest, and serve out of love," and he entices you to the good more than the good inclination! And his intention in this is that certainly a person can't be like this all the time, and therefore it will be completely lost. But if he studies consistently, his good inclination will grow stronger until he comes eventually to study for the right reasons. And then he can profit from what he had studied with selfish motivations in the meantime. This is also a great portal to acting with pure intentions; much greater than not acting at all… Now behold, a person is always going up and down. And at a time of descent, it seems to him as if everything he does, be it Torah study or prayer, is completely without motivation and is unsuccessful. And he wants to rest, and to escape into slumber until that period passes and he can return to his enthusiastic activity. This is well known to those who walk in the way of the Torah. But the truth is not like this. Because a person can more easily climb to his level if he acts—even with some slack—than if he doesn't act at all, since then he would distance himself from Torah, and it will be more difficult from him to get himself going again (*Ruach Chaim* on *Avot* 2:1).

There is a lot to reflect on in this passage, but a few points deserve special attention.

First, notice how Rabbi Chaim of Volozhin speaks about the natural periods of depression experienced by "those who walk in the way of the Torah." He is not saying that such people *also* feel down sometimes; rather, *especially b'nei Torah*, high-performance instruments of divine expression into the world, reach great heights, and then pendulum down. Part of acquiring greatness, making it an integral part of our character, however, is not allowing those downs to overpower us. If a behavior is meaningful to you, defining not just what you do but who you are, you need to do it consistently, whether you feel like it or not.

This is true whether you are a lawyer, or a tennis player, or a writer: if you are going to do some activity so well that it becomes part of your identity, you need to do it consistently. But this is even truer in matters relating to our divine service and our connection to God. Maharal explains, for example, the importance of having a fixed place for prayer (a "מקום קבוע") by noting that the ultimate goal of the encounter is a state of rapture, a fusing with the Divine, דביקות.[36] In this state, the awareness of God's unity becomes fixed in the consciousness of the worshipper, and several customs come to support that psychological posture. Fixed times of prayer and a fixed place for prayer represent and catalyze an unshakeable faith in, and relationship with, God. In addition, God is perfect and unchanging; He is the "unmoved mover"; so if you want to relate to Him, you need to be somewhat like Him— fixed and unchanging, unyieldingly consistent.

Rabbi Chaim of Volozhin suggests that one way to maintain consistency is to bribe yourself with some slightly self-serving motivation, like the praise of people you admire, for coming consistently to class or for taking on an extra study project. Rabbi Chaim of Volozhin teaches this in the context of the Mishnah in *Avot*, "What is the just path that a person should choose—that which is beautiful in his own eyes and beautiful in the eyes of mankind." He explains that when we are still "choosing" our way, and have not yet developed the conviction necessary to be self-sufficient (positive peer pressure), then praise from a teacher or rabbi ("beautiful in the eyes of mankind"), can help you maintain positive momentum.

The wrong reaction to a sudden lack of motivation is to just stay in bed, because once you lose momentum, it is that much harder to get moving again. In fact, the positive momentum of good behavior, for reasons noble or selfish, can help carry you through the nadir until the properly idealistic motivation kicks in again. Behavioral psychologists go one step further and claim that even if you've already stalled in a paralyzing depression, just forcing yourself to get up, get dressed, and get out of the house can help jumpstart the engine of motivation. The Ramchal in *Mesillat Yesharim* ("*The Path of the Just*") refers to this as "an external action [that] awakens an internal enthusiasm," and we will discuss this more in chapter 13.

---

36. Maharal, *Netiv ha-Avodah*, chap. 4.

So if you just make an effort to show up, even though you might not be as productive as you would like, your tenacious grip on continuity will help carry you back to a higher state.

Sefer ha-Yashar: Innovate and Appreciate

Perhaps the most classic source that deals with our issue is the *Sefer ha-Yashar* of Rabbi Yaakov ben Rabbi Meir, more commonly known as Rabbenu Tam.[37] Rabbenu Tam was from the first generation of the *Ba'alei Tosafot*. He was a grandson of Rashi and a younger brother of Rashbam, who completed some of Rashi's commentary to the Talmud after his grandfather's passing. Rabbenu Tam was known for his great saintliness, as well as for his talmudic scholarship and his great wealth (he was a financier). He survived the second crusades, and instituted a communal day of fasting (rarely observed today) on behalf of those martyrs who did not.

Rabbenu Tam's *Sefer ha-Yashar* reflects its author's many interests: a study of the many variant readings of the Talmud demonstrates Rabbenu Tam's great scholarship in this area; a section of halachic responsa, documents his role as a communal leader who received queries from all over the Jewish world. Lastly, the section of *Sefer ha-Yashar* that deals with matters of ethical excellence shows a wonderful combination of sincere piety and psychological sensitivity. Here, Rabbenu Tam recognizes the enthusiasm that naturally accompanies any new endeavor, be it a new hobby, a new course or a new tractate of Talmud. Like a new toy, divine service can also be a subject of early infatuation, which can become boring with time, ultimately being perceived as a burden.

---

37. This traditional attribution may be erroneous, based on the conflation of this work with the halachic work by Rabbenu Tam also titled *Sefer ha-Yashar*. Many scholars now believe that the *Sefer ha-Yashar* from which this passage was taken was actually written by Rabbi Zerachiah ha-Yavani, a Greek-Jewish ethicist of the thirteenth or fourteenth century.

... for whoever begins any action, if he has any pleasure in it, a desire [for it] will enter his heart. For so it is with any action that is pleasurable: at first love will enter his heart, and afterwards it will go away and hatred will enter his heart. And after a while that will go away, and so they will switch on and off constantly: one will go and the

ספר הישר - השער השישי

כי כל מתחיל לעשות שום מעשה, אם יהיה לו במעשה ההוא שום הנאה, תכנס בלבו התאוה. כי כן כל מעשה שיש בו שום הנאה תכנס בלבו האהבה ראשונה, ואחר כן תסור ותכנס בלבו השנאה, ולקץ ימים תסור, וכן יתחלפו תמיד, יסור האחד ויבא השני. אך אם תהיה הנאת העובד בעבודתו גדולה, ויש לו שכל, תעמוד האהבה ימים רבים, והשנאה ימים מספר. ואם לא יהיה לו שכל טוב ואין לו בעבודתו הנאה גדולה, או תבוא עליו ממנה הנאה מצד אחד ומהומה מצד אחר, תעמוד האהבה ימים מעטים, והשנאה תאריך ימים. וכאשר יתחלפו פעמים רבות, אם יתחדשו לאדם חדושים טובים בעבודתו אז תוסיף האהבה ותגדל. ואם יתחדשו דברים רעים תוסיף השנאה, ואם לא תתחדש בעבודה דבר, יהיו שתיהן שוות עד שיבוא השכל ויכריע ביניהן, כי, אם יהיה השכל טוב, תתחזק התאוה בשביל ההנאות הבאות ממנה. ואם תחלש האהבה תחזק השנאה ותלך הלוך וגדל ותתמעט האהבה בכל יום:

other will come. But, if the pleasure that the servant has in his service is great, and he is wise, the love will be sustained for many days, and the hatred for a few days. And if he doesn't have wisdom, and he doesn't have great pleasure in his service, or he has pleasure on the one hand and confusion on the other hand, then the love will be sustained a few days, and the hatred many days. And when this goes back and forth many times, if good innovations are invented in his service, then love will be added and will grow. And if the innovations are bad, then hatred will be added. And if nothing in the service is innovated, then the two will be equal, until the intellect comes and decides between them. Because, if the intellect is good, then the desire will be increased on account of the pleasures that come from it [the service]. But if the love becomes weak, the hatred will become stronger, and will continue to grow, and the love will wane every day (*Sefer ha-Yashar*, 6th Gate).

Rabbenu Tam describes our emotional connection to our Divine service as something of a pendulum, oscillating between enthusiasm and boredom, or worse. We can take some comfort from this description, knowing that, no matter what we do, even if we might be uninterested at any

ספר חסידים - סימן קנח

לכך טוב להתפלל ולכוין בשמחה ובכבוד
להקב"ה, להתפלל בכוונה, שלא תדבר עם
אדם קודם שתעמוד בתפלה, אלא אמור דברים
המכניעים את הלב תחילה ברחמים. וכשתתפלל
תוסיף על כל ברכה וברכה מעניינה לצרכיך,
כי ביותר הם מכינים את הלב. ואם לא תוכל
להוסיף לפי שהקהל סיימו קודם, תוסיף באחת
או בשתים כדי שלא תצטרך למהר בברכה
אחרת, ככל מה שכתבנו בסדר התחינה תוסיף:

particular time, we can keep in mind the advice inscribed on Shlomo ha-Melech's legendary ring: "This too shall pass." But Rabbenu Tam goes further, instructing us not to accept our downturns passively. We can nudge the pendulum back towards enthusiasm by appreciating the pleasure of the experience during the good times, and by making some innovation, a *chiddush*, from time to time.

I recall one of the first times I was personally struck by the power of *chiddush*. As a *ba'al teshuvah*, I only began *davening* seriously when I was 22 years old, during my senior year of college and my subsequent year at Machon Shlomo in Jerusalem. That year was truly inspired and inspiring, and my *tefillot* were filled with sincere appreciation for the treasure I had discovered. Of course, as Rabbenu

Learning to Grow

Tam teaches us, such inspiration cannot last forever. Over the course of the next couple of years, I became increasingly comfortable with the prayer-book, and my *davening* became increasingly routine and uninspired, what the Rabbis in *Pirkei Avot* disparagingly call "*tefillat keva.*" It was then that I began studying at Rabbi Tzvi Kushelevsky's yeshiva, Heichal HaTorah B'Tzion, a relatively traditional yeshiva in the Lithuanian model, in which a strong Ashkenazic pronunciation was the norm for all communal services. I had also been reading the works of the great Zionist rabbis, Rabbi Avraham Yitzchak HaKohen Kook and his successor, Rabbi Yitzchak Herzog, and saw that both of them instructed that traditional pronunciations should be maintained, even as a variety of Jews were returning to the Land of Israel. I was struck that on such varied sides of the Orthodox spectrum, there seemed to be a consensus that I should carefully differentiate between my vowels, (the *patach* and the *kamatz*; the *segol* and the *tzeirei*), so I asked my Rosh Yeshiva, and he concurred.

I had become fluent in my *davening*, but suddenly, I had a new challenge. You might think that this would put an even bigger drag on my *tefillah*, making it even more wooden and "*keva*"; instead, I was surprised that the opposite was true: the new challenge suddenly made it more fresh and exciting. It was only a new pronunciation, but it was a *chiddush* and it re-inspired love.

That experience taught me to look for modest and halachically acceptable innovations at times of disinterest. These innovations don't have to be so technical as a different pronunciation. Instead, they could be purely internal, like davening with a new emphasis of intention—for the sake of a sick child or a poor friend; as a sign of appreciation or as a call for help; with focus on family, or with focus on universal redemption. Sometimes the change in internal focus can also find external expression. For example, the *Sefer Chasidim* of Rabbi Yehudah He-Chasid encourages verbally personalizing the blessings of the *Shemoneh Esrei* (ask a teacher about the laws that regulate this custom).

We see from Rabbenu Tam that an awareness of the pleasurable aspects of our divine service can help sustain enthusiasm, and an innovation can help reignite enthusiasm. But

> **Rabbi Yehudah he-Chasid** ("Rabbi Judah the Pious," 1150–1217) was one of the great teachers of Chasidei Ashkenaz, the Pious of Germany, along with his father Rabbi Shmuel, and his student Rabbi Elazar Rokeach. His principle work, *Sefer Chasidim*, is a rich and popular guide to a religious life full of piety, repentance, and mystically based customs, many of which have become widely adopted.

sometimes innovations seem irrelevant, and the pleasure—if there ever was any—is only a faded memory. Rabbi Shlomo Wolbe, quoting this passage from the *Sefer ha-Yashar*, points to another engine of enthusiasm: the power of the intellect.[38] As your year in yeshiva or seminary continues, you may find that you have fallen out-of-love with a particular course, and you can't think of any innovation to make it fresh and exciting. You might know, in the abstract, that the subject is important, but it just seems dry and underwhelming, not worth getting out of bed for. In such moments, if your intellect is strong enough to appreciate the greatness of Torah, your privileged position to be studying it, and the power it has to improve your life and our broken planet generally, then the intellect can *decide* to love what you are doing, and give you the enthusiasm to continue.

This is how Rabbi Wolbe put it:

> When one's vision is clear and his decision is firm that life without spirituality is not worth living, and that he *must* study Torah and ascend in *mitzvot* and *middot*—with this he swings himself to the side of love, even without innovating anything new and without particular pleasure in his Torah study.

---

38. *Alei Shur* I, pg. 35.

Learning to Grow

The Torah that you learn this year, the *tefillot* that you say… they are saving the world, whether you realize it or not, whether you like it or not. But if you do realize it, then you won't drop the ball, and the sooner your pendulum will swing back towards love.

Chapter 10

Music

Sublime Uses and Vulgar Abuses

A year in yeshiva should be an intense intellectual and emotional experience. You are being confronted by complex ideas in a difficult language, while at the same time challenging fundamental assumptions about the meaning of life itself. All this can be a bit overwhelming, and for many of us a great way to decompress is to relax to some good music, the more familiar the better. This is all the more true because music is a relatively spiritual form of art. It helps to expand our consciousness and settle our souls.

As a developing *ben* or *bas Torah*, however, you may sometimes pause and wonder to what degree are your favorite tunes encouraging that development, and to what degree are they inhibiting it. Upon reflection and after many conversations some accept the approach that all "secular" music is bad, and all "Jewish" music is good and a great purging of MP3s and burning of CDs begins. This may or may not be virtuous, and I hope that this chapter will give you some guidelines for greater selectivity; but this approach also largely misses the point. Without first understanding how music works and why it was created, such censorship is akin to performing surgery with a blunt instrument, and without first studying anatomy. So at the risk of considerable oversimplification, let's first examine what music is, and then we can consider how to use it in our lives.

What is Music?

A close disciple of the Vilna Gaon, Rabbi Yisroel mi-Shklov, reported that his master considered several subjects necessary prerequisites for a proper understanding of Torah, music among them:

> So he said, all the wisdoms are necessary for our holy Torah, and are included in it, and he knew them all completely. He mentioned them: the wisdom of algebra, trigonometry, geometry, and the wisdom of music. And he praised it [music] very much. He would say that most of the reasons of the Torah, and its secrets, the songs of the Levites, and the secrets of the *Tikkunei Zohar* are impossible to know without it. And through it, people can die with a great yearning in its pleasantness. And they could revive the dead with its secrets that are hidden in the Torah. He said that Moshe Rabbenu brought down several melodies and rhythms from Mount Sinai and the rest are derivative[39] (Rabbi Yisroel mi-Shklov, *Pe'at ha-Shulchan*, Introduction).

Clearly, according to the Vilna Gaon, there is more to music than a great beat for working out, or a nice tune so you can chill. Indeed, music opens the heart and touches the soul; it washes away depression and fills us with joy, becoming a catalyst for prophecy itself. This is how *Sefer Orchot Tzaddikim* puts it:

> The Divine Presence only settles upon a joyful state. The prophets could not prophesy whenever they desired; rather, they would focus their minds and sit joyfully and with a good heart and then prophesy, because prophecy does not come through laziness or sadness, but through joy. Therefore

---

39. Vol. 1, pg. 5d.

the disciples of the prophets would have harps and drums and violins before them, and they would attempt to prophesy, as is written, "and as the player played, the hand of God was upon him" (*Sefer Orchot Tzaddikim*, The Gate of Joy).

ספר ארחות צדיקים - השער התשיעי - שער השמחה
אין השכינה שורה אלא מתוך שמחה (שבת ל ב), וכל הנביאים לא היו מתנבאים בכל עת שירצו, אלא מכוונים דעתם ויושבים שמחים וטובי לב ומתנבאים, שאין הנבואה שורה מתוך עצלות ולא מתוך עצבות אלא מתוך שמחה, לפיכך בני הנביאים מביאים לפניהם נבל ותוף וכנור ומבקשים הנבואה, כדכתיב (מלכים ב ג טו): "והיה כנגן המנגן ותהי עליו יד ה'":

Music-lovers know through experience that music can be joyful and uplifting, but how does that work and how does it relate to prophecy? Why does the Vilna Gaon speak about music in the same breath as something so seemingly cold as trigonometry? And why is music associated with the Levites as opposed to the *kohanim*?

Rabbi Shlomo Wolbe taught that true joy results from the balanced connection between opposites. The paradigm for joy is a wedding, in which man and woman are united as one; the ultimate sorrow is that of death, when the soul lives on but leaves the body behind. *Simchah shel mitzvah*—the joy we experience when we learn Torah, or pray, or do an act of kindness well—comes from our being aware of God in our lives, the fusing of heaven and earth in a moment of our making.[40] Rabbi Gershenfeld has pointed out that even infants instinctively clap their hands at times of joy, representing the meeting of the far-right and the far-left in the golden center.

When the stars find their proper place in an ordered universe, when nations of different races and customs dwell in peace, when an individual learns to integrate his body and soul, then we experience

---

40. See *Alei Shur* II, pg. 325.

joy. Not surprisingly, we borrow a word from music to describe such wondrous states of being: we call this "harmony." Our souls resonate with the order that we perceive at these times, basking in a web of interconnection in which everything just fits. Here we find an island of redemption in an otherwise chaotic world.

In contrast, when opposites clash, we are displeased and disturbed. Take a trivial example: you bring home a new device for your computer or audio system. It works great, is shiny and new, you get ready to set it up, but the $2.00 cable has the wrong connector, and it just doesn't fit. Hundreds of circuits are humming away in 21st-century perfection and one dumb connection ruins it all. How frustrating is that?

When otherwise well-functioning nations don't quite fit together we have more than just frustration: we have arms races and wars. And when kids don't get along under the same roof, we have slamming of doors and melt-downs and burn-outs. Often, people can find some way of muddling through that is not quite war, but not quite peace either, and we settle for a passing grade of 65. Think of the cold peace between Israel and Egypt. It is just living life as "good enough." Then there are subjects is in which "good enough" doesn't work, where 99% right is 100% wrong, like math. 2 + 2 is not 3.99999. Not at all. In algebra, we look for the missing variable, and find it *exactly*, and everything fits perfectly. In trigonometry we find *exactly* the lengths and angles that bring the sides together in a perfect polygon. These disciplines teach us to appreciate a world in which 99% is not acceptable, in which a cessation of violence is no substitute for true peace.

That's the theory, at least. Frankly, I'm not much of a math guy, and I've never taken much joy in an equation well solved. So on an intellectual level, I appreciate mathematical precision, but on an emotional level, I remain unmoved.

Music, on the other hand, does move me, and teaches the same lesson. When all the instruments are in perfect pitch and blend together, when the themes move from exposition through development to a climactic recapitulation, and every note is hit just right—well, then we all are in rapture, transported to a world in which all the disorder is resolved and all the pieces fit just perfectly.

This is how a young shepherd named David ben Yishai calmed King Shaul when the latter was in the throes of his depression. Shaul had violated God's command and was told that he would be stripped of his monarchy. He had failed to do the basic mission of a Jewish king: to express the abstract spiritual of God into the physical world of the political. Here were two opposites that he was supposed to unite in harmony, and he had failed. In tragic dissonance, the spirit of God, his joyful enlightenment, left him, and in its place settled a deeply depressing "*ruach ra'ah*," translated by Malbim as "melancholy."[41]

Shaul's servants could have suggested herbs or medicines, but knowing that music settles the soul, they called for a musician. Fortunately for King Shaul, they found not just any professional musician; they found David, who, in addition to the fact that he knew how to play and was handsome, also had the quality of being righteous and God-fearing (unusual even in those times among handsome musicians!).[42]

Shaul's soul was placated not by David's Torah or philosophy or mastery of war, but by his music, which restored a vision of a world as it should be. Tormented by the harsh imperfections of the "real" world and his place in it, King Shaul was comforted by the beauty of an ideal world, in which everything fits. For us as well: when our inner lives are marked by discord—anxiety over the future or depression in the present—music can realign our emotions in an optimistic vision of peace and harmony.

Unless, of course, someone is singing out-of-tune. Like a math problem which is 100% wrong when it is 99% right, one player who

---

41. 1 *Shmuel* 16:15.
42. Malbim on 1 *Shmuel* 16:18.

is off by a beat, or a half-tone, can transform a work of beauty into a cringe-inducing hour of cacophony. Music invites our souls to join in the great cosmic plan, the world as it should be; bad music leaves us frustrated with the anarchy that is.

This is why the Torah commonly associates music with the tribe of Levi. The children of Levi were the guards of the Temple and of the tradition. They maintained order and structure, sometimes by the point of the sword, valuing the laws of the Torah over the bonds of kinship. While the *kohanim* brought down a limitless flow of blessing, and therefore personified the overflowing of kindness (*chesed*), the Levites protected the integrity of the vessels that carried that flow, so that not a drop would be lost. The Levites, therefore, personified strict justice (*din*)—"They shall teach Jacob thy judgments, and Israel Thy law"[43]—sometimes taking their vigilance to an extreme, as their grandfather Levi did in Shechem. Levites, I imagine, never dared sing out of tune.

A visitor to the *Beit ha-Mikdash* would be struck by the structure and order of the divine service, accompanied by the songs of the Levites, and see our human existence acting in harmony with the greater order of the cosmos. At such blessed times, we Children-of-Man join the song of the luminaries in the sky and the angels in heaven, about whom we sing (on *Shabbat*!): שמחים בצאתם וששים בבאום עושים באימה רצון קונם, "they rejoice in their setting and delight in their setting, they perform the will of their Creator with reverence."

As Rabbi Yonason Eybeschutz writes about *Chachmat ha-Musizika*," "how great is the power of this wisdom, which the angels above and the heavenly bodies all intone and sing with a song and pleasant melody according to the good order of tones and half-tones, and they all have a root in the true wisdom...."[44]

---

43. *Devarim* 33:10; See also *Pardes Rimonim* 8:6 and *Sefer ha-Plei'ah*, "Va-yikach lo Lemech."
44. *Ya'arot Devash* 2:7.

Lyrics

When we hear good music, therefore, our souls are captivated by a vision of the universe as it should be, in perfect harmony, where everything fits. This itself can be a tonic for the tired soul, disappointed in the imperfect world in which it finds itself. And this is true whether or not any lyrics are attached. A song with words, however, has a special power: the music opens our soul and tells us "this is the harmonious way the world should be," and the lyrics slip right into our beating hearts.

To be more precise, some music is more upbeat and happy, written in major tonalities, while music in minor keys tends to be more melancholic. The happier music helps us celebrate the greatness of the world as-it-is, while the sadder music makes us long for the world as-it-should-be. In either case, however, the music opens our heart to that vision of perfection—real or ideal—and helps us internalize that vision in ways that cold prose cannot. If I tell you about my worldview, like in a lecture, I'll probably bore you; if I describe it to you in a novel or play, I'll engage you better; but if I *sing* it to you (and if I have some talent) then you will really understand what I'm trying to say, and it will move you.

Rabbi Chaim of Volozhin, based on the Kabbalah, explains the dynamics metaphysically. We humans have three major components to our individual souls: the part of the soul that interfaces, energizes and runs the physical body (the *nefesh*); the part that is the seat of our emotions, where we feel moved (the *ruach*); the part that is the seat of our abstract intellect (the *neshamah*). Similarly, Hebrew words have three parallel components: the physical, written letters; the vowels that tell us how the letters are to be pronounced; the meaning of the word. In Hebrew, the vowels are necessary for the pronunciation of the word, but were traditionally not written (like in a Torah scroll); instead they were passed down in an oral tradition. For example,

ספר נפש החיים - שער ב - פרק טז

כי ידוע שנפש האדם בכללה. היא כלולה מג'
בחי' פרטי'. והם נר"ן [נפש רוח נשמה]. שהם
עצמם הג' בחי' מעשה דבור ומחשבה... וגם
בכל תיבה יש ג בחי' מעש' דבור מחשב'. נר"ן
והם אותיו' ונקודות וטעמי' שבה... האותיות
הם בחי' מעשה כי מציאת אותיות גרידא בלא
נקודות א"א שיהיו אלא בחי' מעשה היינו
מעשה הכתיבה כמו שהם כתובי' בס"ת בלא
נקודו'. כי בדבור א"א להוציא' מהפה אם
לא ע"י צירוף הנקודות אליהם... והנקודות
הם בחי' רוח שלהם. כנ"ל שהנקודו' באים
עם האותי' ע"י הדבור של האדם שהוא בחי'
רוח... והטעמים של התיבות הם בחי' המחשבה
וכונת הלב. שהוא בחי' הנשמה כידוע. כי הם
תנועות והנהגת הנקודות והאותיות ונטייתם
לאיזה צד שהוא דבר התלוי במחשבה...
ולכן נקראים טעמים. כמו שהטעם והפי' של
כל ענין הוא השכל הנסתר שבענין שמתוכו
יוכל האדם להבינו במחשבתו... ולכן העובד
האמיתי בכוונה רצויה. יכין לשפוך ולדבק
יחד בתפלתו כל הג' בחי' נפש רוח נשמה
אשר נפשו כלולה בהם. שבעת שמוציא מפיו
כל תיבה מהתפלה שיש בה כל הג' בחי' נר"ן
באותיותיה ונקודותיה וטעמיה...

without the oral tradition, we would have trouble distinguishing between "חֵלֶב" (milk) and "חֵלֶב" (forbidden fat), and would have difficulty understanding the prohibition of "do not cook a kid in its mother's milk." When written without the familiar vocalization symbols—which are only a recent convention—the word remains ambiguous. Only when the word is spoken does it comes alive with a basic, usable meaning. Now the word has *ruach*—a life force.

In the synagogue, we do not merely read the Torah, adding vowels; we chant it, adding music. This musical addition carries a whole new level of meaning. It gives us a deeper understanding of God's intention by placing emphasis and showing how the words interrelate. The chanting of the Torah is like a punctuation system, but is much more dynamic than just commas, periods, and question marks. It adds drama and pathos, and helps bring the reading to life.

Even were the music only to indicate emphasis, we could see how the meaning would be deeply affected. Consider, for example, the difference between: "do not **cook** a kid in its mother's milk" (implies that mixing is fine); "do not cook *a kid* in its mother's milk" (implies that an adult animal is fine); "do not cook a kid in *its* mother's

ספר חסידים - סימן קנח
ואם לא תוכל להוסיף חקור לך אחר ניגונים, וכשתתפלל אמור אותן באותו ניגון שנעים ומתוק בעיניך, באותו ניגון אמור תפלתך ותתפלל תפלתך בכוונה, וימשוך לבך אחר מוצא פיך. לדבר בקשה ושאלה, ניגון שמכין את הלב. לדברי שבח, ניגון המשמח את הלב, למען ימלא פיך אהבה ושמחה למי שרואה לבבך, ותברכהו בחיבה רחבה וגילה, כל אלה הדברים המכינים את הלב:

milk" (implies that in the milk of a different animal is fine). Same words, but considerably different meaning.

Of course, the music adds emphasis, but also much more. It engages us with emotion, with the imperative of a command or the joy of a hymn. For this reason the musical notations are called "te'amim," which literally means, the "reasons," or the "flavors." The music helps us to grasp the inner meaning and to connect to it, and is therefore considered the *neshamah*—the soul—of the word.

Rabbi Chaim of Volozhin concludes that when we pray, we should try to connect all three part of every word, by visualizing the shapes of the letters, by pronouncing correctly, and by meditating on the deep meaning. This in turn helps us to connect all three parts of our souls in this act of Divine service, integrates the different parts of the physical and spiritual worlds, and creates a conduit to draw blessing from the highest sources down to our parched Earth.

Music helps us communicate to others, and helps us to focus with deep intention on what we read and say. According to the *Sefer*

Chasidim, the use of music, even in personal prayer, can help engage the heart and make our devotion more inspired.

> And if you cannot add [a personal prayer] seek out melodies, so that when you pray you can say them with that melody that is nice and sweet in your eyes: with that melody say your prayer and you will pray your prayer with focus, and your heart will be drawn after the expressions of you your mouth. In a matter of beseeching and request, a melody that prepares the heart. For words of praise, a melody that rejoices the heart, so that your mouth shall be filled with love and joy before the One Who sees your heart, and you shall bless Him with broad love and joy (Rabbi Yehudah he-Chasid, *Sefer Chasidim*, 158).

Rabbi Yisrael Salanter personally used music to help him internalize the truths of the ethical passages he studied. The technique he invented and recommended, termed *limmud musar be-hitpa'alut*, involves the rigorously intellectual study of the topic at hand, followed by singing the passage over and over again. The intellectual component guarantees that you understand clearly what you are buying into—we don't believe in brainwashing. But a clear understanding is not enough to cause an emotional identification, so the music helps create a more profound and personal connection to an otherwise abstract concept. We may not believe in brainwashing, but once we have good reason to accept the truth of the idea, we do believe in heart-washing.

Because the practice of this technique could seem a bit strange, Rabbi Yisrael recommended the establishment of local *batei musar* where students could learn, and sing, and be moved to tears without inhibitions. This is how his student, Rabbi Yitzchak Blazer, described the way in which Rabbi Yisrael would himself study *musar be-hitpa'alut*:

> And our master, the saintly gaon, may his memory be blessed, would himself study works of *musar* with tremendous wonder,[45] with a very pleasant voice that evokes melancholy. And sometimes he would repeat one statement with wonder again and again, and whoever would hear his voice—his heart would melt and become like water... his soul would almost strip away its physicality... and sometimes he would be moved to weeping (Rabbi Yitzchak Blazer, *Sha'arei Or* 9:3).[46]

Be Selective

Music is clearly a powerful tool, and like any tool, we should use it well, and judiciously. When you sing to me, I will more likely accept that this is the way the world is, or at least the way the world should be. Because of this, there are truths I internalize in my childhood that are with me today, and which will probably be with me until the day I die. For example:

Two all beef patties, special sauce,
lettuce, cheese, pickles, onions on a sesame seed bun.

I'm confident that I haven't heard this jingle for a McDonald's Big Mac in well over 25 years, but I still know the ingredients by heart. Just to give equal time to a noble competitor:

---

45. Here, the term is "התפעלות," which is difficult to translate. It is a verb in the reflexive, and can be loosely defined as: actively causing something to impact yourself emotionally.
46. See also *Or Yisroel* 2.

Hold the pickles, hold the lettuce,
   Special orders don't upset us.
All we ask is that you let us
   Serve it your way.
Have it your way, have it your way,
   Have it your way at Burger King.

No, I did not look that up, even though it is a jingle from the 1970s. I didn't have to look it up, because I spent much of my youth in *limmud* burgers *be-hitpaʾalut*. Most likely, you too can recall something that someone tried to sell you with a song. And if you are a fan of most popular music, you've been sold values and ideals of a "good life" that, on some reflection, is not so good after all.

Given the power of music, it makes sense that we need to be selective about what music we choose to enjoy. Not so long ago, this was fairly difficult: you buy an album—three good songs, six mediocre songs, and three toxic songs. But today, with iTunes, Amazon.com, and MP3 players, you can not only delete the bad stuff, you can avoid buying it in the first place.

So it is important to be selective, and today it is easy to be selective. But what should be the criteria for selecting what music to enjoy, and even more—what music can help you with your continued growth?

Rambam: Read the Words

The Mishnah in *Avot* relates the following life wisdom of Rabban Shimon ben Gamliel: "My whole life I have grown up among the Sages and I have found nothing better for the body than silence."[47]

The Rambam, in his commentary to the Mishnah, wonders why this advice is necessary: after all, if the content of the speech is Torah, it should be said, and if it is slander it must not be said; what kind of

---

47. *Avot* 1:16.

speech is at once permissible, but better to avoid anyway? Rambam then explains that there are five types of speech: commanded, desirable, permissible, undesirable, and forbidden.

Commanded speech includes everything which is a mitzvah to articulate, such as words of Torah, the Passover Haggadah, prayer, obligatory testimony, and the like. Since this speech is commanded, there is no reason to limit this kind of speech, and according to the Rambam, Rabban Shimon ben Gamliel was not referring to it.

Forbidden speech on the other hand includes slander and gossip, false testimony, and blasphemy. As forbidden speech, it obviously must not be said, and R. Shimon was not referring to it either.

Desirable speech is not commanded, but since it encourages virtues and discourages vice, praises the wise and the noble, while deprecating the wicked, this kind of speech brings benefit to individuals and society and should not be limited. R. Shimon, again, was not referring to it.

Undesirable speech is the mirror image of desirable speech: it praises the vulgar and discourages the virtuous. It may not be formally forbidden, but since it encourages bad character, it is obviously something to be avoided. R. Shimon ben Gamliel was not speaking about this type of speech either.

According to the Rambam, therefore, Rabban Shimon ben Gamliel was referring only to permissible but value-neutral speech, like business discussions, exchanging recipes, and the like. When he taught that silence is golden, Rabban Shimon ben Gamliel was encouraging limiting such mundane speech as much as is practically possible.

What does all this have to do with music? The Rambam says that the value of a song should be judged based on the same criteria. Without much regard to the language or the author, the Rambam says to judge the song on the merit of the lyrics: is it encouraging virtue, or vice, or is it just plain ear candy:

… Know that the contents of songs, in whatever language they are written, must be evaluated to see how they fit into the categories of speech as I have divided them. I explain this even though it is obvious, since I have seen elders and saints from among the people of our Torah, if they are at a feast, such as a wedding or the like, and someone wants to sing a song in Arabic—even if the subject of the song is praise of courage or generosity, and this is a desirable form of speech, or he wishes to praise the [host's] wine—they will push him away in every direction, and they

רמב"ם פירוש המשניות -
מסכת אבות פרק א
ודע שהשירים המחוברים מאיזה לשון שיהיו צריך שיבחנו בעניניהם אם הם הולכים על דרך הדיבור אשר חלקנוהו, ואמנם ביארתי זה אע"פ שהוא מבואר, מפני שראיתי זקנים וחסידים מאנשי תורתנו כשיהיו במשתה יין כחופה או זולתה וירצה אדם לשיר ערבי אפי' ענין השיר ההוא שבח הגבורה או הנדיבות והוא מן החלק האהוב או בשבחי היין ירחיקו זה בכל צד מן ההרחקה ואין מותר אצלם לשמעו, וכשישורר המשורר פיוט מן הפיוטים העבריים לא ירחיקוהו ולא ירע בעיניהם עם היות בדברים ההם המוזהר ממנו או הנמאס, וזה סכלות גמורה שהדיבור לא יאסר ויותר ויאהב וימאס ויצוה באמירתו מצד הלשון שנעשה אבל מצד ענינו שאם יהיה ענין ההוא מעלה יתחייב לאומרו באיזה לשון שיהיה, ואם יהיה כוונת השיר ההוא פחיתות באיזה לשון שיהיה אסור לאמרו, גם יש לי בזה תוספת כי כשיהיו שני פיוטים ולשניהם ענין אחד מעיר כח התאוה ושבח אותה וישמח הנפש בה והוא פחיתות והוא מחלק הדיבור הנמאס מפני שהוא מזרז ומעורר על מדה פחותה כמו שהתבאר מדברינו בפרק הרביעי ויהיה אחד משני הפיוטים עברי והאחר ערבי או לעז יהיה שמיעת העברי והדיבור בו יותר נמאס אצל התורה למעלת הלשון שאין צריך שישתמשו בו אלא במעלות כל שכן אם יצטרף אליו שישימו בו פסוק מן התורה או משיר השירים בענין ההוא שאז יצא מחלק הנמאס לחלק הנאסר ומוזהר ממנו שהתורה אסרה לעשות דברי הנבואה מיני זמר בפחיתיות ובדברים מגונים.

176

will say it is not permissible to hear. But if a singer wants to sing a Hebrew song, they will not distance him, and it will not seem bad in their eyes, even if the subject is forbidden or undesirable. And this is utter foolishness, since speech is not forbidden, or permitted, or desirable, or undesirable, or commanded based on the language in which it is made, but based on the contents. If the subject is a virtue, it is obligatory to hear it regardless of the language. And if the intention of the song is a vice, regardless of the language, it is forbidden to say it (*Commentary to the Mishnah, Avot* 1).

The Rambam goes on to assert that a song with bad contents is even worse if it is in Hebrew than if it were written in a foreign language, since it abuses the holy Hebrew language. It is outright forbidden to use biblical verses to adorn a vulgar love song.

It's hard to argue with such a reasonable position. Read the lyrics and decide if the message is something that God wants engraved into your brain and heart. If it is ennobling and moving, then by all means use and enjoy it—regardless of who wrote it or in which language it is written. If, on the other hand, it celebrates violence, or superficial romance, or lawlessness or some other vice, then delete it from your device.

Purely instrumental music likely has the status of neutral speech, which may be enjoyed any time, and certainly when useful—like to help you relax, or cheer up, or to help motivate your work-out. Still, Rabban Shimon ben Gamliel would encourage limiting this kind of music. This deliberate pulling back from sensory and sensual pleasures is an exercise in what the *Chovot ha-Levavot* and the *Mesillat Yesharim* call "*perishut*," and it is a way of breaking our addiction to physical stimuli (even if otherwise permissible), so that we can learn to appreciate better the more subtle pleasures of the spirit.

Chovot ha-Levavot explicitly applies the exercise of *perishut* to music. But this is a relatively lofty level of divine service, and I don't recommend working on it without personal guidance from a close teacher.

Of course there are some great authorities who forbid listening to almost any music as a sign of mourning for the Temple and our exile. The more common custom is relatively lenient, forbidding music only if it is accompanied by wine (and it is not at a religious celebration),

ספר חובת הלבבות
שער הפרישות - פרק ה
והשתדל אח"כ לאטום אזניך משמעך
מה שאינך צריך לו ופרוש ממותרי
השמע כפי יכלתך ואל תאזין לשמוע
מה שלא יועילך שמעו ממותרי הדברים
והכזב והרכילות ולה"ר ופרוש ממה
שיביאך להמרות הא-להים ולעזוב
מצותיו במיני הזמר והנגון והשחוק
והרגה הטורדים אותך מן המצות
והמעשים הטובים אבל הט אזנך אל
דברי החכמים היודעים את ה' ואת
תורתו כמו שאמר החכם (משלי כב)
הט אזנך ושמע דברי חכמים ואמר (שם
טו) אזן שומעת תוכחת חיים.

or forbidding the regular waking and going-to-sleep with music. This book is not, however, intended as a book on *halachah*, so you should discuss this issue with your Rabbi.

Chapter 11

Paradigms of Personal Change

Learning to Feel What You Know;
Learning to Live What You Feel

Here is a universal problem: we humans often act in a way that we know is not in own our best interests. Sometimes we make mistakes, we don't know what is bad or good, better or best; but that's not the subject of this chapter. Here I want to discuss something much more frustrating: when you *know* something is wrong, but you do it anyway, or when you know something is good, but you can't get yourself to do it.

Take, for example, the person who never exercises. Unless he has been asleep since 1970, he *knows* that an inactive lifestyle is bad for his health, both short term and long term. I don't have to detail all the problems to you, because *you* haven't been asleep since 1970. And yet, he still cannot get himself to move. Ask him: is exercise good for you; do you wish you could exercise more? He will answer yes to both questions. The problem is he *feels* exercise is bad. His head and heart are not in sync.

Many unhealthy behaviors turn into bad habits because we become "addicted" by the short term pleasures they provide: sweets, fatty meat, sex, flattery... pick your favorite vice.

Learning to Grow

So you may *know* that—for example—an "innocent" teenage romance is a bad idea, since someone is bound to get hurt, sensitivities are going to get calloused, innocence turns to cynicism, and the deepest love often is transformed by break-up into the deepest contempt. Still, when you see the happy ending of a romantic movie where the couple walks hand-in-hand into the sunset to the tune of violins (power of music, again), you don't shout out, "SOMEBODY STOP THEM!" as if it is a horror film. Instead, you sigh with delight, because emotionally it *feels* nice.

Ask a father, "Who are the most important people in your life?" and he will inevitably answer, "My wife and children." Then ask him how many hours he has spent with them this past week (time next to each other in front of the television doesn't count). After all, if these are the most important people in his life, surely he would have earnest conversations with each of them regularly. And yet, according to one statistic I recently read, the average American child watches 19 hours and 40 minutes of television per week, while spending only 38.5 minutes in meaningful conversation with his parents. The busy father *knows* these are the most important people in his life, but he can't get around to talking with them.

Proud Hypocrites

Again, there is a gap between the head and the heart that makes acting on knowledge so difficult. The father knows and says that his kids are important to him, but he acts as if they aren't. In English, we have a term for someone who says one thing and then does another: "hypocrite." If we accept this working definition, that a hypocrite is a person who says one thing and then does another, most of us will have to admit to being hypocrites. I've asked this question to groups of students many times, calling for people to raise their hands if they consider themselves hypocrites. Inevitably, I'll get 99% of the class to raise their hands (which means that only 1% of the class are liars).

Paradigms of Personal Change I

The fact is, we are *all* hypocrites. We all say one thing and do another, and when we stop to think about it we are quite embarrassed. I can get 99% of my classes to admit to being hypocrites, but I can't get anyone to admit to being a *proud* hypocrite.

And that's a mistake, because Rabbi Yisrael Salanter taught that if we are not hypocrites, that's a true tragedy. Yes, let me say that again: we should be proud hypocrites. And let me explain why with an illustration.

Imagine yourself as an adult in the 1940s. Chances are you smoke cigarettes; we all smoke cigarettes. They are perceived as a fairly harmless vice. In fact they calm the nerves and help digestion. They certainly help keep off extra pounds. And they can be quite debonair. Think Humphrey Bogart. Nobody knows about links to lung cancer or emphysema or heart disease.

But you get a cough, and go to a doctor, and to your surprise you are greeted by a pulmonary oncologist transported sci-fi style from the 21st century, together with a suitcase full of x-rays and CAT scans and sevemty years of epidemiological studies. And he wants to have a talk with you.

He has seventy years of data about the dangers of smoking, and pictures to back him up. Tissue samples. Surgeon General reports. He's got on a lab jacket and you have every reason to trust him. How long do you think it will take him to convince you that smoking is, in fact, very, very bad for your health?

One hour? Three hours? Maybe you are quite skeptical and he needs to read through a couple of journal articles with you... a day?

OK, finally you are convinced that smoking is dangerous, toxic, bad. Now, how long will it take for you to actually stop smoking? In fact, this may become a lifetime project. For one, of course, smoking is addictive, but even if it were not, actual change is far more difficult than the learning of new information. We humans can learn something intellectually very quickly, while it takes us much longer to assimilate that new knowledge into our hearts and actions. Long after we discover that something is bad for us, we may still crave it. Our heads change quickly, and our hearts slowly. As we conclude the *Aleinu*: "And you shall know *today*, and you shall place on your hearts...." Real learning is a two-step process, involving a "knowing" that can happen "today," and a placing on the heart that goes on and on.

That's why, according to Rabbi Yisrael, we need to be *proud* hypocrites. Here's the punch-line. Given that our hearts need time and work to catch up to the new ideas in our heads, the only person who is not a hypocrite—the only person who does everything he knows—is the person who has not had a new thought in a very long time.

On the other hand, anyone who is intellectually dynamic will necessarily find a gap opening up between head and heart. The only question is what to do with that gap. Rabbi Gershenfeld has pointed out that people tend to deal with this gap in one of three ways.

The BTD's

Imagine a young Jewish backpacker, Dave, who is overwhelmed with emotion as he approaches the Kotel for the first time. One of the Old City's legendary outreach rabbis, perhaps Meir Schuster or Jell Sidel, puts his arm around Dave and leads him to a yeshiva for *ba'alei teshuvah*. After several weeks of study, debate, and chulent, Dave is convinced: the Torah is divine; the *mitzvot* make us divine. You would think that Dave would be elated with his new discovery and his path to God. For a while he is. But then, inexplicably, Dave becomes depressed and starts to unravel. He has had enough. He's packing his bags.

Dave's *rebbe* calls him in for a chat, "What's gone wrong?"

"Rabbi, this just isn't for me. You tell me that going to the beach on Saturday is bad and that going to services instead is good. And

I *know* that's true, but I still would rather be at the beach. You tell me that being in yeshiva with a bunch of guys is good and having a relationship with my non-Jewish girlfriend is bad. And I *know* that's true, but I would rather be with her than with these guys, at least some of the time. I guess my soul just isn't built for this Judaism stuff, I must be—how do you call it?—*tamei*, impure. Maybe I'm Satan's spawn. I can't take it anymore. I'm leaving."

As Dave studied he grew intellectually and his heart couldn't keep up. A dangerous gap opened up between his head and his heart and Dave fell right in. He came down with a case of—as we say in the business—the "BTD's," or "Ba'al Teshuvah Depression." He blamed himself for a universal phenomenon, experienced by anyone who is intellectually dynamic, especially by yeshiva students (as we saw above in the words of Rabbi Chaim of Volozhin). Dave's only mistake was that he let that gap throw him.

The JOJ's

Others experience the gap between beliefs and actions, but react to it quite differently. Take, for example, an average Orthodox Jewish father who comes home Friday night from synagogue. The table is set beautifully, the family Kiddush cup has a slight patina from decades of blessings. The father fills the cup with his favorite wine and then standing surrounded by family and friends proclaims, effectively, the following:

> *We are gathered here once again to testify and give thanks, that our God created this world from the void, with great wisdom and kindness. We did nothing to deserve this kindness, having not yet been created, but such was His divine desire to give, that He created us so that we could receive His blessings. And so our God created us, and continues to watch over us, and*

perform miracles for us as he did in Egypt. And to help us remember this, God gave us the holy Sabbath, which we guard, and indeed celebrate, as we do now over this cup of wine.

And then he drinks the wine.

Such gorgeous words of testimony. Such a moment of celebration. After washing and breaking bread the father then proceeds to engage in conversation with his company just about everything under the sun *except* for the very profound truths he just pronounced. Perhaps they will discuss sports; perhaps politics or business. They might discuss the movies or a recent play or concert. Just about anything *except* a genuine exploration of the implications of the Kiddush. At some point there will certainly be some formal words of Torah, (*"Quiet everybody, Moshe has a Devar Torah, Moshe speak up, shkoiach, shkoiach, Chana, please pass the brisket, would anybody like some more brisket?"*) but this is more like a ritual than a spontaneous conversation, and often goes nowhere.

Now ask the father, "Excuse me, but didn't you just declare, publicly, over a cup of wine, that you believe that God created the heaven and the earth, and took us out of Egypt, and gave us the Sabbath? Do you actually believe that? If you do, why is this a matter deserving only a formal mention, a toast, and not ongoing discussion and exploration? How can you take more interest in the stock market than in the miraculous universe and the magnificent Torah?"

Do you know what he will tell you?

"Hey, chill out for a minute. Just be normal. What are you anyway, a *ba'al teshuvah*? I know there is a gap between what I know and how I act, between my head and my heart, but that's just how I am, and how my father was, and his father before him. I'll bet Moses himself was like this."

He is one of the JOJ's, the Jaded Orthodox Jews. There is a gap between his professed beliefs and his emotions—what he *knows* is important and what he *feels* is important, but he has given up trying to close that gap, or never learned how. And that's profoundly sad, because he's missing all the joy and pathos of a passionately Jewish life.

Closing the Gap

The third, and unquestionably correct response to a gap between head and heart, is to educate the heart, so that the emotions become synchronized with knowledge. This form of education is rigorous and developed, being a part of several ancient traditions. Unfortunately, it tends to be underemphasized in Western academic systems. Often it is actively discouraged.

Let me explain myself with another example.

Imagine you are in your first semester in a good liberal arts college. One of your core-curriculum courses is a seminar on "Great Books of English Literature" and you are informed on the first day that you will be reading Herman Melville's *Moby Dick*, Charles Dickens' *Great Expectations*, and William Shakespeare's *Hamlet*. You go to the bookstore and heave the first 550-page tome off the shelf and head to the library for many hours of reading. You discover early on that *Moby Dick* is a very large book about a very large fish, and you can't possibly figure out why every student in this college is being subjected to such a tedious story. Boy meets fish; boy loses leg to fish; boy hunts fish for revenge; boy dies and fish lives; *exeunt*. OK, so it was a whale, not a fish—big difference. But 550 pages?! Was Melville, like Dickens, also paid by the word?

Now if you are a real student, an intellectual, and you are confronted with a book like this... after all the frustration and boredom, do you know what you should do?

Read it again.

That's right, read it again. *Moby Dick* is, after all, perhaps the most famous nineteenth-century American novel, and your fine college believes that this book is justifiably worth being read by every incoming freshman. True, you found it wordy, and tedious, and very, very long. But maybe you just didn't crack the code. You didn't get what Melville was trying to say. So you read it again, this time trying to decrypt the symbolism, and find the inner meaning.

You notice that the protagonist is named "Ishmael," an unusual name, clearly invoking the son of Avraham... but the cast away son. The biblical Ishmael was a monotheist, but he was clearly on-the-edge, a monotheist at risk; he was a man of faith, but his faith was vulnerable and insecure. Could Melville's Ishmael be representative of this character type?

Melville knew the Bible well, and had at least some understanding of Hebrew, so it is not surprising that the evil, obsessed captain is named "Ahab," like the biblical idolatrous king of Israel. The ship was the *Pequod*, which in Hebrew (פְּקֹד) means to give reward (or punishment). So somehow, the monotheist-at-risk and the obsessed tyrant are thrown together to get their just deserts by chasing... what does the whale stand for?

Whales are powerful, and elusive. They might represent the powers of the natural world. And the whalers, therefore, might be those who would tame and harness those powers as they journey through the dangerous sea-of-life. *Moby Dick*, however, is more than just a whale, a power; he is *the* great white whale, untamable. He means no harm to those who leave him alone. But for those who have the hubris to control him, to kill him, he has no mercy.

That, therefore, might be the message of *Moby Dick*: that an arrogant attempt to usurp the power-of-powers can only be destructive to oneself, and to fellow journeymen; faith and honesty—even a partial, vulnerable faith—can be redemptive. Ishmael is the only survivor of the *Pequod*'s clash with Moby Dick, while the evil Ahab is dragged to the ocean floor by his own rope.

Paradigms of Personal Change I

Now that you've cracked the code, it seems that this book is not so bad after all. Melville beautifully expressed a deep message, and you suddenly recognize Melville's characters all around you—and within you. You might honestly ask yourself: on even your best days, are you more like Isaac, or like Ishmael. And you might take comfort in knowing that even an Ishmael can be saved from the depths.

If you are a real student, an honest intellectual, what do you do now that you have a better understanding of this story/allegory? There is an inspiring moral message here, but you probably cannot claim to have been truly changed by it. Not yet. So you know what you do?

You read it again.

This time, you know the plot and the characters and the symbolism. So you read it, this time, more thematically, less linearly. You may meditate on a particular passage for a day. And then turn back to an early part of the book to reflect on the way point B was almost inevitable given point A. You reflect on human free will, and its limitations. You dilate on the contrast between fate and faith, on the saving nature of the latter and the deadly nature of hubris that leads to the former. And after a couple of weeks of reading and re-reading, you feel like a changed person: more humble and patient; more tolerant of flaws in others, while sensing a greater responsibility for your fellow passengers on the ship that is our planet. You write an essay about your insights and growth, and you hand it in.

What grade do you think such a student should receive in this course? An "A"? "A+"?

Guess what? You failed first semester freshman English! Yes, you got an A+ on the Melville paper, but while you were re-reading and re-re-reading *Moby Dick* you totally ignored both Dickens and Shakespeare, so you receive a perfect 33.33%. F.

This example may be a bit exaggerated, but it reflects an unfortunate truth. The Western academic system often penalizes those who would prefer to slow down, think deeply, reflect and change. The message we are told again and again is: absorb as much information as possible, as quickly as possible, get tested on it and move on. So we have all been trained to develop our intellects (to some degree), but most of us have never been taught how to use our knowledge to change ourselves. Steven Covey, the bestselling author of *The Seven Habits of Highly Effective People*, makes a similar point: the overly-intellectualized and urbanized worlds of high school, college, business, law, etc., have trained us how to cram for tests. Cramming works: learn it, regurgitate it, and forget it. But imagine how disastrous your harvest would be if you tried to cram on the farm. You can't put off planting until the day before the harvest and expect positive results. Organic things need time to germinate, grow, and blossom. Our hearts and sensitivities are organic too. They too need time to grow and change, and if we try to cram in matters of emotions and ethics, we can expect the same poor results that we would get by cramming on the farm.

Why Can't I Just Muscle Through?

If you are a particularly cold, cerebral type, you might be wondering, "If I know what's right, why do I have to do all this touchy-feely work of engaging emotions and changing sensitivities? Why can't I just muscle through and do what's right based on sheer will power?"

In truth, if you have a strong will, you probably could. For a while. But think of how inefficiently you would be running your life. Trying to give charity, or to go to *minyan* on time, when you are still pulled towards selfishness and laziness, based on the power of an idea and willpower... that's like trying to go grocery shopping with a four-year-old in tow. You can do it, but it's not very efficient. There you are, reading the labels, while the kid is running amok, pulling everything sweet or shiny off the shelves.

Paradigms of Personal Change I

If, on the other hand, the child is ten and not four, you can reason with him and get him on your side. I'm a middle-aged rabbi, so I may be clever, but I don't move so fast. Nevertheless, if I properly motivate my ten-year-old kid, I don't need to move so fast; he'll do it for me. "Listen, kid. You help me out here, and I'll buy you a candy bar when we get to the checkout." All of a sudden my kid, a bundle of energy, is racing down the aisles, bringing me canned corn and lima beans.

That's what life can be like when you get your emotions in sync with your head. You've got something smart but relatively weak, directing all the energy of something less intelligent but far more powerful. Engineers have a term for such relationships: "cybernetics."

An example of a cybernetic relationship is the relationship between the thermostat in your home and the furnace in the basement. The thermostat is very smart, but not very powerful; the furnace is powerful but dumb. If you try to heat your home with only the furnace, you burn you house down. That's what happens if you live your life only on emotions, unguided by reason.

If you try to heat your home with only your thermostat, without the furnace, the results are also sad. You might think that the house just stays cold, but it's worse than that. "Go little thermostat, you can do it. More voltage! More voltage!..." Until you see a spark and a whiff of smoke. You've fried the poor thermostat, trying to get it to heat the house all by itself.

That's what you can do if you try to run your life with only your head and no heart. The results are ugly, and I've seen it happen.

In my third year in Israel I was learning at Kerem B'Yavneh, an Israeli yeshiva with a large American program, near Ashdod. One Shabbat a couple of friends who were one year behind me in my old *ba'al teshuvah* yeshiva came to visit and were impressed with what they saw. I remembered one of them was a top learner, someone who realized early on as a *ba'al teshuvah* that he wanted to go through *Shas*,

189

the entre Talmud, and had little patience for Chumash or *musar* or any of these other kinds of soft, emotional, warm and fuzzy subjects. Everyone thought he was the biggest *tzaddik* in the *beis midrash*. Everyone, except (of course) my Rabbi. He saw this guy as a car crash in slow motion, someone who was only into developing his head, while totally neglecting his heart. This is bad enough for anyone, but for a *ba'al teshuvah*, who is assimilating new information and taking on new behaviors, such neglect is particularly dangerous.

In any case, I remembered him as a star student, so when he suggested that KBY might be the right place for him the next year, I encouraged him. When I later mentioned the possibility to another rabbi of ours, his reaction was utter disbelief, "Oh, him? He hasn't been in the *beis midrash* in weeks. He's a burnt-out shell. He can't go to Yavneh; he can't go anywhere." Last I heard of him, they sent him to Baltimore to live with a nice family and to learn how to be human.

So getting the heart in sync with the head is at least important to help you run at full efficiency, happy in your divine service.

One qualification needs to be added: We are certainly talking about changing how you see the world, about modifying how your spontaneous emotional response system reacts to any situation that might confront you. But I am by no means suggesting that you brainwash yourself, or let others do that for you. That brings us to an important definition and distinction. Brainwashing is when I allow myself to be convinced of something that I have no good reason to believe. I don't believe in brainwashing: it's unethical for a teacher, uninteresting for a scholar dedicated to the pursuit of truth, and doesn't have a lasting effect.

Please don't use the methods in the next chapters to hype yourself into believing something that you have no good reason to believe. That said, I would guess that over the months you've spent at yeshiva or seminary, you *have* genuinely accepted as true at least one new idea, or lesson, or law, and have good reasons for having acknowledged its validity. If that is the case—if you are comfortable with some new concept intellectually but are not yet comfortable with the concept emotionally—we are no longer talking about brainwashing, we are talking about heart-washing. Take that one truth and bring it into your heart. By all means, do some *heart*-washing! Don't let that idea stay cold and abstract until it evaporates, and don't try to bring it into your life with the sheer force of willpower. Instead, use the methods of the next chapters to get your heart in sync with the head, and allow yourself to blossom.

Chapter 12

Paradigms of Personal Change II

Three Methods of Moving the Heart

The previous chapter introduced the problem that confronts anyone who has been learning new ideas: the more we learn intellectually, the more we sense a gap opening up between what we know and what we feel. Our internal sense of right and wrong, good and bad, sweet and bitter, has been shaped by years of education, acculturation, practice, and habit, and that internal sense is very slow to change. We can learn things overnight—that the Earth orbits the sun, for example, and not the opposite (despite all appearances); and yet, when we wake up early one morning and see the sky brighten, we still experience, emotionally, that to which we've become accustomed: a sunrise.

This emotional stickiness is not just true for things astronomical; it holds true, and is far more important, for things moral as well. For example, many of us have developed a certain fashion aesthetic, a sense of what is beautiful, from years of acculturation. Later, in yeshiva or seminary, we might learn and intellectually accept that more modest dress is better, and that what we are used to is sometimes a bit unrefined. But we remain emotionally attracted to our old familiar aesthetic and are uninspired by flowing skirts and long-sleeve blouses.

The gap that opens between the head and the heart presents a formidable challenge in the growth of any intellectually dynamic person, and that challenge was the subject of the previous chapter. Fortunately, Judaism has a set of powerful solutions to help us bridge that gap, and that's the subject of this chapter.

Method 1 – Contemplation

Towards the beginning of his *Mishneh Torah*, the Rambam asks, "What is the method for achieving love and awe of God?" One might think that such a sublime and elusive state would be a life-long project. Not so, says the Rambam:

What is the method for achieving love and awe of God? When a person contemplates God's wondrous actions and creations, and perceives in them His boundless wisdom, he immediately loves and praises and glorifies and profoundly longs to fathom His great name. As King David said, "My soul is thirsty for the Lord, the living God." And when one considers these things, immediately he is shaken backwards, and fears, and knows that he is a small,

רמב"ם יד החזקה - הלכות יסודי התורה פרק ב' הלכה ב'
(ב) והיאך היא הדרך לאהבתו ויראתו בשעה שיתבונן האדם במעשיו וברואיו הנפלאים הגדולים ויראה מהן חכמתו שאין לה ערך ולא קץ מיד הוא אוהב ומשבח ומפאר ומתאוה תאוה גדולה לידע השם הגדול כמו שאמר דוד צמאה נפשי לא-להים לא-ל חי וכשמחשב בדברים האלו עצמן מיד הוא נרתע לאחוריו ויפחד ויודע שהוא בריה קטנה שפלה אפלה עומדת בדעת קלה מעוטה לפני תמים דעות כמו שאמר דוד כי אראה שמיך מעשה אצבעותיך מה אנוש כי תזכרנו ולפי הדברים האלו אני מבאר כללים גדולים ממעשה רבון העולמים כדי שיהיו פתח למבין לאהוב את השם כמו שאמרו חכמים בענין אהבה שמתוך כך אתה מכיר את מי שאמר והיה העולם:

base, opaque creature, who stands with frail knowledge before the One with perfect knowledge. As King David said, "When I behold Thy heavens, the work of Thy fingers, the moon and the stars, which Thou hast ordained; what is man, that Thou art mindful of him, and the son of man that Thou visitest him?" (*Hilchot Yesodei ha-Torah* [*Laws of Torah Fundamentals*] 2:2).

Here, the Rambam claims that love and awe of God can be attained *immediately*, and he even uses this term twice!

It is helpful to think about this statement of the Rambam (actually, a *halachah*, a law!) in context. This is from the second chapter of the Rambam's magnum opus, the *Mishneh Torah*. What was the *first* chapter about? The first chapter of Rambam's great code of law deals with matters of theology: the existence of God; the fact that He is one; that only His existence is necessary existence (as opposed to the rest of us who exist, but who did not *have to* exist); everything depends on Him; He depends on no one. This is all very important stuff and worthy of serious study, and someone who understands it well would be appropriately considered wise and a theologian. But he wouldn't necessarily be devout and saintly; he would not necessarily be an *ohev Hashem*. How, then, can one translate theology into emotion? How can you translate *knowledge* of God into *love* of God?

That's the Rambam's chapter 2, and his method is useful for the translation of any abstract idea into a very real emotion.

As a great believer in the power of the human mind, the Rambam has a relatively cerebral answer to this question: contemplation, deep thought, can take an otherwise abstract concept (the unity of God, for example), make it real and bring it down into the heart. In the Rambam's own example, the study of God's creations help inspire us to fall in love with their Creator. But "study" is not enough, since as we all know too well, many biologists, botanists, and physicists can get so lost in their microscopes or telescopes that they lose sight of the Creator behind it all.

The kind of thought required is more poetic and holistic. The scientific study of the creation is important because it brings out the detailed structure and design; only the poetic reflection, however, can bring out the "wow" and engender love.

The Hebrew word for "reflection" or "contemplation" is "התבוננות" from the language of "לבנות"—to build—but in the reflexive form. Literally, the term could be understood as, "to build yourself," which is appropriate because that's was deep thought does. It takes the abstract blueprint of your ideals and reshapes your emotions, and through them your life, in its image.

Let me give you an example of how this could work.

My father was a three-pack-a-day smoker for as long as I knew him. He grew up in the 1940s and 1950s, so that's not such a surprise. When I was growing up, he would come downstairs in the morning, have a cup of coffee and a cigarette, and read the *New York Times*. Throughout the day, he would have a cigarette with him as often as not. The times changed, but he held onto his ways. Smoking was found to be very harmful and fell out of fashion. My father adjusted to this reality by stepping outside more often and by avoiding going to the doctor at any costs. He just didn't want to be preached to.

At some point he just couldn't avoid going to the doctor any longer. I think maybe he got a cold or something, or maybe my step-mother just talked him into having a checkup. After examining him, Dr. Wenglin said something to the effect of:

"Nate, good news, your health is just fine. For now. But you are a heavy smoker and you hate coming to me. So I'll give you two options. Like in a Chinese restaurant: you can choose Column One or Column Two. Okay, option one is you continue to smoke, and if you ever get sick, I'll take care of you. Fortunately, I'm a great doctor, I'm associated with the best hospital in New York, which is one of the greatest cities in the world. You are fairly well off, and you have great medical insurance, so if you do get sick, I you will be able to get the best medical care Western medicine has to offer. That's option one.

"Option two is a bit less complicated. You quit smoking and never see a doctor again for the rest of your life. You might find this attractive, because you hate doctors. Don't worry, I don't take it personally. Anyway, if you get sick, don't go to a doctor. If you get strep, don't go to a doctor, don't take any medicine. It will resolve. Break your leg... don't go to a doctor.

"I guarantee you that you will be happier, healthier, and live longer with option two than with option one. Because if you keep smoking... well, even I am limited in what I can do. Well, what's it going to be?"

And my dad stopped smoking. Just like that. (Well, okay, he does still chew some nicotine gum. We'll work on that.) He turned away from a forty-year-old habit and hasn't looked back.

Now my father didn't learn anything new from this speech. It's not like he suddenly sat up straight and said, "Wait a minute! You mean smoking is dangerous? Why didn't anyone ever tell me!" So there was no new information there. But there was reflection; a realization that these are not just bold type warnings on the side of the pack. Dr. Wenglin managed to put my father into the picture, to give him a clarification of implications, that this is not just an academic study, that this is for real. And thank God, he hasn't smoked ever since.

Like the Rambam says, contemplation is very powerful, transformative, and it can happen "immediately."

Rabbi Moshe Chaim Luzzatto ("the Ramchal") takes this one step further in his work *Derech Etz Chaim*. Ramchal was an extraordinary scholar and kabbalist and close to the end of his short life he wrote

one of the most
important works
of Kabbalah of
the 18th century,
the *Klach Pitchei
Chochmah* (literally
the *138 Gates of
Wisdom*). As an
introduction to this
work, he authored
a short treatise of
ethical instruction,
for kabbalists,
by a kabbalist, in
the spirit of the
Kabbalah. You
can't get the highest
levels of wisdom,
the Ramchal
teaches, with a
corrupt character.
If the Kabbalah
itself is that highest
wisdom, the actual
"Tree of Life" (as
in the famous work
Etz Chaim of Rabbi
Chaim Vital, based
on the teachings of
the great Arizal),
then excellence of

רמח"ל – דרך עץ חיים

וזה תראה, כי שנים הם בתבונה אחת נבראו: שכל
האדם, והתורה המשכלת אותו. על התורה נאמר
"הלוא כה דברי כאש נאם ה'". והודיענו בזה, כי אמת
הדבר, שהתורה היא ממש אור...

וכנגדה שכל האדם עשוי כן, כי גם כן יש לו כח
השגה רבה אך כאשר יתלהט בכח התבונות. ועל זה
כתיב (משלי ב ו): "כי ה' יתן חכמה מפיו דעת ותבונה".

...הנה על כן חוב הוא מוטל על האדם לשים עצמו
להתבונן, כי אם אינו מתבונן ומחשב, הנה לא תבוא
חכמה לבקש אותו, ונשאר בחושך בלא ידיעה. והולך
בדרכי ההבל ובאפילה, וסוף דבר יתן דין וחשבון לפני
מלך מלכי המלכים הקדוש ברוך הוא, על שלא נשתמש
מן החכמה ומן הכח אשר הטביע בו לעשות חיל. זה
ודאי פיתוי היצר, הסיטרא אחרא, אשר ישתדל בכל
עוז להפילו בזה ובבא, כי כבר ידע אם נפל בזה מעט
נשאר לו לשוב ולהתקומם, כי ידיעת האמת מחזקת
הנשמה ומרחקת ממנה היצר ודאי, ואין דבר מחליש
הנשמה לפי היצר כחסרון הידיעה:

ואם היתה הידיעה רחבה ועומדת על לב בני האדם
לא היו חוטאים לעולם, אך לא היה אפילו היצר קרוב
אליהם ושולט עליהם, כמו שאינו שולט במלאכים.
ולהיות שהקדוש ברוך הוא רצה שהאדם יהיה בעל
יצר, שיוכל להיות מנוצח או נוצח בשיקול אחד, לכן
שם בהם הידיעה, אך סגורה כגחלת, ושתוכל להתפשט
כשלהבת, והבחירה ביד האדם. וחכמינו זכרונם
לברכה, אמרו (בבא בתרא עח ב): "על כן יאמרו
המושלים בואו חשבון" (במדבר כא כז), "המושלים"
- אלו המושלים ביצרם, "בואו חשבון" - בואו ונחשוב
חשבונו של עולם! כי מי שאינו מושל ביצרו, לא ישים
עצמו לזה לעולם - אך המושלים ביצרם הם יעשו את
הדבר הזה, וילמדוהו לאחרים לעשות אותו

character is the *Derech Etz Chaim*, the *path* to the Tree of Life. The Ramchal recommends contemplation as the ultimate method for refining—perfecting!—character:

> Note that these two things were created in the same manner—the human mind, and the Torah that enlightens it. About the Torah it is said, "Behold, all of my words are as fire, says Hashem." It is also compared to fire, because all of its words and letters are like coals, that if left alone will appear to be plain dim embers. But if one should work on them, they will ignite. This is like the human mind: it also has a great capacity for understanding when excited through the power of contemplation. Therefore a great obligation is placed upon humanity to contemplate....
>
> If knowledge were broad and sustained in the heart of humanity, we would never act improperly. Even improper thoughts could not approach to control us. Since God wanted us to have temptations, in order that we should conquer or be conquered, God gave us knowledge, but shut inside like a coal, that could be released like a flame, and the choice is in our hands.

We have all appreciated the beauty of a campfire. At some point, the fire dies down and the coals get covered with white ash, and the fire looks like it is extinguished. But if you blow on it, it comes to life again, revealing warmth and multicolored lights. You don't need a new match, or new fuel. All you need is to focus concentration on the energy that is hidden inside. The mind also has God-given information locked inside, all in potential. You don't need new information or external stimulation, all you need is to appreciate the truth of what you already know. The Ramchal reveals that the oxygen that releases the warmth and transformative illumination of the mind is the power of contemplation.

This is an incredible formulation. It turns out, the Ramchal teaches, that true "free will" is *not* whether to act properly or not; true "free will" is whether to be a deep thinker or whether to be superficial, whether to be poetic or whether to be prosaic. What a promise! One who thinks deeply will never sin, while one who is shallow may have lots of information, but it all remains in potential, its transforming energy locked inside, like an oxygen-starved flame is locked inside a dim ember.

We will deal with some other methods for internalizing intellectual knowledge shortly, but for now I want to point out some of the powerful benefits of this method in particular. For one, as I mentioned above, this method can be immediately transforming. It can lift you off of a dangerous path, point you in a new direction, and restart your life. In addition, because it is so cognitively based, you internalize not just the main point, but all the subtleties. Let me give you an example: a selfish person might internalize the importance of charity by reflecting on the blessings that God showers on all His creations, and then wanting to emulate this divine model. Because he thinks so deeply about the life-giving qualities of charity, he will always give that which will bring more life. Sometimes this will be a gift of money; but if he suspects that the money will be spent by an alcoholic on drink, he will deliberately give only food. Later we will see more behaviorally based methods of change which—although powerful in their own ways—may not generate such subtle discrimination.

The disadvantage of this method is that it requires serious and profound thought, and some very good, sincere people are just not so deep and poetic. However, the very fact that you are reading this sort of book probably makes you a good candidate for the method suggested by the Rambam and Ramchal.

Method II – Consistent Thought

Let's learn about the transformation of one of the Mishnah's most famous *ba'alei teshuvah*, Rabbi Akiva.

> What was Rabbi Akiva's beginning: It is said that he was 40 years old and had not learned any oral law. Once he was standing by the mouth of a spring and asked, "Who carved this stone?" They replied, "The water that constantly falls on it every day." They said, "Akiva, didn't you read, 'stones that are carved by water'" (Job 14:19). Immediately Rabbi Akiva inferred: if something soft can hew something hard, obviously words of Torah—that are hard as iron—can hew my heart of flesh and blood. Immediately he returned to study Torah (*Avot de-Rabbi Natan,* Chapter 6).

When Rabbi Yisrael Salanter examined the details of this famous story, he discovered that it hinted to Rabbi Akiva's larger biography. Notice, for example, that Rabbi Akiva was standing at the spring after never having studied any "*oral*" law (in Hebrew, "לא שנה" from the language of "משנה"). This implies that he had studied some of the more basic *written* Torah, just not the more difficult oral Torah. In addition, at the end of the story we are told that he "*returned*" to study Torah, implying that he had been studying earlier, but quit. What's going on here?

Rabbi Akiva grew up a practically illiterate shepherd, the son of a convert. He was unlearned in the extreme. But even in his ignorance, he displayed enough character that Rachel, the daughter of a prestigious family, decided to marry him and send him to learn Torah. As he learned the written principals of Judaism he experienced the classical *ba'al teshuvah* problem: a discouraging gap was opening wide between his head and his heart.

Paradigms of Personal Change II

We can imagine the conversation between the (not yet) Rabbi Akiva and his teachers:

AKIVA: Rabbi, I know I should be focusing more during the lectures, taking fewer breaks, using my Shabbat afternoons to review the week's lessons... but I can't. I want to take walks. I miss the open pastures. On Shabbat afternoon I'm exhausted and want to nap. Why do I *know* that Torah is good, but I *want* something else?

RABBI (YEHOSHUA?): Akiva, very often when people are exposed to new ideas, they find a gap open between their heads and their hearts. The Rambam and the Ramchal will deal with this problem many centuries from now. They will recommend that you contemplate. Think deeply about the power of Torah, its ability to improve your life and rectify all of creation. Try to be less superficial and more poetic. Reflect on the truths that you are learning.

AKIVA: Excuse me, but I'm a simple shepherd. I try to think deeply, but I can't. My head hurts. I'm going out for a walk.

And he exits the yeshiva. As he is walking through the forest, Rabbi Akiva comes across a spring dripping water on a rock. The years of consistent dripping have eroded a channel into the hard granite and Rabbi Akiva has an insight.

Q: What do you get if you take a reservoir of water and dump it all on a hard rock?

A: You get a wet rock.

Q: What do you get if you take that water and drip-drip-drip it onto the rock over months and years?

A: You start to erode a channel into the rock.

Armed with his new insight, Rabbi Akiva returned to the yeshiva, to study patiently and consistently, giving time for the Torah he was learning to effect a sea-change. It took Moshe forty days to bring Torah down to Earth. It may take forty consistent days for us to bring any character trait down from abstract knowledge and into our lives.

אבות דרבי נתן פרק ששי
מה היה תחלתו של רבי עקיבא. אמרו בן ארבעים שנה היה ולא שנה כלום. פעם אחת היה עומד על פי הבאר אמר מי חקק אבן זו אמרו לא המים שתדיר [נופלים] עליה בכל יום אמרו [לו] עקיבא אי אתה קורא אבנים שחקו מים. מיד היה רבי עקיבא דן קל וחומר בעצמו מה רך פסל את הקשה דברי תורה שקשה כברזל על אחת כמה וכמה שיחקקו את לבי שהוא בשר ודם. מיד חזר ללמוד תורה.

In the previous method, we learned about the power of contemplation, deep thought. But that isn't for everyone. A more universal method is that of regular, *consistent* thought. You don't need to be such a deep thinker; all you need to do is to remind yourself of the idea over and over again. Our hearts, like our bodies, grow and change slowly over time. If you want to build your muscles, if you want to move from ten chin-ups to eleven, you need to do ten chin-ups a day, every day, for a week. Then you get the eleventh. That eleventh chin-up was not the result of the most recent exercise, but was the result of the hidden incremental growth that was almost invisible.

Because this method takes time, it can be frustrating. Like dieting, you don't see immediate results. You can go on a diet and every day the scale might continue to read "150 pounds." Monday: "150." Tuesday: "150." Wednesday: "152"! Yes, sometimes the needle even seems to move in the wrong direction. This can be discouraging, and you might give up. Ask anyone who has ever gone on a diet—consistency over the course of weeks and months is very difficult. But with perseverance, exercise, dieting, and personal development, it all pays off.

Paradigms of Personal Change II

Say for example that you know that you are not as careful with *halachah* as you should be. The regular study of a work like Ramchal's *Mesillat Yesharim* can be dramatically transformative even if you engage in it for as little as fifteen minutes a day. The very act of opening the book reminds you of the project, of the importance of self-awareness, and that reminder leaves a mark.

This method is at the heart of the "*musar seder*" that has become commonplace in most yeshivas. Traditionally, students close their Talmuds to spend about half an hour in front of some ethical work, usually in the afternoon before *Mincha* or *Ma'ariv*. Personally, this *musar seder* left me frustrated. I've always enjoyed the more philosophical parts of our Torah, so I welcomed the daily opportunity to close my *gemara* and open a *Kuzari* or a Maharal. But it takes me about ten minutes just to settle into a book, to shut out any internal or external distractions, and become fully absorbed. Then I could sit there for hours. But after twenty minutes there is a sudden *klop* on a table and everyone is beginning the evening *Ma'ariv* service, and I feel like they are clearing away my plate with the main course only half-finished.

It took me a while to understand that not everyone enjoys this genre as I do, and that not everyone could be expected to put hours dedicated to such study to good use. But everyone can benefit from opening up works of *musar* if only for half an hour. They get plugged into a way of thinking, reminding them of some topic deserving of consistent thought and work, and drip-drip-drip, they are slowly transformed.

You too can apply this by regularly and consistently engaging in the study of a personally challenging topic. Like a program of exercise or dieting, it's difficult to stay committed, and you won't notice any dramatic change from one day to the next. But be assured that after forty days, you will be emotionally and spiritually leaner and meaner.

Method III – Visualization

Sometime during the eighth or ninth century, the king, nobility, and much of the general population of Chazaria converted to Judaism from their pagan religion. Bordering the Black Sea in what is now Ukraine, Kazachstan, and Russia, a sovereign Jewish state then existed until the middle of the tenth century. The conversion of this country's elite was a source of much Jewish pride during a time of anti-Semitic persecutions elsewhere, and during the later middle ages, and the story formed the literary basis of one of the great works of medieval Jewish philosophy, Rabbi Yehudah ha-Levi's *Kuzari*.

This work describes the king as a humble, truth-seeking, ethical man, who had a familiarity with the philosophy of his day and a sharp critical intellect. Guided by a Rabbi (the *"chaver,"* who may have been Rabbi Yitzchak Sangari), the king slowly repudiated his pagan beliefs in a multitude of competing gods and the myths that attributed to them human attributes and flaws. He came to believe in the one God of the Jews, the source of all existence, infinite and perfect, without physical form and ultimately unknowable.

> **Rabbi Yehudah ha-Levi** (1075–1141), "ריה״ל‎," was one of the greatest Jewish philosophers and poets of the middle ages. Born in Spain, he was educated in the popular neo-Aristotelian philosophy of the time, but turned his back on it, preferring a theology more rooted in the Tanach and *siddur*. Many of his poems express a longing for the Land of Israel and have been included in our liturgy. He died shortly after his arrival there.

But then he read Tanach. Surprisingly, Tanach depicts not the infinite, unknowable, abstract God of Jewish philosophy, but a God who has "a strong hand and an outstretched arm" and "eyes," who rests His "legs" on a footstool of sapphire, who has emotions like "wrath" (in literal Hebrew, His "nose was on fire"), and whose image can be perceived. Puzzled, the king asked his rabbi the following question:

Paradigms of Personal Change II

THE KING: Once the matter of the dominion of God, and His unity and His power and His wisdom enters the heart of man, along with the knowledge that everything derives from Him and is dependent on Him, and that He needs nothing, both awe and love of God will be engendered. Why then do we need such anthropomorphism?

The king's question sounds a lot like the passage from the Rambam we saw in the first method—deep thought about even an abstract theological concept can engender strong emotions. But Rabbi Yehudah ha-Levi's *chaver* is not so certain.

THE RABBI: This is the claim of the philosophers. Nevertheless, we see from experience that the human soul is more frightened by the perceived presence of a frightening object than by its description. Similarly, the human soul is more attracted by a beautiful form than by its description (*Kuzari* 4:4-5).

Our emotions, after all, are more affected by what we see than by what we are told. If I tell you a ghost story, you'll feel eerie; but if I sneak up behind you and shout "boo!" you might leap right off you seat and into the campfire. If I describe a beautiful person of the opposite gender to you, you might be intrigued; but if that person were to walk into the classroom... well, I may as well end the day's lesson right then.

If I'm an advertiser, and I want to get you to buy a hamburger, or a pair of shoes or a new car, I'll want you to see them. That's one reason why television advertisements are so much more expensive than radio ads. True, the audience is bigger, but the media itself is also much more impactful. You'll never see a McDonald's ad in which a grey-haired man comes on screen in a lab jacket to describe the benefits of the burger; they *show* you the Big Mac and that's what moves you. Even if you can't use pictures, even if you are writing an essay or story, the rule is the same (remember ninth-grade creative writing): don't tell me; show me.

It is, of course, for that reason that ethically sensitive people are very selective about what images they let into their minds and hearts.

The Torah also uses powerful imagery on almost every page. It doesn't just tell you about ultimate reward and punishment, but it gives graphic images describing the attributes of God. It seems that according to the *Kuzari*, the Torah is less concerned with theological precision than it is with helping to develop moral excellence. If anthropomorphic terms (giving God a human form) help us develop love and fear of the Almighty, then the Torah will use such terms, even if they are not so philosophically precise.

Elsewhere, the *Kuzari* describes how saintly individuals apply the power of imagery in their own divine service to help them reinforce their faith or internalize virtues of character.

> The saint then commands his imagination to visualize a desired spiritual concept—a most precious image stored in his memory—such as the receiving of the Torah at Sinai, or the binding of Yitzchak by Avraham on Mount Moriah, or the Tabernacle of Moshe and the divine service and the settling of the Heavenly Presence on the Tabernacle (*Kuzari* 3:5).

The biblical stories of Divine intervention and communication, of the heroism of the patriarchs and the miracles of Moshe, should be a source of tremendous inspiration. A creative imagination can give life to the words on the page, make the concepts less abstract and more vivid, and generate the energy necessary to translate the lessons from dry history into passionate motivation.

Visualization is used not just by Rabbi Yehudah ha-Levi's saintly individuals. It is used by football coaches ("imagine yourself running for the ball, imagine yourself catching the ball and running for the touchdown") and zen golfers ("be the ball"). And it can be used by you.

If, for example, you *know* that you should quit smoking, but just can't generate the motivation to resist your cravings, go visit a cancer ward and see people sucking oxygen into their disease-ravaged lungs. Look at x-rays of emphysema and photographs of nicotine addicts taking a drag through their tracheotomies. Such vivid images speak directly to the heart and affect us far more powerfully than a clinically cold Surgeon General's warning.

A positive action that you find difficult can be rehearsed in your mind's eye, again and again, until it becomes less daunting. In my neighborhood, for example, poor individuals come to the door nightly, requesting charity for themselves or institutions they represent. If you find this intrusive, as many people do, you can rehearse in your imagination jumping from your comfortable chair to open the door with a smile and a compassionate greeting. Imagine, as well, the applause of the angels.

On a deeper level, this positive use of imagination is something shocking in its spiritual effect. The Rambam (and after him both Rabbi Ovadiah Sforno and Rabbi Yisrael Salanter) identified the power of imagination as nothing less than the *yetzer hara*—the evil inclination—itself.[48] Jews often refer to the basic conflict between the human *yetzer hara* and *yetzer tov*, but these concepts are often left too vague to be of much practical help. At best we view them as a miniature good angel and bad demon perched on our shoulders, whispering conflicting advice in our confused ears. The Rambam

---

48. *Guide for the Perplexed* 2:2; Sforno on *Bereshit* 3:1; *Iggeret ha-Musar*.

helps us by defining quite clearly what part of the human personality is this "little demon," and that is the power of imagination. After all, most of the time our imagination places us in a fantasy world in which everything is possible, sin is sweet and (the greatest fantasy!) there is no punishment. An abstract temptation can rarely cause a healthy person to stumble, but give that temptation a picture, a fantasy, and even a saint is in jeopardy.

That's how our imagination usually functions. But when it can be enlisted in the service of our intellect (the *yetzer tov,* according to the Rambam), to create a picture of how the world should and can be, to motivate us to act our best, then we are actually serving God with our *yetzer hara*! It is for this reason that we teach our children to have active, creative imaginations. And it is for this reason that, according to the Rambam, the power of imagination is a necessary component of prophecy: imagination takes a divine, abstract idea and gives it a shape, a metaphor, a means of communicating the idea to the masses and making it practical.[49]

This holy use of the imagination is, perhaps, hinted to in the *Shema,* "You shall love God with all your heart." Rashi points out that "heart" is written "לבבך" with the letter *bet* used twice, meaning both of your hearts, your good and evil inclinations. By enlisting our otherwise liberated and libertine power of imagination in our ethical development, we are truly serving God, loving God, with both our *yetzer tov* and our *yetzer hara.*

---

49. *Guide for the Perplexed* 2:32.

Chapter 13

Paradigms of Personal Change III

Moving the Heart by Modifying Behavior

Sefer ha-Chinnuch was written anonymously in thirteenth-century Spain as a primer for the author's young son. It systematically details all 613 commandments as they are divided by Maimonides, although it follows the order of the weekly Torah reading. The *Chinnuch* presents an overview of the basic laws, together with their rationale, as understood by the author. It is often printed with the *Minchat Chinnuch*, the penetrating analysis of the nineteenth-century scholar R. Yosef Ben Moshe Babad.

The previous chapter outlined the problem many dynamic thinkers face: that their emotional sensitivities often lag behind their intellectual growth. In the previous chapter I detailed three strategies for overcoming this problem: deep contemplation; consistent reflection; imagination and visualization. In this chapter I would like to conclude the topic by describing a fourth classical method that lies at the heart of many of our commandments and which has been echoed by behavioral psychologists: by changing our behavior, we can change our feelings.

Sefer ha-Chinnuch notes that many of our commandments seem to be redundant, since they each remind us of the Exodus from

Egypt. Indeed, the Exodus should never be forgotten, by can't we just keep the memory alive by meeting once a year, at the Seder, to tell over the story? Surely that alone would preserve the historical memory. Why do we also need the following commandments, all explicitly for the sake of "a remembrance of the Exodus": Shabbat; *tefillin*; *mezuzah* (according to Ramban); all of the holidays; the laws relating to firstborn animals; and, of course, all the particular commandments of Passover? The *Sefer ha-Chinnuch* concludes that this question is based on a mistaken premise regarding the function of the commandments. God gave us the commandments not to keep historical memories alive, but rather to cause those memories to animate our present lives:

> And if you consider, my son, jumping on my words to ask: and why did God command us to do all these as a remembrance of that same miracle; after all, with one remembrance the matter will be recalled and will not be forgotten by our children? You would not be asking wisely, and it is childish thinking that leads you to this. And now my son, if you are wise, hear this, turn your ear and hear: I will teach you useful matters about Torah and commandments. Know that a person is influenced by his actions, and his heart and all his thoughts constantly follow the acts he does whether they are good or bad. Even one who is completely wicked in his heart, whose thoughts and desires are only for bad, if he is inspired for the better and puts his effort and involvement with consistency in Torah and commandments, even if it is not for the sake of Heaven, immediately he will turn towards the good. And through the power of his actions, he will kill his Evil Inclination, since the heart follows one's actions. Similarly, even if one is a completely righteous person, and his heart

is just and pure, who desires Torah and *mitzvot*—if perhaps he should involve himself consistently in impure matters, for example the king forced him into a vulgar career, in truth if he were to be constantly involved in that job, after a certain amount of time he will become turn from the righteousness of his heart to be a completely wicked person. For we know, and it is true, that every man is affected by his actions.

ספר החינוך - מצוה טז

ואל תחשוב בני לתפוש על דברי ולומר, ולמה זה יצוה אותנו השם יתברך לעשות כל אלה לזכרון אותו הנס, והלא בזכרון אחד יעלה הדבר במחשבתנו ולא ישכח מפי זרענו, כי לא מחכמה תתפשני על זה, ומחשבת הנער ישיאך לדבר כן. ועתה בני אם בינה שמעה זאת, והטה אזנך ושמע, אלמדך להועיל בתורה ובמצוות. דע כי האדם נפעל כפי פעולותיו, ולבו וכל מחשבותיו תמיד אחר מעשיו שהוא עושה בהם, אם טוב ואם רע, ואפילו רשע גמור בלבבו וכל יצר מחשבות לבו רק רע כל היום, אם יערה רוחו וישים השתדלותו ועסקו בהתמדה בתורה ובמצוות, ואפילו שלא לשם שמים, מיד ינטה אל הטוב, ובכח מעשיו ימית היצר הרע, כי אחרי הפעולות נמשכים הלבבות. ואפילו אם יהיה אדם צדיק גמור ולבבו ישר ותמים, חפץ בתורה ובמצות, אם אולי יעסק תמיד בדברים של דופי, כאילו תאמר דרך משל שהכריחו המלך ומינהו באומנות רעה, באמת אם כל עסקו תמיד כל היום באותו אומנות, ישוב לזמן מן הזמנים מצדקת לבו להיות רשע גמור, כי ידוע הדבר ואמת שכל אדם נפעל כפי פעולותיו, כמו שאמרנו:

The *Sefer ha-Chinnuch* strongly believes that people can change. We may or may not be hard-wired in a certain direction, but that nature is very plastic, and can be profoundly molded by nurture. This plasticity is both a blessing and a curse, because good and bad actions alike will be self-reinforcing. Good choices lead to better choices and bad choices lead to still worse choices—as we see in *Avot* (4:2), "a mitzvah leads to a mitzvah and an *aveirah* leads to an *aveirah*." The purpose, therefore, of all the commandments that recall the Exodus is not to keep the historical memory alive, but rather to reinforce the faith that the Exodus teaches through continual symbolic actions.

As I mentioned above, contemporary behavioral psychologists echo this belief in people's ability to change in general, and to change by way of repeated actions in particular. John B. Watson, the founder of American behaviorism, has been widely quoted as saying: "Give me a dozen healthy infants, well formed, and my own specified world to bring them up in and I'll guarantee to take any one at random and train him to become any type of specialist I might select—doctor, lawyer, artist, merchant-chief, and, yes even beggarman thief, regardless of his talents, penchants, tendencies, abilities, vocations, and race of his ancestors" (Watson, *Behaviorism*, 1930). Today, many psychological maladies are regularly treated with Cognitive Behavioral Therapy (CBT), through which a person's regular and controlled exposure to otherwise uncomfortable situations and actions slowly adjusts the person's character.

Say, for example, a person is oppressively scared of heights. With CBT, we would explain to him (this is the cognitive part) that his fears are disproportionate to the actual danger, and that we can get him more comfortable with heights through therapy. We would then take him to the foot of the Empire State Building and ask him look to up. Should he faint, we will catch him, and then take him home. On the next day, he would be taken to the lobby and then brought home. Day 3: step into the elevator and step out. Day 4: step in and then let the doors close; doors open and then out and home. Doors close, elevator goes up, elevator goes down and home. By the end of a couple of weeks, we might have him leaning over the rail, counting the yellow taxi cabs. This might seem extreme, but as we saw in chapter 5, we want to counterbalance his extreme fear with a bit of extreme courage for a while, so that the "golden mean"—a healthy respect for heights, but without paralyzing fear—is able to stick.

Paradigms of Personal Change III

CBT is useful for people who are unwell, to help them function normally. Commandments work similarly for people who are well-adjusted (remember *derech eretz kadmah la-Torah*), to get them to excel. The Rambam expressed this idea very strongly in his introduction to *Pirkei Avot*, which is worth studying at length:

> The Law forbids what it forbids and commands what it commands only for this reason, i.e., that we move away from one side as a means of discipline. God therefore enjoined the following upon us: the prohibition of all forbidden foods, the prohibition of forbidden sexual intercourse, the ban concerning the prostitute, the requirement of a marriage contract and betrothal, and even so [sexual intercourse] not always being permitted but forbidden during the periods of menstruation and birth, and the further limitation upon sexual intercourse instituted by our elders who prohibited it during the daytime, as we explained in *Sanhedrin*. The purpose of all this is that we move very far away from the extreme of lust and go a little from the mean toward insensibility to pleasure so that the state of moderation be firmly established within our souls.
>
> The same applies to everything occurring in the Law with respect to the paying of tithes, the gleanings of the harvest, the forgotten sheaves, the corner of the field, the fallen grapes, the gleanings of the vineyard, the decree of the Sabbatical year and the Jubilee year, and charity sufficient for what the needy lack. These come close to prodigality so that we move very far away from the extreme of stinginess and approach the extreme of prodigality, the purpose being to establish generosity firmly within us.

Learning to Grow

If you consider most of the commandments in this way, you will find that all of them discipline the powers of the soul. For example, they eliminate revenge and vengeance by His saying: "You shall not take revenge nor bear a grudge," "You shall surely release it," and "You shall surely help to lift them up," etc.; these aim at weakening the power of rage and irascibility. Similarly, You shall surely bring them back, aims at removing the state of avarice. Similarly, the following aim at removing the state of impudence and instilling that of modesty: "You shall rise before the aged and honor the old man," "Honor your father," and "You shall not turn aside from the thing they shall tell you." Moreover, He also moves [us] away from the other extreme, i.e., shyness, for in order that shyness be eliminated and we remain in the middle way, He said: "You shall surely rebuke your neighbor and not bear sin because of him and You shall not fear the face of any man."

In this passage, the Rambam teaches his famous psychological approach to the rationale behind many of our commandments. Elsewhere, he elaborates in more detail, describing some *mitzvot* as directed to maintaining civil society (e.g., the prohibition against theft), and other *mitzvot* as teaching proper theology (e.g., praying only to G-d). Here he focuses on the many *mitzvot* that are directed at improving our character. Like *Sefer ha-Chinnuch* and behavioral psychologists, the Rambam understands that repeating an action over and over impacts the emotions and scripts the soul.

For this reason, the Rambam elsewhere points out that (all things being equal) it is better to give one dollar one hundred times than to give a hundred dollars once.[50] The very act of reaching into your pocket one hundred times scripts the soul and makes you more

---

50. Commentary to *Avot* 3:15.

generous. Remember this as you encounter beggars this year—each one of them is training you in generosity, and it is well worth a shekel or two to acquire such an elusive virtue.

The last sentence of the Rambam's passage is particularly important and worth expanding on: some commandments train us to be humble and meek (for example), while others train us to be brave and even brazen; together they make us well-balanced, noble people, comfortable bowing low when appropriate and comfortable putting up a courageous fight when appropriate. Now think about what would happen to someone who picks and chooses which commandments to keep and which to ignore. That approach could easily create a lopsided personality. A coward who is too scared to keep the commandments that require and reinforce bravery will keep only those that teach meekness, and he will become even more cowardly; an arrogant man who refuses to keep the commandments that require and reinforce humility will keep only those that require brazenness, and he will become still more arrogant.

This is not to say that Torah and *mitzvot* are an all-or-nothing proposition; certainly something is better than nothing, if only because it shows a modest level of commitment to the system that will, hopefully, flourish into something more well-rounded. But we should acknowledge that the Torah is remarkably well-balanced, and that there is a danger inherent in applying it inconsistently.

This is especially true since the way in which people "pick and choose" among *mitzvot* tends to reflect pre-existing imbalances and will reinforce those imbalances. Let's take, for another example, a glutton. Which *mitzvot* will he claim "work for him" and which will he ignore? Presumably he will love the feasting on Shabbat and holidays, and the drinking on Purim. You will find him at the Kiddush table and the wedding buffet. But *kashrut* and fasting and not eating before morning prayers? ... Not so much. So he ignores the laws that are supposed to train him in temperance, while he feasts with exuberance at every opportunity. This lopsided approach to *mitzvot* will only reinforce his character flaws instead of curing them.

Because of this phenomenom, you can actually use the system of Torah and *mitzvot* diagnostically. You see, many people know that they are imperfect and claim that they are willing to "work on themselves," but don't quite know what needs fixing. Someone who is physically ill can compare himself to the healthy people around him and realize that if he is having problems walking and they don't, then he needs to see a doctor for his legs. But someone who is surrounded by the infirm no longer has a clear point of reference to determine normalcy. If you grow up in a hospital, where one person uses a cane to help his sick legs and another uses a hearing-aid to help his sick ears, you might go to the doctor and say, "Doc, give me something for my sick arms—as hard as I flap, I can't fly!" To some extent, we are all growing up in a moral infirmary, where no one is truly healthy; so how do we determine what needs fixing?

The Rambam teaches that a healthy, well-balanced person should be able to perform the commandments fairly naturally, since "its ways are pleasant, and all its paths are peace." Therefore, if you find certain *mitzvot* particularly challenging, that should be a warning sign that you need work precisely in that area and you need to see a "doctor of the soul," Rambam's term for a Rabbi. He will likely tell you that the *mitzvot* that you most want to ignore are probably those that you most urgently need.

This work needs to be gradual, however. The same way that the person who fears heights should not be taken straight up to the top of the Empire State Building, but should be led there gradually, so the glutton should not be immediately placed on a diet of bread and water. The Rambam does teach, earlier in this same chapter, that we heal a sickness of the soul by going to the extreme. The glutton *should* spend some time on a bread and water diet, and the slothful person *should* train himself by getting out of bed early. But as we discussed in Chapter 5, they shouldn't jump to that extreme immediately.

The efficacy of this method of change—behavioral modification— has been echoed by the Ramchal in his *Mesillat Yesharim*:

Furthermore, just as zeal can result from an inner burning, so too can it create one. That is, one who perceives a quickening of his outer movements in the performance of a mitzvah conditions himself to experience a flaming inner movement, through which longing and desire

ספר מסילת ישרים - פרק ז - בבאור חלקי הזריזות

ואמנם, התבונן עוד, שכמו שהזריזות הוא תולדת ההתלהטות הפנימי, כן מן הזריזות יולד ההתלהטות. והיינו, כי מי שמרגיש עצמו במעשה המצוה כמו שהוא ממהר תנועתו החיצונה, כן הנה הוא גורם שת- בער בו תנועתו הפנימית כמו כן, והחשק והחפץ יתגבר בו וילך. אך אם יתנהג בכבדות בתנועת איבריו, גם תנועת רוחו תשקע ותכבה. וזה דבר שהנסיון יעידהו:

will continually grow. If, however, he is sluggish in the movement of his limbs, the movement of his spirit will die down and be extinguished. Experience testifies to this.

By acting *as if* we have enthusiasm, we truly acquire enthusiasm. The best way to get up on time regularly is to get up on time regularly. (Actually, Rabbi Shlomo Wolbe pointed out to me that zeal—*zerizut*— in waking begins with *zerizut*—in going to bed on time). The best way to enjoy prayer or study is to get there early, focus while there, and stay until the end. Please note, however, that this acting "as if" is different than that of the cold intellectual in Chapter 11 who claimed that he can just do what's right without trying to change his heart.

That individual was in danger of burning out by trying to act on his ideals without working to affect his emotional sensitivities. Here, the whole purpose of the action is in order to change our emotions, and we must continually monitor ourselves to be certain that we are building ourselves up and not breaking ourselves down.

Of all the methods of personal change we've discussed—deep thought, consistent thought, imagination, and behavioral modification—this behavioral method is probably the easiest. That's why it is highlighted in the *Sefer ha-Chinnuch* (written for a bar-mitzvah boy) and is towards the beginning of Ramchal's *Mesillat Yesharim*. Please excuse the comparison, but… you can train a dog this way.[51] As I mentioned briefly in the previous chapter, this method does have a relative disadvantage: since it is less intellectually based, it's not very subtle. After all, if you train yourself to be charitable by giving to everyone who asks, you may develop a reflexive generosity in which both the deserving and the undeserving are treated equally.

Fortunately, these methods are not mutually exclusive. You can mix and match and find the cocktail that works best for you. The important thing is to identify some new idea that you have learned and have good reason to believe, and realize that this knowledge only gets you half way. If you want your year in yeshiva or seminary to be more than just an intellectual exercise, if you want to take home something more valuable than a souvenir, you have some work to do. Fortunately, you also have some new tools in your toolbox.

---

51. See also, Isa. 1:3.

Chapter 14

Chanukah

The War Against the Greeks

You chose to come to yeshiva or seminary this year, perhaps deferring matriculation to university to do so, and that is wonderful. Torah is great and it deserves at least one year of intense, passionate immersion. My certainty that Torah study is amazing does not, however, motivate me to bash secular studies in general or university in particular. All wisdom, if it is true wisdom, is great. The decision whether and how to pursue your secular studies is very personal. It should be based on your goals and talents, and should be considered carefully with your parents and with a teacher you trust.

That said, you should be aware that the western academic tradition does stem from Athens, and Jerusalem and Athens have been in competition for well over two thousand years. The very word "academic" is based on the name of a wealthy Greek landowner, Academus, who allowed the students of the philosopher Plato to study in his estate. As you pause your academic studies to grow and change in Torah, you might want to reflect on the differences between these two traditions, and there is no better time than Chanukah to consider the differences between the wisdoms of Jerusalem and Athens.

There is, after all, a rhythm to the Jewish year, and each season is infused with its own special spirit. Although you should by all means enjoy the jelly doughnuts and the Chanukah parties—perhaps even a vacation for a day or two—Chanukah clearly is a time for great reflection. The lights of the *menorah* represent wisdom, and throw into relief the contrast between Greek and Jewish wisdom, for all the greatness that these two traditions share.

It is interesting that the traditional Jewish term for a heretic, "*apikorus*," is also Greek word. But what does this obscure word mean? The Talmud teaches, "What sort of person is an *apikorus*? Like those who say, 'what good are the Rabbis?'" (*Sanhedrin* 99b). Clearly, the definition of *apikorus* is not dependent on explicitly articulating this question. Instead, *apikorsut* is an attitude—a philosophy—from which such articulations can stem. By studying Chanukah, the festival which celebrates the Jews' victory over the philosophy of *apikorsut*, we can understand what was and remains the central point of conflict, and how the Chanukah victory reinforces our convictions against the

mistakes of the Greeks. Only after the danger of the Greeks' challenge is clear to us can we attempt to eat the fruit of secular wisdom while throwing away its dangerous shell.

"What is Chanukah?"

The essence of Chanukah is discussed in the following talmudic passage:

What is "Chanukah?" The Rabbis taught: The days of Chanukah are eight, beginning

תלמוד בבלי שבת כ"א:
מאי חנוכה? דתנו רבנן: בכ"ה
בכסליו יומי דחנוכה תמניא אינון,
דלא למספד בהון ודלא להתענות
בהון. שכשנכנסו יוונים להיכל
טמאו כל השמנים שבהיכל,
וכשגברה מלכות בית חשמונאי
ונצחום, בדקו ולא מצאו אלא
פך אחד של שמן שהיה מונח
בחותמו של כהן גדול, ולא היה
בו אלא להדליק יום אחד, נעשה
בו נס והדליקו ממנו שמונה ימים.
לשנה אחרת קבעום ועשאום
ימים טובים בהלל והודאה.

on the 25th day of the month of Kislev, and on them one must not eulogize or fast. When the Greeks entered the sanctuary, they defiled all the oil in the sanctuary, and when the kingdom of the Hasmonean house became strong and defeated them, they checked and found only one flask of oil remaining with the seal of the High Priest. And there was only enough in it to burn for one day, and a miracle occurred and it burned for eight days. The next year, they established them, and made them days of celebration, for giving praise and thanks (*Shabbat* 21b).

Commentators discuss which element of the holiday is most central: the oil that lasted for eight days, the military victory, or the rededication of the altar. Rabbi Isaac Alfasi (the "Rif") teaches that we should say the blessing on the miracle of Chanukah, "*she-asah nissim,*" on every night of the holiday, implying that the main miracle was the repeating miracle of the oil. Since the oil burned miraculously every day, we say the blessing *she-asah nissim* on each of the eight nights; after all, were the main

Rabbi Isaac ben Jacob Alfasi ha-Kohen (the Rif, 1013-1103) was born near Fez, Morocco. He studied under Rabbenu Nissim Gaon and Rabbenu Chananel and conceived of the idea of compiling a comprehensive work that would present all of the practical conclusions of the Talmud in a clear, definitive manner. To achieve this goal, he worked for ten consecutive years in his father-in-law's attic. The Jewish community in Fez undertook to support him and his family so that he could work undisturbed. The most famous of his many students is Rabbi Yehudah ha-Levi, author of the *Kuzari*; he also taught Rabbi Joseph ibn Migash (the Ri Migash), who was in turn a teacher of Rabbi Maimon, father and teacher of Maimonides. In 1088, the Rif left Fez for Spain, eventually becoming head of the yeshiva in Lucena in 1089. In a sense, the Rif brought the geonic period to a close—the last of the Babylonian Geonim, Rav Hai Gaon, died when the Rif was 25 years old.

miracle to be the military victory or the rededication of the altar, each of which happened only once, we would only say this blessing once at the beginning of the holiday. We universally accept the Rif's opinion and repeat the blessing *she-asah nissim* each night, focusing our attention on the miracle of the oil.

There are a few points worth noting here. One is that unlike the Babylonians and the Romans, the Greeks did not destroy the Temple. Nowhere is it mentioned that they tried to, or even wanted to destroy it. They only entered it. Similarly they didn't destroy the oil; the defiled it. It was as if they went around opening one bottle after another, but leaving the contents undisturbed. (Haven't you always wanted to do that to all the ketchup bottles in the grocery store?) What was the point? Lastly, why did they leave the flask with the seal of the Kohen Gadol undisturbed? Most oil was sealed by the local people who produced or supervised the oil. What does the rare oil sealed by the Kohen Gadol represent?

To answer these questions I would like to have the Greeks speak for themselves.

Although Socrates and Plato are among the most-remembered Greek philosophers, they were not the most popular at the time. In fact, the Senate in Athens effectively executed Socrates for poisoning the minds of the youth with his radical philosophy. And Plato was his student who led an elite academy. Aristotle, on the other hand, had a profound impact on popular Hellenism.

Aristotle and Epicurus

Aristotle was born in 384 BCE (about 200 years before the Chanukah confrontation). From 342 to 336 he tutored the teenage Alexander the Great. Aristotle wrote and taught on physics, ethics, and theology. He was a most profound thinker, and his yardstick for accepting or rejecting any theory was physical evidence and his own sharp logic. In building his view of reality he rejected that which seemed incomprehensible and embraced that which seemed most reasonable.

And so in his *Metaphysics* (XII 7) Aristotle argued that, "There is something that is always being moved in an incessant movement, and this movement is circular (as is evident not only from argument but also from observation); and so the first heaven will be eternal." Aristotle looked at the unceasing revolution of the heavens around the earth and saw a movement that, like a circle, has no beginning and no end. In other words, Aristotle concluded that creation *ex nihilo* (the creation of the world from nothing, at a particular moment in time) was a logical impossibility.

Similarly, Aristotle reasoned that a perfect God would not bother Himself with matters that are base or coarse or vulgar. A perfect God would be uninterested in the very imperfect, ephemeral objects and moments of our material world. Instead a perfect God would only reflect eternally on the most refined of things, on perfection… that is, on Himself: "The mind, then, must think of itself if it is the best of things, and its thought will be thought about thought" (*Metaphysics* XII 9). Aristotle believed in an ultimate deity, an "unmoved mover," but with clever argument Aristotle ruled out the possibility of divine creation, supervision, and providence. This cold theology echoed through and from Athens ever since.

In the century of the Chanukah confrontation even Aristotle was overshadowed in popularity by the philosophy of Epicureanism, named after the philosopher Epicurus. He was born in 342/1 BCE, and he opened his school in Athens in 307/6 (150 years before Chanukah). If you were a Hellenist at the time of Chanukah, you were probably an Epicurean. Extending Aristotle further—Aristotle rejected that which he could not comprehend—Epicurus denied all abstract truths, even mathematics, considering them uncertain. He argued that one can only be certain of his perceptions, internal or external. Thus, "the criteria of truth are the senses, and the preconceptions, and the passions." And, "if you fight against all your sensations, you will have no standard to which to refer and thus no means of judging even those sensations which you pronounce false."[52] Since for an epicurean, sense perceptions are the most certain of things, the "good" will be defined by that which has the most pleasure and the least pain. Epicureanism is the most classical hedonist philosophy.

Epicurus' physics similarly described a world "due to mechanical causes and there is no need to postulate teleology [the purpose of the world].... The evil with which human life is afflicted is irreconcilable with any idea of divine guidance in the universe."[53] The gods dwell in the "intermundia" (eating and drinking and speaking Greek, one historian of philosophy quips), separated from the world of man. Epicurus therefore "freed" man from the fear of the gods, and the world from divine providence.

In summary, these two seminal philosophers taught that we humans cannot influence the spiritual, and the spiritual cannot influence the world. There may be a God in Heaven; but He is trapped there by virtue of His own greatness. God demands nothing from us; and we can hope for nothing from Him.

Our Rabbis formulated this attitude simply:

"And darkness" — this is the Greek exile that darkened the eyes of Israel with decrees saying, write for yourselves on the horn of the ox, "we have no part in the God of Israel" (*Bereshit Rabbah* 2).

מדרש רבה בראשית פרשה ב פסקה ד

"וחושך": זה גלות יון שהחשיכה עיניהם של ישראל בגזירותיהן שהיתה אומרת להם כתבו על קרן השור שאין לכם חלק באלהי ישראל:

---

52. Diogenes Laërtius, 10,31 and 10,146 in F. Copelston, *A History of Philosophy*, vol. 1, pp. 402 - 403.
53. See Copelston.

In other words, the Greek bumper sticker would be: There may be a God, but we don't have any "part" in Him; nor does He in us. Our wheat grows because of nature, and because we have harnessed the power of the ox. We do what is wise, perhaps even what is considered by humans to be moral. But we are not spiritual.

That was the world of Hellenism in general and the world of the most popular Hellenistic philosophy, Epicureanism in particular. These doctrines are clearly antithetical to the Torah, which is why we refer to a follower of Epicurus as an *apikorus*, the classical rabbinic term for a heretic, and to this most intellectual, most "enlightened," of exiles as "darkness."

The irony involved in referring to philosophic enlightenment as "darkness" is obvious, but it also quite symbolic and profound. Notice that when you look up at the night sky from a busy city street, you will be able to find very few stars. Even without smog or obstructing buildings, the bright city lights obscure the more subtle and refined light of the stars. This is a phenomenon known as "light pollution" and astronomers take it very seriously. In many ways, the bright light of human, Greek wisdom obscured the more subtle prophetic light of the Torah, creating a spiritual darkness that was considered an "exile" even as we continued to live on our land. Wherever the radiance of secular wisdom threatens to eclipse the allure of Torah, we can safely refer to such intellectual enlightenment as a spiritual blackout.

That's accurate even when the secular wisdom is true; the competition between Athens and Jerusalem is challenging even where the two cities do not stand in open contradiction. The Hellenists, however, were "proving" and "demonstrating" with sharp wit and keen argument that the truths of the Torah—like prophecy, providence, and creation—were not just untrue, but logically impossible.

The intellectual posture of the great Greek thinkers made the prospect of winning them over and changing their minds daunting in the extreme. To the epicurean Hellenist, only seeing is believing.

To the Aristotelian Hellenist, only man's logic is the judge of all truth and the final arbiter of all reality. Our records and traditions, our claims of historical divine revelations and interventions, were all inadmissible evidence in their court of human reason. They had proven our histories not just incorrect, but impossible myths—so how could we bring these myths in our favor? For all our greatness, we had few weapons sharp enough to pierce the armor of such intellectual hubris. As the Ramban writes on his commentary to *Vayikra* 16:8 about Aristotle:

I cannot elaborate since I would need to contradict the investigators of nature who are influenced by the Greek who denied anything that is not apparent to him, and was so arrogant—he and his evil students—to doubt the truth of anything that was incomprehensible to his reason.

רמב"ן ויקרא פרק טז פסוק ח
ולא אוכל לפרש. כי היינו
צריכים לחסום פי המתחכמים
בטבע הנמשכים אחרי היוני
אשר הכחיש כל דבר זולתי
המורגש לו, והגיס דעתו
לחשוב הוא ותלמידיו הרשעים,
כי כל ענין שלא השיג אליו הוא
בסברתו איננו אמת:

One of the most important lessons of the yeshiva experience is the intellectual humility we develop after being confronted, again and again, with the infinite, prophetic wisdom of the Torah. Rabbi Gershenfeld, certainly no intellectual lightweight, once summarized how humbling yeshiva can be as follows: "I thought I understood what the Chumash was saying until I learned the Mishnah; then at least I understood the Mishnah, or at least I thought I did until I learned the Gemara; once I learned the Gemara, everything seemed clear, until I learned Rashi; Rashi gave me new insight on the Gemara... until I learned Tosfos...."

The Decrees of Antiochus IV Epiphanes

The Greeks, however, were reluctant to sit down with Matisyahu over a Gemara with Rashi and Tosafot; instead, they sent armies on elephants. Giving political muscle to the teachers' doctrines, Aristotle's and Epicurus' cultural descendant, the Seleucid king Antiochus IV Epiphanes decreed in 169 BCE a set of laws that would deny human communication with, and influence over, the spiritual world. According to tradition,[54] these decrees specified a ban on circumcision (the sanctification of even the most base human passion), a ban on the Sabbath (testimony to divine creation and providence), and a ban on the dedication of the new moon (our control over the spiritual ramifications of time). In the Midrash quoted above, the Rabbis referred to these decrees as "darkness"—not death or physical destruction, but the severing of the physical from the spiritual world.

Similarly, when the Greeks entered the Temple, they did so with the same intention, violating the sanctity of the place, not the physical structure, as if to say, "What a lovely building; we can come and go as we please, because there is nothing holy about it." They opened the flasks of oil, defiling them but leaving the contents alone, indicating that the light of human wisdom is disconnected from any supernatural source. They claimed that there is no such thing as prophetic light: God doesn't communicate; God doesn't care.

There was one flask, however, that they left untouched. The Greeks did not feel threatened by the single flask of oil sealed by the High Priest. In their view, the High Priest and the flask that represented his wisdom were too removed from the world, too spiritual. After all, they didn't deny that spirituality exists; only that it is not connected in any useful way to our physical existence. It can't illuminate anything down here. The rarified single flask of the High Priest—representing the most abstractly spiritual—was too aloof to have much earthly

---

54. See both *Pri Tzaddik* and *Sefat Emet* to *Parashat Miketz*.

effect, so they left it unmolested, a symbol of hopelessly remote spirituality. Place it on a pedestal, if you like; but you will never get significant light from it.

Then a wondrous thing happened. That rare oil that was supposed to be too spiritual to illuminate the physical world burned for eight days! There is nothing that can disprove the Greeks' heretical thesis more than a miracle—clear divine intervention. And God did it with the very object that they left as a symbol of the spirit's inability to influence the physical.

Historians of science say that because Aristotle lacked a microscope, his biology was flawed; because he lacked a telescope, his cosmology was flawed. We Jews can add: because he lacked prophecy, his theology was flawed. God does know, care, and act. And if we can't understand how that can be... that just doesn't matter, because we experience it. Similarly, we can act with confidence, knowing that everything we do to bring more of God's light into the world rectifies creation, prevents suffering and disease, and helps win wars.

The students of Epicurus will continue to ask, rhetorically, "What good are the Rabbis?" Keeping Chanukah in mind, we can respond that the Rabbis and their teachings connect us to the cause of all reality, and help us influence the unfolding of that reality at its source. Although this is a conviction that we need to have burning inside of us all the time, during Chanukah we can place it in our windows and on our doorsteps to share with friends and publicize among our neighbors.

Most of all, an awareness of Athens' blessings and challenges should inform our decisions regarding how we might best eat from the fruit of secular wisdom. The natural world is a remarkable creation and it is deserving of serious and careful study—but don't forget that the natural rests on the hidden supernatural, and that our Torah gives us special access to the mysteries behind the curtain.

Chapter 15

Asarah B'Tevet

The Day the Lights Went Out

And the word of God was upon me in the ninth year, in the tenth month, on the tenth of the month saying: Son of Man, write for yourself the name of the day, this very day the king of Babylon pressed upon Jerusalem, on this very day (Ezek. 24:1-2).

ספר יחזקאל פרק כד

(א) וַיְהִי דְבַר ה' אֵלַי בַּשָּׁנָה הַתְּשִׁיעִית בַּחֹדֶשׁ הָעֲשִׂירִי בֶּעָשׂוֹר לַחֹדֶשׁ לֵאמֹר: (ב) בֶּן אָדָם כְּתָב לְךָ אֶת שֵׁם הַיּוֹם אֶת עֶצֶם הַיּוֹם הַזֶּה סָמַךְ מֶלֶךְ בָּבֶל אֶל יְרוּשָׁלַם בְּעֶצֶם הַיּוֹם הַזֶּה:

So began the siege on Jerusalem, the beginning of the destruction of the first temple and the Babylonian exile. Given that we commemorate these tragedies on several other fast days as well, we should reflect on the unique loss of the Tenth of Tevet. What should we be thinking about and how can we use the spirit of this day to help us develop in our *avodat Hashem*? As we will see, the loss that we suffered on this day continues to permeate our religious consciousness—obstructing our access to the spiritual, undermining our respect for the Torah, and chilling our relationship with our creator. When we look into the world today, 2,600 years later, we still look at it through the eyes of the Tenth of Tevet.

Learning to Grow

As much as we should examine the meaning of any fast or holiday, this is particularly important for the Tenth of Tevet. After all, this day gets relatively little consideration, being overshadowed—perhaps for good reason—by the intense period of mourning that stretches from the 17 Tammuz (Shivah Asar b'Tammuz) until the Ninth of Av (Tisha b'Av). Those "Three Weeks" give us an entire season in which to consider our exile and grieve over our loss. The customs of that time help us to focus our attention and build to the cathartic climax of a 25-hour fast. Compared to those days, the Tenth of Tevet seems something like an afterthought, a gesture to a moment in history whose tragedy has been eclipsed by the greater tragedies that followed. One might convincingly argue that we need not fast in Tevet: since we will mourn the actual destruction in the month of Av, isn't the beginning of the siege truly superseded by those later events? The question becomes even sharper when we remember that the city continued to hold out for another three years!

The Tenth of Tevet also has some unique laws that, at first glance, are difficult to understand. For example, the Tenth of Tevet is the only public fast day that ever falls out on a Friday. In theory, were it to fall out on the Sabbath, we would have to fast even then, whereas other rabbinic fasts would be suspended until Sunday. The *Beit Yosef* brings:

> The great Rabbi David Abudraham wrote... the Tenth of Tevet is different from other fasts, since if it were to fall out on the Sabbath, we would not be able to suspend it until another day, because about it is written

בית יוסף אורח חיים סימן תקנ
וה"ר דוד אבודרהם כתב בהלכות
תענית (עמ' רנד) שעשרה בטבת
הוא משונה משאר תעניות שאם
היה חל בשבת לא היו יכולים
לדחותו ליום אחר מפני שנאמר
בו (יחזקאל כד ב) בעצם היום
הזה כמו ביום הכפורים ולא
ידעתי מנין לו זה. וכתב עוד
דעשרה בטבת חל לפעמים בששי
ומתענין בו ביום ושאר צומות
לעולם אין חלים בששי:

230

(see above) "on this very day," like on Yom Kippur. And I don't know where he got this from. He continued writing that the Tenth of Tevet does sometimes fall out on Friday, and we fast then; and other fast days never fall out on Friday.

Although the Tenth of Tevet is recorded in the books of the Prophets, since it does not originate from Sinai it has the authority of a rabbinic fast. As such, however, it is unique, falling sometimes on Friday and— in theory at least—having the power to force fasting on the Sabbath. This may seem like a somewhat technical point of legal trivia, but celebrating the Sabbath is a cornerstone of Judaism. The Sabbath almost *demands* to be celebrated, and its celebration will override every other fast day but Yom Kippur. What is so powerful about the Tenth of Tevet that it can do what even the Ninth of Av cannot?

In addition, another reason we fast on the Tenth of Tevet is in commemoration of the passing of Ezra the Scribe on the ninth of Tevet. Again, however, we can ask why this *yahrzeit* is worthy of a public fast. We don't have a public fast commemorating the death of Moshe or Aharon. Some especially righteous individuals may take upon themselves a day of fasting on such dates, but these are not communal fasts. What is different about the passing of Ezra?

Lastly, we fast on the Tenth of Tevet because during the time of the Second Temple, the Torah was translated into Greek in Alexandria. This translation, known as the Septuagint, was completed on the eighth of Tevet, and we are told that darkness immediately descended on the world for three days. But we can wonder why this translation was such a terrible event. Moshe himself translated the Torah into seventy languages before our ancestors crossed the Jordan, and certainly one of those languages was Greek! The Rabbis tell us that a *Sefer Torah* written with Greek letters (and only Greek letters!) has *kedushah* and can be used in communal readings (Mishnah, *Megillah* 1:8). So what was so tragic about this translation?

Learning to Grow

The Septuagint

Of the three events that we commemorate, the translation of the Torah is the one closest to us historically, and the one to which we can most relate. The three days of darkness the translation caused—from the eighth until the tenth of Tevet—also bracket the three events and therefore can best inform them. So let's start our study of this fast day with the history of this third century BCE translation, as it is described in one of the earliest historical sources we have, Josephus' *Antiquities* (Book XII, chap. 2).

When Alexander had reigned twelve years, and after him Ptolemy Soter forty years, Philadelphus then took the kingdom of Egypt, and held it forty years within one. He procured the law to be interpreted, and set free those that were come from Jerusalem into Egypt, and were in slavery there, who were a hundred and twenty thousand. The occasion was this: Demetrius Phalereus, who was library-keeper to the king, was now endeavoring, if it were possible, to gather together all the books that were in the habitable earth, and buying whatsoever was anywhere valuable, or agreeable to the king's inclination (who was very earnestly set upon collecting of books), to which inclination of his Demetrius was zealously subservient. And when once Ptolemy asked him how many ten thousands of books he had collected, he replied, that he had already about twenty times ten thousand; but that, in a little time, he should have fifty times ten thousand. But he said he had been informed that there were many books of laws among the Jews worthy of inquiring after, and worthy of the king's library, but which, being written in characters and in a dialect of their own, will cause no small pains in getting them translated into the Greek tongue; that the character in which they are written seems to be like to that which is the proper character of the Syrians, and that its sound, when pronounced, is like theirs also; and that this sound appears to be peculiar to themselves. Wherefore he said that nothing hindered why they might not get those books to be translated also; for while nothing is wanting that is necessary for that purpose, we may have their books also in this library. So the king thought that Demetrius was very zealous to procure him abundance of books, and that he suggested what was exceeding proper for him to do; and therefore he wrote to the Jewish high priest, that he should act accordingly.

On the face of it, this initiative of Ptolemy Philadephus and his librarian hardly seems pernicious. Here they are, freeing Jewish slaves and respectfully gathering Jewish books as they build the most famous library in the ancient world. To be sure, they consider the Hebrew tongue "peculiar" (it sounds like Aramaic!), but their charming lack of Jewish literacy is a far cry from the pillage and plunder of Nebuchadnezzar or Antiochus!

Nevertheless, you don't need to be so sensitive to realize that the translation of Philadelphus was driven by a vastly different motivation than that which brought Moshe to translate the Torah *"be'er heiteiv"* on the eastern bank of the Jordan. At best, Philadelphus was little more than a bibliophile. As he rounded the corner on half-a-million volumes, he thought that it would be nice to have the laws of the Jews as well. Instead of being The Book, the Torah became... well, just another book, complete with a Dewey Decimal Number (it is, by the way, 221.0), in the section on Semitic religions.

The seventy elders called upon to translate the Torah realized that their project was sponsored by a pagan king for the consumption of a polytheist culture. Philadelphus' motivation might have been charming, but it was also superficial; the elders justifiably feared that the Septuagint would be read superficially as well. Unless they were careful, their translation of our mysterious and sometimes cryptic Torah might accidently reinforce the Greeks' polytheism. Miraculously, they consistently and creatively managed to translate potentially problematic passages in a way that were less likely to be misunderstood.

The Talmud[55] gives many examples of the seventy elders' miraculously creative translation together with the back-story.

"Once Ptolemy the king gathered seventy two elders and placed them in seventy two chambers and did not reveal to them why he had gathered them. He went into each one and said to them, 'Write for me the Torah of Moshe your Rabbi.' G-d placed counsel into the heart of each of them and they agreed on one conception and they wrote for him: 'G-d created in the beginning; *I shall make man in a form and image…*'"

All seventy sages independently agreed to the same important changes in a miraculous way, leading to an incredible *kiddush Hashem*. Still, the Sages refer to this day as one comparable to that on which

תלמוד בבלי מסכת מגילה דף ט/א - ב
דתניא מעשה בתלמי המלך שכינס
שבעים ושנים זקנים והכניסן בשבעים
ושנים בתים ולא גילה להם על מה
כינסן ונכנס אצל כל אחד ואחד ואמר
להם כתבו לי תורת משה רבכם נתן
הקדוש ברוך הוא בלב כל אחד ואחד
עצה והסכימו כולן לדעת אחת וכתבו
לו א-להים ברא בראשית אעשה אדם
בצלם ובדמות ויכל ביום השישי וישבות
ביום השביעי זכר ונקבה בראו ולא כתבו
בראם הבה ארדה ואבלה שם שפתם
ותצחק שרה בקרוביה כי באפם הרגו
שור וברצונם עקרו אבוס ויקח משה
את אשתו ואת בניו וירכיבם על נושא
בני אדם ומושב בני ישראל אשר ישבו
במצרים ובשאר ארצות ארבע מאות
שנה וישלח את זאטוטי בני ישראל ואל
זאטוטי בני ישראל לא שלח ידו לא חמד
אחד מהם נשאתי אשר חלק ה' א-להיך
אתם להאיר לכל העמים וילך ויעבוד
א-להים אחרים אשר לא צויתי לעובדם
וכתבו לו את צעירת הרגלים ולא כתבו
לו ואת הארנבת מפני שאשתו של
תלמי ארנבת שמה שלא יאמר שחקו בי
היהודים והטילו שם אשתי בתורה:

55. See also מסכת סופרים א:ז-ט.

the Golden Calf was made. Like the construction of the Golden Calf, the Septuagint was miraculous, but tragically so. The elders certainly inoculated the Torah against polytheistic misunderstandings, but at the same time, they emptied it of much of its wonder and majesty, making it—in many ways—just another book of laws and stories appropriate for the library of a pagan king.

When we read the Torah in the original, we are (or should be) shaken by the fact that while we might understand the wise surface layer, beneath that surface rages a storm of infinite meaning, theological mystery, and Divine revelation.[56] We are meant to be provoked by strange phrases and difficult texts into a search for a fuller meaning that always lies just beyond our grasp. Presumably the translations of Moshe, carved into stone on the eastern bank of the Jordan, captured some of that wonder and mystery; but the translation in Alexandria avoided it all, deliberately producing a "Torah" that was flat and sterile.

Let's look at three important examples.

1. "Let us make man..."

The Torah reports G-d commanding: נעשה אדם בצלמנו כדמותנו, "let us make man in our form as our likeness." The Sages wonder: to whom was God speaking? They answer that he was consulting with the ministering angels. Of course, these angels would never disagree (or would they?) with the Divine plan, so why bother asking them? The Rabbis learn from God's incongruous statement, "let us make man" that even the greatest leaders should humbly consult with their subordinates.[57] Since we are expected to model God's character, the Torah emphasized divine humility here, even though this statement carried a risk of being misunderstood polytheistically—as if God were conferring with his equals. Given that Judaism is radically monotheistic, the

---

56. Rabbi Abraham Isaac ha-Kohen Kook dilates poetically on this idea at the beginning of *Orot ha-Torah*.

57. *Sanhedrin* 38b; Rashi to *Bereshit* 1:26.

risk of misinterpretation was small, and the importance of the moral lesson was great, so God commanded the Torah be written without concern for the potentially dangerous ambiguity.

When translating the Septuagint, however, the Sages could not rely on the Greeks filtering their reading through monotheistic presumptions. In fact the opposite was the case: they assumed that the Greek reading would be manifestly polytheist. Rightly fearing that the important moral lesson would be lost in a theological misinterpretation, the Sages preferred to flatten the translation and jettison the moral lesson. Their translation: "I shall make man."

2. "... in our image, as our likeness."

The continuation of the same verse contains a similarly dangerous ambiguity. God teaches that we humans are made in the divine image, uniquely endowed with an ability to make free will choices,[58] to think abstractly,[59] and to create and destroy the universe.[60] At the moment of our birth, God communicated to us the ominous potential which is our essential identity. As the Mishnah teaches, "Beloved is man who was created in the Divine image; especially beloved being informed that he was created in the Divine image."[61] It is not enough to be given this divine identity; we need to know about it, otherwise we would be in a truly tragic position.

Rabbi Noah Weinberg, the founding Rosh Yeshiva of Aish HaTorah, used to share the following analogy:

> ... imagine a group of homeless people who have taken up residence on a cold, noisy, and grimy street. Each has his own dilapidated shopping cart, spilling over with the most meager belongings imaginable. They beg for money; they sift

---

58. Seforno.
59. Rashi and Rambam.
60. *Nefesh ha-Chaim.*
61. *Pirkei Avot* 3:18.

through garbage pails for a piece of bread. It's a miserable existence.

Now suppose, in a flight of benevolence, you decide to give a million dollars to one of them. Imagine what he would do with all that money! He would buy a warm home, a comfortable bed, new clothes, a kitchen-full of groceries, etc.

There's only one problem. You hide the money in the bottom of his bag and he doesn't know a thing about it. He's schlepping around a million dollars, but he lives with the same misery, the same hopelessness, because he doesn't know what he has. What a tragedy.

The Sages are teaching us that while it's great to be created in the image of God, if we don't know what we have then we're basically living the life of a mule.[62]

Unfortunately, the translators of the Torah into Greek had a problem. Were they to translate the Torah literally, accurately, then the polytheist Greeks would completely misinterpret the verse. Instead of understanding that the Creator endowed man with divine qualities, they would interpret this verse, "Let us make man in our image" as attributing human, physical form to the Olympian gods! So what did these Sages do? Once again, they flattened the translation, safely resolving the ambiguity by jettisoning the important moral lesson. Their translation: "I shall make man in an [i.e., not *our*] image and a likeness." We may have a million dollars in our carts, but we wouldn't know it from reading the Septuagint.

3. "In the beginning..."

Sometimes the Torah hints to secrets that are truly mysterious and difficult. Nowhere is this more true than in the very first verse, "In the beginning God created the heaven and the earth." This beginning of

---

62. Rabbi Noah Weinberg, *What the Angel Taught You*, 2003, p. 121.

all beginnings, recounted with such understatement, is so loaded with esoteric wisdom that we have an entire mystical work, the *Tikkunei Zohar*, dedicated to unpacking this verse, with seventy different explanations in all. But when the seventy elders in Alexandria approached this verse, they couldn't think about preserving the secrets it contained until they first disarmed its potential theological misunderstandings.

The first potential misunderstanding of "בראשית ברא אלקים" is that God, the third word of the sentence, placed after the verb, is actually the object of the sentence and not the subject. The blasphemous misreading could be, "The primordial created god with the heavens and the earth." This would be a natural reading for someone in the Hellenistic world, being not unlike the Greek creation myth according to which light, sky, and earth all came from chaos. The seventy elders disarmed this potential misunderstanding by moving "God" to the start of the sentence: "God created in the beginning," clearly making the divine the creating subject of the sentence and not a created object.

The problem with this solution is that, according to at least one interpretation in the *Tikkunei Zohar*, אלקים really *is* the object of the sentence, indicating not God, but an archangel!

... This is Metatron who the Holy One, Blessed is He, created primordially and at-the-head ("בראשית"!) of all the multitudes of the heavens below, and this is the diminutive *Adam* that *Ha Kadosh Baruch Hu* made in the image and form of the above without adulteration...

תיקוני זוהר תקונא שתין ושבע
בראשית ברא אלקי"ם דא מטטרו"ן
דברא ליה קודשא בריך הוא קדמון
וראשית לכל צבא השמים דלתתא
ודא איהו אדם הקטן דקודשא בריך
הוא עבד ליה בדיוקנא וציורא דלעילא
בלא ערבוביא

According to this ancient mystical tradition, God himself, the true subject of the sentence, is unmentioned. The unmentioned God— or more accurately, the system of *sefirot* emanated to represent God—created an angel in the image and form of the *sefirot* to govern the lower worlds. Elsewhere our Rabbis teach that this archangel Metatron "is called by the name of his master" (*Sanhedrin* 38b).

The astonishing interpretation that God Himself is not actually mentioned in the Torah's first verse make more sense in light another mystical tradition, recorded by the anonymous author of *Sefer Maarechet ha-Elokut* (chapter 7) that God Himself, the *Ein Sof*, is nowhere mentioned by name in the Chumash, the Prophets, or in the Talmud; only the *sefirot*, emanated from the *Ein Sof*, are indicated through the divine names. And this surprising teaching of the *Tikkunei Zohar* is not unique. It echoes a similar teaching of the *Sefer ha-Bahir* (8:10), according to which the name *Elokim* indicates the *sefirah* of *Binah*, emanated from the *sefirah* of *Chochmah*, which is itself indicated by the word *"bereshit."* According to the kabbalist Rabbi Joseph Gikatilla in his *Shaarei Orah* (eighth gate), the name *Elokim* in this verse indicates not only the *sefiriah* of *Binah*, but two other of the lower *sefirot* as well.

Phew… now the object of this book is not to teach Kabbalah, so if much of the above leaves you confused, that's fine. Just understand that the first verse of the Torah is deep and mysterious and a bit confusing. It was crafted by God Himself to be able to tell a narrative of creation while hinting to metaphysical secrets, and those secrets are at once thoroughly baffling and wholly monotheistic. As a believing Jew, you can tolerate some confusion with intellectual humility; knowing that there are layers of Genesis that are beyond your grasp—for now— should leave you with a sense of the Torah's glory and a desire to continue learning.

All of this was, of course, lost on those who opened the Septuagint to the words, "God created in the beginning...."

In summary, our Ptolemy II Philadelphus coerced our Sages to translate the Torah into Greek. The Septuagint that they produced was a safe work of literature, masquerading as the wisdom of the Jews. It had been simplified and sanitized and then opened to the world for it to scrutinize and criticize. The *Sefer ha-Todaah* brings a striking analogy: it is like lion that was trapped and locked in a cage—while it roamed free everyone feared it and fled before it; and now anyone can approach and stare at it, saying, "It doesn't seem so mighty to me."

If our Torah can be dissected and critiqued in the hallowed halls of academia, if it can been treated as just another book of fables, if it can be poked at by archeologists, or feminists, or capitalists, or Marxists, or sociologists, or political scientists... we should know that this is because it was translated in Alexandria over two thousand years ago. And that's a tragedy worthy of mourning.

The Death of Ezra

Ezra the scribe died on the ninth of Tevet and his passing is commemorated on the tenth as a communal fast day. Earlier, I wondered what is so significant about the death of Ezra that justified a day of fasting; after all, we don't fast on the anniversaries of the deaths of other great leaders, not even Moshe.

Our Rabbis teach us that Ezra was also called Malachi (*Megillah* 15a),[63] and we know that Malachi was the last of the prophets. So when we mourn the death of Ezra, we are mourning not just the loss of a great individual; we are mourning the loss of prophecy.

During the age of the prophets we enjoyed an access to the realm of the holy that is difficult for us to imagine today. In a time when God spoke to us directly, we were aware of the entire creation being

63. See also Rashi to *Malachi* 2:11.

a form of divine communication. It is not accidental that the Hebrew word for an object, "דבר," is the same word for a "word." In a time of prophecy, even those among us who have not achieved active prophecy are acutely aware of the holiness of the world, that every mundane object is in truth a *devar Hashem*.

That heightened spiritual awareness during the age of prophecy had a negative corollary: people were drawn towards idolatry. Perceiving the spirituality iridescent within every brook, tree, and mountain, they were only one small mistake away from worshiping these creatures themselves. If we find idolatry difficult to comprehend, it is because with the close of the prophetic age our world has become more opaque and the objects in it seem wholly material and dull, without any spiritual core. In a world of prophecy, one might be a passionate idolater, but atheism would have seemed an absurd denial of the obvious and ever-present holy spirit that speaks through all existence.[64]

But then the lights went out. We are taught that with the death of Ezra/Malachi, the holy spirit (*ruach ha-kodesh*) left the Jewish people (*Yoma* 9b).

This marked an entirely new era, and demanded a new approach to God. After the death of prophecy, God was hidden and the world seemed flat, secular, and lonely. Atheism became possible as never before. It is perhaps no coincidence that the two most famous materialist, determinist philosophers of the ancient world, Democritus (known as "The Mocker") and Epicurus (from whose name we derive the term for a heretic, *apikorus*) lived at and just after the time of Ezra's death.

So while the death of a prophet, even one as great as Ezra, might not justify a day of public fasting, the death of prophecy certainly does.

---

64. Rabbi Jeremy Kagan has expanded on this idea in his profound book, *The Jewish Self*.

Learning to Grow

The Siege on Jerusalem

And it was in the ninth year of his rule, in the tenth month, on the tenth of the month, that Nebuchadnezzar, the king of Babylon, came with all his army against Jerusalem; and they camped against it and built siege towers around it. And the city

סֵפֶר מְלָכִים ב פֶּרֶק כה
(א) וַיְהִי בִשְׁנַת הַתְּשִׁיעִית לְמָלְכוֹ בַּחֹדֶשׁ הָעֲשִׂירִי בֶּעָשׂוֹר לַחֹדֶשׁ בָּא נְבֻכַדְנֶאצַּר מֶלֶךְ בָּבֶל הוּא וְכָל חֵילוֹ עַל יְרוּשָׁלַם וַיִּחַן עָלֶיהָ וַיִּבְנוּ עָלֶיהָ דָּיֵק סָבִיב: (ב) וַתָּבֹא הָעִיר בַּמָּצוֹר עַד עַשְׁתֵּי עֶשְׂרֵה שָׁנָה לַמֶּלֶךְ צִדְקִיָּהוּ: (ג) בְּתִשְׁעָה לַחֹדֶשׁ וַיֶּחֱזַק הָרָעָב בָּעִיר וְלֹא הָיָה לֶחֶם לְעַם הָאָרֶץ:

came under siege until the eleventh year of King Tzidkiahu. On the ninth of the month the famine became strong in the city and there was no bread for the people of the land (2 *Melachim* 25:1-3).

Four hundred and ten years after King Solomon celebrated the Temple's dedication, his descendant King Tzidkiahu looked down from the walls and witnessed Jerusalem under siege. Surrounding the city on the tenth of Tevet, the Babylonians built watch towers and posted continuous guards to ensure that nothing and no one would enter or exit. On the level of pure physical suffering, the Babylonians inflicted years of horrifying misery. According to the Midrash's descriptions, otherwise pampered young women were driven by hunger into the empty markets, hopelessly to search for any scrap of food. Finding only starving friends, the women embraced and stumbled together through the desolate city, until finally exhausted, they slid to the ground and died in the streets. Their famished toddlers, abandoned, emerged from the shadows and crawled among the bodies looking for their mothers, only to perish while pitifully sucking their cold, dry breasts.

Asarah B'Tevet

Yirmiyahu, mourning over the destruction, noted the tragic irony of Jerusalem under siege. After all, he lamented, "The kings of the land, all the inhabitants of the world, did not believe that an oppressor and enemy could enter the gates of Jerusalem" (Lamentations 4:12). Jerusalem was perceived as invincible, and not just for military reasons. It was the throne of not just the Davidic dynasty, but the earthly throne of God himself. This was the place where heaven and earth kissed, where blessing flowed out into the world in response to the prayers and sacrifices offered in its Temple. How could the conduit of divine blessing be overrun and the earth continue to exist?

Nebuchadnezar sent Nebuzaradan the chief butcher to destroy Jerusalem, and he worked at it for three and a half years. Every day he would circle Jerusalem and he could not conquer it. He considered retreating when God gave him an idea: he began measuring the wall and found that it was sinking two and a half handbreadths every day until it sank completely. Once it sank, the enemies entered Jerusalem. On that time is written, "The kings of the land, all the inhabitants of the world, did not believe that an oppressor and enemy could enter the gates of Jerusalem." Since they sinned they were exiled, and since they were exiled Yirmiyahu wailed over them, "*Eichah*"!

> **איכה רבה, פתיחתות ל**
> ושלח נבוזראדן רב טבחים להחריב
> את ירושלים ועשה שם שלש שנים
> ומחצה, בכל יום מקיף את ירושלים
> ולא היה יכול לכבשה, בקש לחזור
> נתן הקדוש ברוך הוא בלבו התחיל
> ממדד בחומה והיתה שוקעת בכל יום
> טפחיים ומחצה עד ששקעה כולה,
> וכיון ששקעה כולה נכנסו השונאים
> לירושלים, על אותה שעה הוא אומר
> לא האמינו מלכי ארץ וכל יושבי תבל
> כי יבא צר ואויב בשערי ירושלים,
> כיון שחטאו גלו וכיון שגלו התחיל
> ירמיה מקונן עליהם איכה.

Rabbi Moshe Shapira, reflecting on this passage, noted that anyone who is sensitive to what Jerusalem represents should be provoked by the image of *measuring the walls* of Jerusalem. This royal city of divine light and blessing was in many ways beyond all material measure. This could be seen most obviously in the teaching of the Rabbis that pilgrims to the Temple could be standing shoulder-to-shoulder, but when it came time to bow prostrate, miraculously, everyone had ample room around them (*Avot* 5:4). Similarly, the Rabbis point out that that the open floor space of the Temple's Holy of Holies was not diminished by the presence of the Ark of the covenant; the Ark, miraculously, did not take up any space (*Megillah* 10b).

When Nebuzadaran measured the walls, he was in effect trivializing the unique greatness of this city. He was expressing that this city—once the seat of infinite divine overflow—is in actuality quite finite, with walls so high, so wide and so deep; that this eternal city is actually within the bounds of history, with a beginning, a middle… and an end.

Of course, this is precisely the definition of a siege—it limits the surrounded city. Nothing goes in and nothing comes out. This would be horrific for any city, but in the case of Jerusalem, it opposes its very nature. Jerusalem, after all, is the city of divine overflow. It is the place where prayers go in and energy comes out. That is Jerusalem's essential function. Choking off Jerusalem is truly undermining its most basic essence, while choking off the flow of divine light into the world. God would not permit our planet to wither and die, so He continues to provide life even after the Tenth of Tevet. But that life comes into the world in ways that are darker and polluted, without the illuminating clarity that we once had and tragically squandered.

Asarah B'Tevet

Summary

In summary, whether we consider the divine wisdom once obvious in Torah, the prophetic energy once iridescent in the world, or the life-giving blessing that once flowed through Jerusalem and out into the universe, all our points of contact with God have become fundamentally distorted, and they did so on the Tenth of Tevet. The three days of darkness following the translation of the Torah on the eighth of Tevet bracket the eighth, ninth, and tenth, and represent a *chazakah*, an established new way of relating to God, not through the clarity of light, but in darkness.

We express this in the *Selichot* prayer that we say on this fast day:

In the month of Tevet
I have been greatly afflicted,
and all the pathways
have been distorted...

Obviously, the siege on Jerusalem happened before the breach of the wall or the destruction of the Temple. The Tenth of Tevet was the beginning of the tragic downfall. It represents the day that the lights went out. Afterwards, everything else happened in the vague darkness of our spiritual eclipse. Rabbi Shapira explained that this is the reason why if the Seventeenth of Tammuz or the Ninth of Av fall out on Shabbat, we can move the fast to

סֵדֶר סְלִיחוֹת לַעֲשָׂרָה בְּטֵבֵת
אֶזְכְּרָה מָצוֹק אֲשֶׁר קְרָאַנִי. בְּשָׁלֹשׁ
מַכּוֹת בַּחֹדֶשׁ הַזֶּה הִכַּנִי. גִּדְּעַנִי הֲנִיאַנִי
הִכְאַנִי. אַךְ עַתָּה הֶלְאָנִי:
דְּעָכַנִי בִּשְׁמוֹנָה בּוֹ שְׂמָאלִית
וִימָנִית. הֲלֹא שְׁלָשְׁתָּן קְבַעְתִּי תַּעֲנִית.
וּמֶלֶךְ יָוָן אֲנָסַנִי לִכְתּוֹב דָּת יְוָנִית. עַל
גַּבֵּי חֲרָשׁוּ חוֹרְשִׁים הֶאֱרִיכוּ מַעֲנִית:
זֹעַמְתִּי בְּתִשְׁעָה בּוֹ בִּכְלִמָּה וְחֵפֶר.
חָשַׁךְ מֵעָלַי מְעִיל הוֹד וָצֶפֶר. טָרוֹף
טֹרַף בּוֹ הַנּוֹתֵן אִמְרֵי שֶׁפֶר. הוּא
עֶזְרָא הַסּוֹפֵר:
יוֹם עֲשִׂירִי צֻוָּה בֶּן בּוּזִי הַחוֹזֶה.
כְּתָב לְךָ בְּסֵפֶר הַמַּחֲזֶה. לְזִכָּרוֹן לְעָם
נָמֵס וְנִבְזֶה. אֶת עֶצֶם הַיּוֹם הַזֶּה...
יָרֵחַ טֵבֵת מְאֹד לְקִיתִי בוֹ. וְנִשְׁתַּנּוּ
עָלַי סְדָרֵי נְתִיבוֹ. סָרַרְתִּי פְּשָׁעְתִּי
יִגְלֶה לִי טוּבוֹ. הָאוֹמֵר לַיָּם עַד פֹּה
תָבֹא:

a different day, because after the siege everything became fuzzy. This vague nature is expressed by the Bible's referring to these fast days by the months in which they fall: the fast of the fourth month, the fast of the fifth. They are referred to by their "moon," the fuzzy luminary of the dark night. If we fast on the ninth of Av or the tenth, it doesn't make such a big difference—the important thing is that we get the month, the moon, right.

This is not true of the Tenth of Tevet. After all, everything was sharp and clear until the lights went out, so we know exactly when that happened, and we are told to remember that clarity we once had and to mourn that clarity we once lost: "Son of Man, write for yourself the name of the day, this very day the king of Babylon pressed upon Jerusalem, on this very day!"

If life seems sometimes fuzzy and without direction, if we sometimes find Torah dry and God distant, if our valleys are dark and our eyes lack vision, we can attribute that to the Tenth of Tevet. And that's worth mourning.

But we can also work to correct the mistakes that brought about these tragedies in the first place. We can look for the signs of God's blessings even in the darkness of exile, we can see the physical world as a means to a greater end—and not as an end in itself—and we can certainly look for the light in the Torah, to treat it with reverence by showing up on time and focusing our attention, particularly during your precious time in an environment of growth.

Chapter 16

Chanah's Prayer

Modeling Ourselves on a Master

Jewish prayer should be uplifting and inspiring. Unfortunately, many people consider it a burden and a chore. At best, they use their time in synagogue to daydream or mentally plan their next vacation or business deal. I once heard a successful businessman marvel, "I don't know how people who don't pray succeed in business; when else do they think about long-term tax strategies?"

Without question, some services seem to drag on and on. But I've come to realize about myself that this perception is really more a function of my inner life than it is of the service itself. There are some days that the morning prayer takes only 45 minutes, but it feels like two hours; and on other days the service can take an hour, and feel like it ended way too soon. I find that if I arrive on time, truly concentrate, and am wholly present, then the time seems to fly. But if I avoid being psychologically and emotionally engaged, then it truly is a burden, and that's a shame on so many different levels. After all, as an observant man I will continue to spend a significant amount of time in prayer—or at least physically present at a service of communal worship—so I might as well enjoy it.

Learning to Grow

Your year in yeshiva or seminary can be a laboratory for you to explore this aspect of your inner life. There are ample opportunities, and often obligations, for you to enjoy considerable amounts of time in prayer, and those opportunities give you space to experiment and to get the advice of those around you.

"Experiment" might sound like a strange verb to use with a service that seems so rigidly structured, but, actually, that structure is only intended to set certain parameters and to guide. Ultimately, for prayer to be enjoyable and meaningful, it must be personalized. You may have been introduced to prayer by your parents or by your teachers, but you will never flourish if you only pray with your father's heart.

We have previously seen the statement of the *Sefer Chasidim* that urges the personalization of prayer, to the point where we are allowed to insert personal requests right into the middle of the *Amidah*.[65] The Rabbis teach, "Whoever prays in a fixed way (קֶבַע), his prayer is not a supplication (תחנונים)" (*Berachot* 28b). Apparently it is not enough to personalize prayer in a fixed, unchanging way; rather it is important that this personalization adapt to reflect our changing emotions, hopes, and fears.

One year I had the privilege of praying close enough to a great Rosh Yeshiva, and I was able overhear his private *Amidah* every day. Consistently, he took quite a while to finish this prayer, but he was very inconsistent in how he did it. Usually he went through the blessings at a fairly normal pace until he got to one that would be the focus of his attention that day. He would then totally lose himself in that one blessing, often repeating one or two phrases over and over again. He would then finish up, almost racing through the remaining blessings. The next day, he would dilate on a different blessing, although he did

---

65. I suggest you speak to a teacher knowledgeable in *halachah* before practically acting on this idea, because there are important details that must be followed.

have his favorites. This is far from a "fixed" prayer, and also far from most people's conceptions of what Jewish prayer should be like.

Prayer in general is a universal phenomenon. Our tradition teaches that it is shared even by the members of the plant and animal kingdoms (as is obvious from even a simple reading of *Tehillim* or *Perek Shirah*). It is certainly practiced by religiously inclined humans of many faiths. Having so much in common, it would be easy to confuse our particularly Jewish approach to prayer with those of other traditions, and perhaps for that reason even Jews who have little connection to Yiddish often prefer to speak of "*davening*" rather than "praying." If our awareness of the unique Jewish approach to prayer ends with that linguistic idiosyncrasy, however, this would be a distinction hardly worth making. Instead, we should truly learn to *daven*—to pray as Jews—from a master.

One of the most famous prayers in Tanach was that of Chana, the wife of Elkanah, and the mother of the prophet Shmuel. In fact, it was Chana's prayer that brought this great prophet—compared in leadership to Moshe and Aharon combined! (*Berachot* 31b) —into the world. Clearly worthy of close study, the Rabbis of the Talmud learned lessons and laws from almost every phrase, and although we will not go into all the detail here, I do want to point out some important lessons that we can learn from Chana.

The first thing we can learn from Chana is that when we want something good and noble, we need to take the high road to get it. Anything worthwhile will necessitate focus, attention, and work; so although money might buy you opportunity (tuition to a great school, a fantastic coach, or a dinner seat next to a world leader) you can't purchase greatness itself.

The Rabbis learn this lesson from the following story:

Every day a heavenly voice would explode across the world and say, "in the future a righteous one will rise, and his name will be Shmuel." Every woman who gave birth to a son would call him "Shmuel," but when people saw his actions they would say, "This Shmuel is not that Shmuel." And when this one was born, people saw his actions and said, "it seems that this is the one."

מדרש שמואל פרשה ג
רבי ירמיה בשם ר' שמואל בר רב יצחק אמר, בכל יום ויום היתה בת קול יוצאה ומתפוצצת בכל העולם כולו, ואומרת, עתיד צדיק אחד לעמוד ושמו שמואל. וכל אשה שהיתה יולדת בן היתה מוציאה שמו שמואל, וכיון שהיו רואין את מעשיו היו אומרים זה שמואל אין זה אותו שמואל. וכיון שנולד זה, ראו את מעשיו, אמרו, דומה שזהו. וזהו שאומר, אך יקם ה' את דברו...

Calling your son "Shmuel" in response to a heavenly voice is a quick fix, a superficial attempt to purchase greatness on the cheap. The reaction of these women seems almost comical—until we admit that we all tend to react a bit superficially to the attention-grabbing news of the world (or the more private news in our lives). Whether we are confronted by "explosive" sounds of war, or "explosive" developments in communication technology, our increasingly interconnected world presents us with global events and movements, positive and negative, deserving of sustained consideration and reflection. More personally, important life cycle events such as a bar or bat mitzvah, a graduation, or certainly a marriage or birth of a child all call for potentially life-changing contemplation. Instead, however, we often fall back on predictable reactions and empty slogans. Chana was unusual, in that she did the hard work that should have been obvious to all her friends: she introspected, and considered what her relationship would have to be with her creator in order to merit not just a "Shmuel" in name only, but rather the truly righteous Shmuel the Prophet.

Step 1: Take Charge

Chana's introspection grew into Chana's prayer, a prayer that changed not only the course of Chana's life, but the course of Jewish history.

1 *Shmuel* 1:9-15

And Chana rose up after they had eaten in Shiloh, and after they had drunk. And Eli the priest sat upon a seat by the doorpost of the Temple of God. And she was upset, and prayed to God, and cried very much. And she vowed a vow, and said, God of hosts, if you will look on the pain of your handmaid, and remember me, and not forget your handmaid, and will give your

שמואל א פרק א
(ט) ותקם חנה אחרי אכלה בשלה ואחרי שתה ועלי הכהן ישב על הכסא על מזוזת היכל ה': (י) והיא מרת נפש ותתפלל על ה' ובכה תבכה: (יא) ותדר נדר ותאמר ה' צבקות אם ראה תראה בעני אמתך וזכרתני ולא תשכח את אמתך ונתתה לאמתך זרע אנשים ונתתיו לה' כל ימי חייו ומורה לא יעלה על ראשו: (יב) והיה כי הרבתה להתפלל לפני ה' ועלי שמר את פיה: (יג) וחנה היא מדברת על לבה רק שפתיה נעות וקולה לא ישמע ויחשבה עלי לשכרה: (יד) ויאמר אליה עלי עד מתי תשתכרין הסירי את יינך מעליך: (טו) ותען חנה ותאמר לא אדני אשה קשת רוח אנכי ויין ושכר לא שתיתי ואשפך את נפשי לפני ה':

handmaid the seed of man, then I will give him to God all the days of his life, and no razor will come upon his head. And as she continued praying at length before God, Eli noted her mouth. And Chana, she spoke from the heart; only her lips moved, but her voice was not heard, and Eli suspected that she was drunk. And Eli said unto her: How long will you be drunk? Remove your wine from yourself. And Chana answered and said: No, sir, I am an unhappy woman I have not drunk wine or strong drink, but have poured out my soul before God.

Elkanah, Chana's husband, was famous for his devotion to the Temple, then situated in Shilo. Every year he would take his family to the Temple's temporary site by a different road, in order to encourage the people on route to join him in his pilgrimage. He was a man of great initiative, and it seems that Chana relied on his merit and enterprise in her hopes for a child. But this year, Chana saw that Elkanah gave up hope. He asked her, "Why do you cry, why don't you eat, why be so upset; aren't I dear to you like ten children?"

Elkanah was trying to comfort her, but instead—like a slap in the face—his response to her childlessness had the opposite effect. Chana realized that she could no longer rely on any one else and that she would have to petition God herself. So, as Malbim points out, Chana "got up" and turned directly to God.

Perhaps this is the first lesson we can learn from Chana's prayer. For prayer to be effective, it must be a direct and full-throated expression of an immediate, personal reliance on God. It certainly can't be just a way of hedging your bets.

Of course, it is always a good thing to have a particularly saintly person pray on your behalf as well. This has always been part of the job description of great Jewish leaders ever since Moshe (see Ramban on *Shemot* 18:15), and presumably Chana was relying on Elkanah for this kind of intercession. But the prayer of a *tzaddik* should never be *in place* of personal petition, but only a supplement. After all, often the reason why God withholds His blessings in the first place is in order to bring us to connect to Him more profoundly,[66] so an exclusive reliance on intermediaries would entirely defeat this plan. Chana had been relying too much on Elkanah and did not sufficiently build her own relationship with her divine source of all blessings. When Elkanah despaired, Chana took initiative, with miraculous results.

---

66. See *Yevamot* 64a: "Why were our forefathers childless? Because God desires the prayers of the righteous", and Maharal's *Commentary to Aggadah* there.

Step 2: The Four Elements of a Successful Prayer

According to Malbim, verses 10 and 11 above teach us four elements of an effective prayer. For prayer to be effective, you need to:

1. Feel the need and get upset;
2. Pray with deep intention towards God alone;
3. Cry real tears;
4. Make a vow.

1. Feel the need and get upset

God doesn't intervene in the course of history, and certainly doesn't perform miracles, for the sake of your self-indulgent luxuries. We have many examples of wealthy individuals in the Bible, but I can't think of a single biblical prayer for wealth. (According to one Chasidic master, Yitzchak Avinu did pray for wealth, but this was really a hidden prayer for children.)[67] On the other hand, God will intervene for the sake of a basic necessity. Verse 10 describes Chana as being "מרת נפש"—terribly upset. Were Chana upset over some trivial matter, that would have been a selfish temper tantrum; but Chana wanted to help build the Jewish nation and pass her ideals to another generation. Chana wanted something essential: Chana wanted a child. If you realize that God's own honor is blemished when the righteous are denied their basic physical and spiritual needs, and if that realization becomes translated into the world of emotion as deep upset, then God is likely to respond for the sake of his own honor as much as for you.

How can you tell the difference between a tantrum over a luxury as opposed to a deep upset over something essential? That's easy.

---

67. *Sefer Maor va-Shemesh, Parashat Toldot*. Many *machzorim* for Rosh Hashanah and Yom Kippur have optional prayers that can be inserted while the *shaliach tzibbur* is saying the *kedushah*: one for forgiveness, one for extreme wealth, and one for righteous children. There is not enough time to say them all, leading me to the conclusion that the choice between them is itself a test of priorities.

You are, after all, asking God to intervene here. If your friend or neighbor were in this situation, would you intervene to help him or her? I have often taken time and made an effort to help friends and acquaintances find a job, or a spouse, or wisdom, or spiritual fulfillment. I've even helped relative strangers who are struggling with such challenges, because these things are essential needs of any human, and we should intervene when we see someone suffering because they lack these things. But if you call me and tell me that you just *have to* get your hands on a luxury automobile, or yacht, or handbag... I'm likely to be a bit under-whelmed. If you get emotional because the room at your five-star hotel doesn't have the view you wanted, your upset is really just a tantrum, and you can't expect other people, or the Almighty, to intervene.

Chana emphasized that her request was not for something unusual or luxurious by praying for "זרע אנשים"—literally, the "seed of *men*," in plural. The Rabbis explain that she was asking for just a child of average ability, who would not stand out in a crowd of men, not too tall and not too short, not too smart and not too dull. In other words, she wasn't looking for fame and fortune; she was upset only because she did not have the basic tools necessary to express her ideals into the next generation.

When you are lacking the basic tools you need to care for yourself and your family, or tools that you need to express your ideals into the world in a beautiful way, you have the right—and perhaps the obligation—to speak out against the *chillul Hashem* implied by the God's withholding his grace. To be clear: being upset about lacking such basics in no way contradicts the famous dictum of Ben Zoma, "Who is wealthy? One who is happy with his lot." As Rabbenu Yonah explains:

"Who is wealthy? One who is happy with his lot" — One who says, "It is enough for me to have my portion, since I am able to provide for myself and my household and be involved in Torah. Why do I need more money; I only need enough for my needs and to keep God's word" … And he is called wealthy since God gave him that which he needs for his livelihood and to be involved in Torah and *mitzvot*. For what is the benefit to man of all his labors—only to keep the Torah and *mitzvot*.

פירוש רבינו יונה על אבות
פרק ד משנה א
"איזהו עשיר השמח בחלקו" - האומר
די לי בחלקי אחר שאני יכול לפרנס
את עצמי ואת ביתי ולעסוק בתורה. מה
לי לממון אחר אך להיות לי כדי צרכי
ולהקים את דבר ה'... והוא הנקרא
עשיר אחר שהשם ית' נתן לו במה
שיתפרנס ויעסוק בתורה ובמצות כי מה
יתרון לאדם בכל עמלו אך לקיים את
התורה והמצות:

Rabbenu Yonah clearly implies that the virtue of being "happy with your lot" begins only when your basic physical, emotional, and spiritual needs are covered. Until then, you have the right to be distressed. Direct those emotions in faithful prayer to the One who can truly answer them.

2. Pray with intention to God alone

Notice that verse 10 does not just say that Chana prayed; rather, it says that she prayed *to God*, and this is no trivial detail. For our prayers to be most effective, we need to know to whom our petitions are addressed, to the best of our limited human understanding.

It is for this reason that the *Amidah* prayer begins with praises of God, because through those praises we focus our attention on God as He actually is. In fact, the act of reconnecting intellectually and emotionally to our source of blessing may be the most important part of the prayer—as I mentioned above, God often withholds blessing just so that we will reconnect with Him—and it for this reason that if you lose focus during any other part of the *Amidah* you have still fulfilled your obligation, but if you lose focus during the first blessing, you need to repeat the service.[68] In the first blessing we define our perception of God's identity. Establishing theological clarity helps us "address" our prayers correctly. As my friend Rabbi Eli Pielet once pointed out, if you smudge a thank-you note, it still does the job, even if it lacks some elegance; but if you smudge the *address*, it will never arrive.

To some degree, this insight turns our conceptions of prayer on its head. We might have believed that the requests are the central part of prayer and that the praises are just a flattering introduction. But God can't be flattered. Instead, the praises have to be genuine, because the reconnecting is the central core of any prayer, and the deprivation, leading to a need to petition, is really just a catalyst to help us restart that relationship.

Still, prayer should be more religiously emotional than theologically intellectual. Theological clarity by itself is too cold to be considered devotion or worship. Only when that clarity informs the emotions, and is then expressed out into the physical world through speech, does your entire personality—thought, emotion, and body—resonate in prayer. We see this movement from the world of thought to the world of feeling in verse 13, "And Chana spoke from the heart." Actually, the literal translation should be "And Chana spoke *to* the heart," implying that Chana began her petition of God by dictating to her heart what it should feel. Unrestrained religious passion can easily slip into various forms of ecstatic paganism; by beginning the prayer with theological clarity—by praying "to God"—we can allow ourselves to become emotional without fearing that our prayers are superficial or misdirected.

---

68. *Shulchan Aruch, O.C.* 101:1, but ask a rabbi for practical guidance.

3. Cry Real Tears

The Tanach reports that "Chana cried very much" and this contributed to the success of her prayer. According to the Talmud, after the destruction of the Temple the gates of prayer are

תלמוד בבלי מסכת ברכות דף לב עמוד ב
ואמר רבי אלעזר: מיום שחרב בית המקדש נגעלו שערי תפלה, שנאמר: (איכה ג) גם כי אזעק ואשוע שתם תפלתי, ואף על פי ששערי תפלה נגעלו שערי דמעה לא נגעלו, שנאמר (תהלים ל"ט) שמעה תפלתי ה' ושועתי האזינה אל דמעתי אל תחרש.

locked and only the gates of tears remain open, so if crying was helpful for Chana, it is even more essential in our post-Temple world. What are tears, and why do they work wonders?

The Vilna Gaon points out that the word for "tears" in Hebrew is "דמעה" which is relates to a term for a mixture. We cry when we are "mixed-up," when we feel powerless and confused. Similarly, "crying" is "בכי" from the word "נבוך"—confused. This emotional state evokes mercy from G-d, as well as from other people, because it indicates utter humility and dependence on others.[69] So long as someone feels—rightly or wrongly—that he can persevere on his own, he will not cry. Only when he stands face-to-face with his hopeless situation will he cry. The tears melt away the hubris that created the barrier between man and God in the first place.

Of course, tears of *categorical* hopelessness, otherwise known as despair, indicate a lack of faith. Despair is not an appropriate emotion for one who believes in the Almighty. It has been asked: if the gates of tears are never locked, why does there need to be a "gate" in the first place? One famous answer is that the gate keeps out tears of despair. Only tears of hope, tears of *prayer*, are answered.

Chana cried tears of helplessness and tears of humility. These were tears of true prayer and they succeeded in bringing the soul of Shmuel ha-Navi into the world.

---

69. See also Maharal to *Bava Metzia* 58a.

4. Make a Vow

There is an ancient custom for Jews to make small vows at the time of *Ne'ilah* as the sun sets on Yom Kippur.[70] Although we generally discourage vows, and we introduce Yom Kippur by nullifying vows, they do have a positive place in the life of a Jew if used judiciously. At this moment in her life, Chana had the clarity to understand the purpose of her life, the blessings she had already received, and the future blessings for which she was praying. One way she locked in her commitment to use her blessings only to bring light and life into the world, for the sake of that world and its creator, was by taking the extreme step of dedicating Shmuel's entire life to the service of God and the nation.

Prayer, when done correctly, should bring us to approximate Chana's clarity of vision, answering the basic existential questions of life: why am I here? what do I require in order to fulfill my mission? what do I need to change about myself in order to deserve those tools? Once we have that clarity, we need not take a vow as extreme as Chana's, but we might make a smaller gesture to ensure that this moment of insight and inspiration continues to inform the more mundane moments of life on a regular basis. On Yom Kippur, for example, Jews pray for life itself. We therefore make almost trivially small vows that force us to reconnect to the powerful feelings of *ne'ilah*—if only for a moment—every day of that renewed life.

At time of crisis, we often achieve a clarity of vision, perspective, and priorities that will certainly fade as the daily events of "regular" life relentlessly distract us from more ultimate issues. When you turn to God at a time of a humbling crisis, consider taking a small, symbolic vow, which will later remind you of that moment you stood before God, head bowed low and heart open wide.

---

70. *Mishnah Berurah* 623:3.

Step 3: Understand What Prayer Is and What It Is Not

Rav Hamnuna said: how many great *halachot* (laws) we can learn from the verse about Chana. "And Chana, she spoke from the heart," from here we learn that one who prays must direct his heart. "Only her lips moved," from here we learn that one who prays must pronounce with his lips. "But her voice was not heard," from here we learn that it is forbidden to raise one's voice in prayer. "And Eli suspected that she was drunk," From here we learn that one who is drunk is forbidden to pray. "And Eli said unto her, how long will you be drunk," Rav Elazar said, from here we learn that if one sees something improper in his friend, that he must inform him (*Berachot* 31a).

תלמוד בבלי מסכת ברכות ל"א עמוד א'
אמר רב המנונא: כמה הלכתא גברוותא איכא
למשמע מהני קראי דחנה: (שמואל א א) וחנה
היא מדברת על לבה - מכאן למתפלל צריך
שיכוין לבו. רק שפתיה נעות - מכאן למתפלל
שיחתוך בשפתיו. וקולה לא ישמע - מכאן,
שאסור להגביה קולו בתפלתו. ויחשבה עלי
לשכרה - מכאן, ששכור אסור להתפלל,
ויאמר אליה עלי עד מתי תשתכרין וגו' - אמר
רבי אלעזר: מכאן, לרואה בחברו [דף לא
עמוד ב] דבר שאינו הגון צריך להוכיחו:

Pray from the Heart

The synagogue is not a fashion show or a social club. Rabbi Yishmael ben Elazar reports that one of the two "sins" that brings death to boorish people is that they call the synagogue a "בית עם" – the "House of the People" (a Jewish Community Center perhaps?).[71] Now this mistake is not one of the formal 613 *mitzvot*, so R. Yishmael must be criticizing an attitude in which loutish people dishonor an

---

71. *Shabbat* 32a.

opportunity to connect with God on an emotional level, turning it into something that takes care of only their social or physical needs.

The irony, of course, is that if you want a social hang-out, or place to impress your friends and neighbors with your new car or well-dressed kids, there are far better and more comfortable places to do that than standing upright with your feet together at 9:00 a.m. on a Saturday morning. No wonder why so many people who grew up thinking of the synagogue as a place to go three times a year, dressed in their holiday finest, have checked out of *shul* altogether.

Instead, prayer should be seen—indeed *felt*—as an opportunity to get emotional about our spiritual quest within the safety and guidance of a prophetically inspired framework. The Midrash on the second paragraph of the *Shema* calls prayer "service of the heart." The emotional impact on the self is what Jewish prayer is about, and that truth is apparent in the verb we use to describe it. Like the verbs להתרחץ (to wash oneself) and להתלבש (to dress oneself), the verb for prayer, "להתפלל" is reflexive; it is something you do *to yourself*. The root of the verb "פלל" means "to judge"[72] and therefore "להתפלל" literally means "to judge oneself." At a time of need, I stand before my God and I judge *myself*. I ask: Why am I in this situation? what is my relationship to my Creator and his people? what must I do to improve? and, perhaps the most terrifying judgment of all: who am I really?

The very act of confronting these questions changes us, humbles us, and opens us up to more blessings. If you think you are nearly perfect—a full vessel—then you have left little room in your life for God to overflow his blessing into you. On the other hand, if you recognize the humble condition you share with all of humanity, you've removed the "lid" that has sealed you off. You've invited God to shine more light into your life. That's what prayer does, and this approach answers a classic philosophical question about the "justice" of prayer.

---

72. See *Metzudat David* on *Yeshayahu* 28:7.

Chana's Prayer

It has been asked: why pray? Doesn't God know what's best for you? The Almighty is all-kind; He obviously believes what He has already given you is the best and most just for you. You certainly don't want to ask Him for something which—in His infinite wisdom—is *not* best for you![73]

Now that we understand prayer to be an act of self-evaluation, we can agree that before prayer you truly did *not* deserve what was being withheld, and perhaps it would have been even counterproductive for you. But after prayer, after you've judged yourself and changed yourself, perhaps you are now a different person, and perhaps you are now deserving of the object of your petition.

Rabbi Leon of Modena (Venice, 1571–1648) elucidated this idea with an analogy. Imagine, he writes, that someone is traveling in a small boat down a river. He throws a rope to a stake on the shore and he pulls in the rope, hand over hand. An unsophisticated observer might think that he is pulling the shore towards the boat, but anyone sensible knows that it is not the land that is moving towards the boat, but rather the man is pulling the boat towards the shore. The same is true of prayer, writes Rabbi Leon of Modena: more than prayer is intended to move God, the "unmoved mover," prayer is intended to move the one who prays.[74]

Certainly, you can't expect the fixed, perfect, and unchanging Almighty to be more affected by your prayer than you are. And if you are unmoved by your own prayer, don't be surprised if God is similarly unaffected.

The biggest blessing, therefore, is not the object of the petition, but the change itself. The perceived object of desire is mostly a catalyst to get each of us to reflect, reach out to, and pull ourselves towards the Almighty. If you are interested in pursuing this line of thought, I

---

73. Maharal, *Netivot Olam, Netiv ha-Avodah* 2.
74. *Sefer Ari Nohem.*

recommend you look at the *Chovot ha-Levavot* (*Duties of the Heart*) by Rabbenu Bachya ibn Pakuda, in the Eighth Gate (שער חשבון הנפש), chapter 5. There, you will see that the true focus and goal of prayer is not the formulated text, nor is it the object of petition, but rather the emotional reflection of God and your relationship to Him.

Pronounce With Your Lips

The centerpiece of Jewish prayer, the *Amidah*, is often wrongly referred to as the "silent meditation" or the "silent devotion." I guess we need some way of signaling the congregation, in high English, that this is a moment of relative reverence. But in truth, such a description is all wrong, both in terms of the law, and in terms of the spirit behind the law. Of course, there is a place in Judaism for silent meditation, but that's called *hitbonenut*, not *tefillah*. Jewish meditation is as powerful as it is neglected. It is certainly worthy of both study and practice. But it is not prayer.

Hitbonenut is about internal reflection that builds and strengthens the self (as the root of the word implies). It is, therefore, essentially self-centered, although in a constructive way. Prayer, in contrast, is certainly about judging the self, but it is directed towards God, who is outside of the self, and who serves as both an external standard of reference and as an external source of blessing. The goal of prayer is also to affect the world and not just to change the self (although self-change is an early rung in the causal chain).

We express the outward direction of prayer by articulating our petitions out through our lips and into the world. At the end of the day, in prayer we try to break ourselves out of our lonely and limited, solipsistic selves. We reach out to God for assistance and we pour our hopes out into a world desperate for healing.

Don't Raise Your Voice

In prayer we petition and beseech and beg; but as people of faith, we never panic. The Talmud instructs us that one who makes his voice heard in prayer is one "of little faith."[75] Rashi explains that by raising his voice he demonstrates his doubt that God can hear him. Prayer should engender a mindful humility, a recognition that the universe existed before we got here, and will continue to exist long after we are gone. We ask in prayer for the tools necessary for us to play a modest role in this cosmic drama to the best of our ability, while acknowledging that God alone is the divine playwright who will never abdicate his position for another. In prayer we strike a balance between active self-assertion and devout acceptance. Raising our voices would disrupt the tension in which a majestic creature encounters its Creator.

Maharal adds that for prayer to work, we must connect with God quietly and profoundly. Prayer is not performing arts; it is not a show. To connect to God we need to emulate Him: since God is hidden, exquisitely modest, we need to cultivate modesty in order to approach Him.[76]

Don't Pray Drunk

We use wine to sanctify the Sabbath and to commence our momentous life-cycle commandments because wine opens us up emotionally.[77] One would think that wine might be a great catalyst for us to engage in "service of the heart." Why then is prayer forbidden even after a single cup of wine, considered like an offering of "foreign fire"?

Maharal explains that although wine certainly opens our emotions, it does so at the expense of our higher intellect. A drink or two might lead us to a more passionate prayer, but instead of praying for wisdom, world peace, or redemption, we might end up praying

---

75. *Berachot* 24a.
76. *Netivot Olam, Netiv ha-Avodah* 2.
77. See *Pri Tzaddik, Lech Lecha* 3.

for a pizza. When we take something that should be used for the most lofty of purposes and we instead use it for more base and personal pleasures, that act is then categorized as a "תועבה," sometimes translated as an "abomination." For this reason, the Talmud calls a drunken prayer a תועבה, because the object of such a prayer is likely to be something relatively physical, instead of being appreciated as an opportunity to connect to God himself.[78] For the same reason, *Mishlei 28*

> **ספר נתיבות עולם, נתיב העבודה, פרק ב**
> וענין זה כי תועבה נקרא כאשר האדם נוטה אל ענין זר... ומפני כך תפלת שכור תועבה כי השכור כבר סר ממנו השכל עד שנעשה גופני, וכאשר מתפלל אל השם יתברך לעשות צרכיו, וכאלו הוא רוצה שהשם יתברך יתן לו שאלתו למלאות תאותו הגופנית כמו שהוא עתה שכור בעל גוף בלא שכל והרי תפלה הזאת בודאי תועבה היא אל השם יתברך. כי ראוי שיתפלל האדם שיתן לו השם יתברך צורכו כדי שיעבוד השם יתברך וילמוד תורה ואז תפלתו בודאי רצויה אל הקדוש ברוך הוא, אבל השכור בעת אשר נטה אל ענין הגוף ביותר ומתפלל אל השם יתברך שיתן אליו צרכו, והתפלה היא כמו שהאדם הוא בשעת תפלה שהוא בעל גוף לגמרי ויתן לו עוד שיהיה נמשך אחר הגוף לגמרי ודבר זה הוא תועבה בודאי.

teaches: "One who turns his ears from hearing Torah, his prayers are also *to'evah.*" After all, were such a person really interested in connecting to God in prayer, he would also be interested in hearing the word of God, and learning God's will. From the fact that he doesn't study Torah, we understand that he is uninterested in the relationship. Like a rebellious teen, he only calls God when he wants to borrow the car keys.

So although liquor or drugs might make us feel more "spiritual," they in fact dull our higher intellect and make us less lucid. Spirituality, in Judaism, is less about feeling close to God and more about being *like* God. God heals the sick and feeds the poor. In the same way, we

78. *Eruvin* 64a.

can be most spiritual only when coherent enough to perform surgery and care for the needy. You should be able to be spiritual behind the wheel of a car.

Chana was passionately spiritual in her prayer, and lost herself in her reverie to the point that Eli suspected she was drunk. But her emotional fervor wasn't artificially induced and in no way contradicted her intellectual lucidity. She knew exactly what she needed, what the world needed, and she knew exactly to whom her petition should be addressed. Chana's prayer brought the soul of Shmuel into a difficult world, at difficult time. We have often needed our prayers answered, but the challenges we face today as individuals and a people most certainly require almost miraculous divine intervention; may we all learn from Chana to make our prayers worthy of divine consideration and a favorable reply.

Chapter 17

Torah Study

Good, Great, and Greatest

This chapter is a long time in coming. I've held myself back from a discussion of the importance of Torah study for a couple of reasons. Firstly, I suspect that many of your teachers spend a good amount of time encouraging your growth in Torah study, as they should, and I therefore preferred to elaborate on other topics that might get less attention, or which might be addressed differently than I've presented them here.

But mostly, I've wanted to emphasize, perhaps through omission, that although Torah may be necessary for dramatic and sustained personal growth, it is not sufficient, at least not in our generation. To be sure, idealistic *Torah lishmah* can by itself purify already refined individuals. This principal was taught by the Vilna Gaon[79] and was the basis for the early opposition to the introduction of *musar* into the traditional yeshivas. But as Rabbi Shlomo Wolbe asked rhetorically in his *Alei Shur*: how many of us truly achieve the level of *Torah lishmah* called for by the Gaon? Decades earlier, Rabbi Yisrael Salanter founded the *musar* movement in response to that same rhetorical question, emphasizing that for most of us, personal

79. See his *Kol Eliyahu* to *Bava Batra* 51b.

growth must be its own focus of study, just as deliberate and rigorous as Torah study itself.

In some ways, I've followed the lead of Ramchal's *Mesillat Yesharim*. Ramchal structured his work around a *baraita* that begins, "Torah brings to watchfulness; watchfulness brings to zeal; zeal brings to cleanliness…." Ramchal wrote chapters detailing watchfulness, zeal, cleanliness, and the other "steps" listed in the *baraita*, but against expectations he did not include a chapter on "Torah," seemingly the very first step. No one can say for certain why Ramchal omitted a chapter on Torah, but one possible explanation is that he wanted to prevent people from making the mistake of getting stuck on "Torah"—much like today people get stuck on "watchfulness"—and never moving on to the next steps. He perceived that his generation's Torah scholars should have been working directly on character issues instead of relying on their Torah studies for perfection. He therefore skipped the "step" of Torah and moved straight to watchfulness.

I know you've come to yeshiva or seminary to learn Torah, and I'm confident that your teachers are guiding you in the importance of Torah study daily, through their classes and their example. I hope that I've drawn your attention to some other potentially critical topics for your year (and beyond), and added insight to those topics covered by your teachers as well.

But ultimately, a book about a year in yeshiva without some serious treatment of Torah study would be like a book on human anatomy that neglects to mention the head. "Decapitated" is no way to go through life, or a year in yeshiva. So it is time to discuss the importance of Torah study, in the spirit of personal growth.

Mystical Methods of Change

A few chapters ago, you read about four major methods for effecting change: contemplation; consistent thought; visualization; and behavioral modification. These are all reasonable and intuitive. Our

Torah teaches, however, that there are other methods that are less intuitive. Indeed, they are almost magical in their power. Perhaps the strongest of them is Torah study.

Rabbi Yisrael Salanter learned this from the Talmud itself. The Talmud discusses the supernatural punishment that would befall the unrepentant adulteress (the *sotah*) and her consort[80] at the time of the Temple. Refusing to confess and preferring to drink a magical potion concocted according to a biblical recipe to test her innocence, her eyes would bulge, her belly would swell, and they would quickly remove her from the Temple before she died. There were, however, certain causes that would delay or prevent the potion from working and one of them was the merit of Torah study:

Rava said: Torah study, when you are involved in it, protects you and saves you; when you are not involved in it, it protects you, but does not save you. *Mitzvot*, whether you are involved or after you are involved, they protect you but do not save you.

תלמוד בבלי מסכת סוטה דף כא/א
אמר רבא תורה בעידנא דעסיק בה מגנא
ומצלא בעידנא דלא עסיק בה אגוני מגנא
אצולי לא מצלא מצוה בין בעידנא דעסיק
בה בין בעידנא דלא עסיק בה אגוני מגנא
אצולי לא מצלא:

Rashi explains the difference between "protection" and "salvation." "Protection" means a defense against afflictions, an externally imposed challenge; "salvation" is far deeper, it relates to a defense from one's own *yetzer hara*, a fortification of one's own free will against temptation. These types of help are supernatural, beyond what would be intuitive based on the psychological, educational, or social effects we would expect from even the most intense Torah study. After all, they protect even from an ancient, Torah-formulated potion.

---

80. See Mishnah, *Sotah* 5:1.

Torah Study

Rabbi Yisrael Salanter pointed out that this supernatural power of Torah study has effect regardless of the particular subject being studied, so long as that Torah is being studied in accordance with the Torah's own rules. The intense study of the laws of Shabbat, for example, will unexpectedly strengthen a person's commitment to the laws of usury, and blunt his temptations for non-kosher food. That being the case, you don't need to give so much thought to this magical type of protection when choosing a subject to be studied; you just have to study, intensely, in accordance with the laws that govern the mitzvah of Torah study (like studying in a clean environment with clean hands).

There is a more prosaic psychological and social impact that Torah study will have on a person as well, and here too, the study of one subject will affect the student's commitment to other subjects as well. Because the serious study of Torah engenders reverence for the Torah in general, the effects of Torah study are broader than one might imagine from any particular topic. For example, the study of the laws of Temple sacrifice might make you more honest in business or a more sensitive spouse, because the study impressed you with the depth and precision of the Torah system in general, and you know the Torah also wants you to be honest in business and a sensitive spouse.

In general, the natural effect generated by such serious engagement in Torah study can be described as *"yirah"*—awe and reverence—and it is that *yirah* which is the expected and intuitive healing force of Torah study. Rabbi Yisrael discovered this effect in the following passage:

Rava said: Iyov wished to acquit the entire world from judgment. He said, "Master of the Universe, You created the ox with split hooves and the donkey with cloven hooves; You created the Garden of Eden and You created Gehinom; You created the righteous and You created the wicked. What can hold You back!?" What did his friends answer him: 'you are denying *yirah* and are underestimating prayer before God. The Holy One indeed

תלמוד בבלי מסכת בבא בתרא דף טז/א
אמר רבא בקש איוב לפטור את כל העולם
כולו מן הדין אמר לפניו רבונו של עולם
בראת שור פרסותיו סדוקות בראת חמור
פרסותיו קלוטות בראת גן עדן בראת גיהנם
בראת צדיקים בראת רשעים מי מעכב על
ידך ומאי אהדרו ליה חבריה [דאיוב] אף אתה
תפר יראה ותגרע שיחה לפני אל ברא הקדוש
ברוך הוא יצר הרע ברא לו תורה תבלין:

created the evil inclination, but He created for it the Torah to temper it."

Iyov, in his suffering, felt as if he were trapped in a Greek tragedy, inevitably fated to his bad fortune by the unassailable will of the Omnipotent. He questioned how the flaccid free will of frail humanity could possibly stand up against the forces—both internal and external—that seemingly compel him to sin. His friends answered him that we humans are indeed subject to strong influences, including personal passions and vices, and social pressures; but we have also been given a gift that strengthens our resolve and enhances our ability to make healthy, free will choices. According to the verse, we have *yirah*—awe and reverence. As they often do, the Rabbis translate this into practical advice: when Iyov "denied *yirah*" he was forgetting the power of Torah study that engenders this *yirah*.

As I mentioned before, this *yirah* is natural and intuitive (what Rabbi Yisrael terms a *bechinah gashmit*, a "physical aspect"), not the supernatural effect might even save the Sotah from the biblical potion. And unlike that supernatural effect, it seems not to require the highest halachic level of Torah study. Note that according to many opinions, Iyov was not even Jewish; it seems, however, that he could still derive *yirah* from those aspects of Torah that are relevant to gentiles. Certainly, this *yirah* aspect of Torah study is as relevant to women as it is to men despite the technical differences between them in their levels of obligation.

As powerful as the *yirah* you get from Torah study is in general, it can also be fine-tuned and focused by a careful attention to your choice of subject. The deep and sincere study of any aspect of Torah will naturally affect the student in at least three ways: (1) it will give you a sense of reverence for the depth of Torah generally; (2) it will impress you with the Torah's concern over the details of behavior; (3) it will give you a confidence that answers to life's questions can be uncovered through a careful investigation of Torah texts. But some subjects in Torah more clearly develop one of these aspects, while other subjects more clearly develop the others. Depending on which of these three effects you are looking to emphasize, you could prefer texts which are analytically difficult talmudic tractates, or aspects of *halachah* in which the granular detail is particularly apparent, or laws (and their inner meanings) that are deep and mysterious.

In fact, according to Maharal, God wished to strengthen the Jewish people before Sinai in these three ways, and therefore He gave them three types of Torah to study in Marah just after they crossed the Red sea (see *Shemot* chapters 15-16). They spent the weeks leading up to Sinai learning monetary law (known for being analytically difficult), the laws of the Sabbath (detailed and precise), and the laws of the red heifer (deep and mysterious).[81] These subjects parallel a standard yeshiva curriculum (Talmud, often in *Nashim* and *Nezikin*; *halachah*; *musar* and *machshavah*) in ways that are hardly accidental.

In addition, Rabbi Yisrael taught that the *yirah* of Torah can be focused even more precisely. If one has a problem with honoring parents, for example, one should study the Torah related to that mitzvah, both law and philosophy, with exhausting passion and

---

81. See *Gur Aryeh* to *Shemot* 15:25.

precision. Rabbi Yisrael compares this to medicine: the more severe the illness, the more intense the study should be. The very act of investing so much in that study will naturally impress upon the student the importance of that mitzvah, to the point where his character will be improved permanently.

This might sound a bit obvious, but as with anything, we tend to gravitate to the Torah subjects with which we are comfortable, and we typically avoid those subjects that we find practically challenging. It's not so comfortable for someone with a girlfriend to study the laws of *yichud* or for someone who can't get out of bed on time to study the laws relating to the morning *Shema*. Rabbi Yisrael encourages us to be brave and not to avert our eyes from that we might find embarrassing. If you know you should be doing a mitzvah, but just can't get yourself motivated, don't avoid this subject. Rather, dive into it, and allow the study to help you live up to your ideals. This does require a faith in the truth and goodness of *halachah* in general. But it does not require a perfect faith. A rigorous study of any mitzvah will help strengthen your commitment to its practice, and a studied practice of that mitzvah inevitably will engender an appreciation of its truth and goodness, because ultimately Torah is really true and good.

Study with Selfish Intentions

So what I am suggesting here is the study of Torah, even if you are not fully committed to practice that which you are studying. This may not get you the kind of supernatural assistance promised in the case of the *sotah*, but it certainly will contribute to your appreciation for the tradition generally and to the subject you are studying in particular. In some ways, this is a restatement of that famous talmudic dictum: מתוך שלא לשמה בא לשמה, the study of Torah and the performance of commandments without pure intention will lead to their performance with pure intention. At any given moment, we are motivated to study Torah for a variety of reasons, some more honorable than others.

We want the approval of friends or teachers. We want to cultivate a reputation that will lead to a good *shidduch* or a teaching position in a yeshiva. Or, quite simply, we might be acting virtuously in order to earn divine reward, in this world or the next. One could argue that at certain stages in our lives, pure intention is quite rare. And even then, it vanishes quickly.

That being the case, it is worthwhile to discuss what "pure intentions" really are, what impure intentions are, and how we can move the latter to be more like the former. When discussing pure intentions, the Rabbis use the term "לשמה," which is a term borrowed from the laws of sacrifice and divorce. The Mishnah derives that a bill of divorce must be written with a particular woman in mind.[82] In the words of the verse, the man shall "write for her," which the Mishnah interprets as "לשמה," literally, "in her name." The first Mishnah in *Zevachim* also teaches that sacrificial animals must be slaughtered "לשמן" — with the intention of them fulfilling the obligation of a particular sacrifice.

We see from these sources that the idea of לשמה is that there should be a coherence between the act being performed and the true intention behind the act. Kabbalists bring a homiletic that "לשמה" is shorthand for "לשם ה" — for the (rectification of the) name of God.[83] But while such lofty intention is transcendent, basic religious intention can be much more prosaic and at the same time still noble. At the end of his *Hilchot Teshuvah* ("Laws of Repentance"), the Rambam effectively identifies the idea of לשמה with serving God because you love Him. This again sounds out-of-reach, but then pay attention to his surprising formulation:

> One who serves from love is involved in Torah and *mitzvot* and walks in the paths of wisdom, not because of any worldly

---

82. *Gittin* 3:3.
83. The Arizal opens his *Sha'ar Hanhagat ha-Limmud* with this teaching, which was already hinted to in the *tikkunim* of the *Zohar Chadash*.

reason, and not because he fears bad tidings, and not in order to inherit benefits, but he does what is true because it is true, and in the end benefits will come because of this. And this level is a very great level, and not every sage acquires it, and it is the level of Avraham our father.

הלכות תשובה פרק י

(ב) העובד מאהבה עוסק בתורה ובמצות והולך בנתיבות החכמה לא מפני דבר בעולם ולא מפני יראת הרעה ולא כדי לירש הטובה אלא עושה האמת מפני שהוא אמת וסוף הטובה לבא בגללה ומעלה זו היא מעלה גדולה מאד ואין כל חכם זוכה לה והיא מעלת אברהם אבינו...

When you pay your worker on time because it is the right thing to do, because this is virtuous behavior and you are a virtuous person, you are acting *lishmah*. This doesn't sound so elusive after all. You are doing what is right, because it is right, and your values are in sync with those of the Torah. It is important to free ourselves from a common misconception: some people believe that the study of Torah is most noble when you are overcoming inertia, when you are learning diligently despite the fact you don't really enjoy it. Enjoying Torah, they think, makes it more selfish and less *"lishmah."* The Rambam, again, disagrees:

The third commandment is the commandment that we have been commanded to love God. And this is that we should reflect and understand his commandments and actions, so that we should apprehend Him and take pleasure in our apprehension of Him with ultimate pleasure. This is the love which is obligated. And this is the language of the *Sifri*: "And as it is written, 'you shall love Hashem your God' (*Devarim* 6:5). Do I know how to love God!? The verse continues, 'and these words that I command you today shall be on your heart,' that through this you will recognize the One who spoke and brought the world into existence." It has already been explained to you that investigation will make true the apprehension, and will bring to pleasure, and love will necessarily follow...

> **רמב"ם ספר המצוות – מצוה עשה ג**
> היא שצונו לאהבו יתעלה וזה שנתבונן ונשכיל מצותיו ופעולותיו עד שנשיגהו ונתענג בהשגתו תכלית התענוג וזאת היא האהבה המחוייבת ולשון ספרי לפי שנאמר ואהבת את ה' א-להיך איני יודע כיצד אוהב את המקום תלמוד לומר והיו הדברים האלה אשר אנכי מצוך היום על לבבך שמתוך כך אתה מכיר את מי שאמר והיה העולם כבר בארו לך כי בהשתכלות תתאמת לך ההשגה ויגיע התענוג ותבא האהבה בהכרח...

According to the Rambam, enjoying Torah study is not a "problem" of selfish motivation; it is actually a fulfillment of the mitzvah to love God! If you don't enjoy learning Torah so much, but you know that by pushing yourself you will develop more fluency with the ideas and the language, and that such fluency will make future study more enjoyable, you are climbing the ladder of love.[84]

A similar misconception is to identify pure "*lishmah*" as the dedicated performance of a commandment that makes no sense to you. You might think that the less it makes sense to you, the more you are doing it because God said so, and what could be higher than that?

In fact, there is something higher: understanding that God's commandments are not arbitrary and that His Torah is infinitely wise. To whatever degree we understand the wisdom behind the commandments and internalize that wisdom, we are behaving with ever greater religious virtue.[85] A study of the rationale behind the

---

84. See also the introduction to the *Eglei Tal* of Rabbi Avraham Borensztain (1838-1910), the first Rebbe of the Sochatchover Chasidic dynasty.
85. See chapter 6 of Rambam's *Eight Chapters*, where he distinguishes between commandments that have a clear rational basis and those that do not.

commandments (טעמי המצוות) is not an exercise in apologetics or motivational psychology; rather, it is an attempt to discover some of the ways in which each commandment is good for us so that we can synchronize our own intentions with those of our Commander.

Thinking About "Levels"

Why then does the Rambam consider serving out of love such elusive behavior? Don't we all often do "what is true because it is true." Oftentimes, yes; but not always. We may participate in *lishmah* from time to time, but I think most of us would be kidding ourselves were we to claim this is our *level*. After all, most of us continue do the *wrong* things for the *wrong* reasons; certainly we are far from always doing the right thing for the right reasons. So while we may dabble in *lishmah*, we are still far from being on a level of *lishmah*.

I find Ramchal's *Mesillat Yesharim* so useful because it helps me to identify my level and to transition to the next. Rather than showering us with a whole bewildering constellation of virtues, Ramchal leads us through them systematically, one at a time, from the more basic "watchfulness" to the most sublime "holiness." As we acquire each virtue, we make it our new level, from which we can reach up to the next. You carefully climb the ladder, and like any ladder, the climb can be smooth so long as you don't try to skip any rungs.

Someone who is working on Ramchal's "alacrity" can sometimes have a moment of "purity" (that's where we actively work on being *lishmah*), or "saintliness," or even "holiness." For example, one Shabbat during my first year in yeshiva we were gathered around the table for the third meal (*seudah shelishit*), listening to Torah from the rosh yeshiva and singing the traditional songs. Shabbat was waning as the sun set behind the golden Jerusalem hills. Having come from a secular university just a few months earlier, I was genuinely moved by being in a place of such warmth, wisdom, and *kedushah*.

Torah Study

Kedushah, in the scheme of Ramchal, is when the highest aspect of the spirit connects to the physical world, and when that physical object is then transformed into spiritual energy by being used for holy purposes. Overwhelmed with gratitude for being blessed with wonderful friends, teachers, Torah, Jerusalem, Israel… I felt an urge to eat a rugelach. Yes, a chocolate rugelach from Angel's bakery in nearby Givat Shaul, and fortunately a pile of such rugelach was on a plate right in front of me. I was grateful for that too.

So I reached over and took a bite of this rugelach, and as the sweetness filled my mouth I knew that this was just a fraction of the ultimate sweetness that God had created, in His pure kindness, for all of us. Later I would learn that the Baal Shem Tov would call this connecting to the *olam ha-ta'anug.*

Kindly indulge me, be generous and allow me that perhaps I did experience at that magical moment a flash of holiness, the highest rung on Ramchal's ladder. But if you were to tap me on the shoulder at that sublime instant and ask me on what *level* I was holding, I would only be deluding myself if I were to answer anything but the most basic watchfulness—making sure not to violate gross, blatant transgressions. I might have been momentarily *participating* in "holiness," and I cherish that inspirational moment and carry it with me; but still, in those early months I was *working* on "watchfulness." We need to be aware of our typical and likely challenges, and we need to work on ourselves appropriately. But just because you may still be working on the basic performance of fundamental *mitzvot,* that does not mean that you shouldn't beautify the *mitzvot* that you are doing. True, *hiddur mitzvah* is a form of higher "saintliness," and until you are halachically correct across the board, working on saintliness is premature, perhaps even presumptuous. But you can still touch saintliness, and even holiness, drawing inspiration and energy from those moments, even if you are not honestly holding there.

Similarly, you can have plenty of *lishmah* moments (*taharah* in the scheme of Ramchal's *Mesillat Yesharim*), doing the right thing because it is right and the true thing because it is true, even if you are still struggling with more basic Torah observance. You can and should be doing some Torah *lishmah* every day, and that's far more powerful than you might think.

The Motivating Power of Self-Interest

One of the leading students of the Baal Shem Tov ("the Besht") was Rebbe Yaakov Yosef of Polnoye, who was the first to publish teachings of the Besht. In the spirit of the *Tikkunei Zohar* and the Safed kabbalists, the Besht used the most critical language against studying Torah for reasons of personal gain or heavenly reward. Like a dog, such a person demands "*hav! hav!*" (that's the way dogs bark in Hebrew), meaning literally, "give! give!" The performance of the commandment for selfish reasons is not divine service. This is hardly a mitzvah; in fact it is the abuse of a mitzvah, equivalent to a transgression! And yet, we have seen the Talmud teach that we should continue to do the right thing for the wrong reasons, since ultimately we will end up doing the right thing for the right reasons.

Rabbi Yaakov Yosef ha-Kohen of Polnoye (1710–1784) was a great kabbalist and talmudist. As Rabbi of Shargorod, he was originally opposed to the nascent Chasidic movement of the Besht. He reports that the Besht won him over by teaching him how to overcome distracting thoughts during prayer. His commentary *Toldot Yaakov Yosef* was the first Chasidic book ever published, and it quotes the Besht hundreds of times.

Rebbe Yaakov Yosef explained that one must indeed use the motivating power of self-interest. He gives the example of waking up before dawn to pray and learn. This isn't easy, so bribe yourself with a cup of hot chocolate—get up for something sweet, and then go learn. Learn for applause. Learn for reward. One day, all these rehearsals will finally pay off. Having habituated yourself (for whatever reasons) to perform noble actions, you will be inspired. You will have the kind of moment I had with my chocolate rugalach at third meal, and you will act *lishmah*.

ספר תולדות יעקב יוסף פרשת בראשית: דהא התוס' הקשו מהא דפסחים, לעולם יעסוק בתורה שלא לשמה וכו', ומשני התוס' דוקא לקנתר אסור אבל שיתקרי רבי שרי וכו' יעו"ש. וכ"ת רשות, זה אינו, שאני הוכחתי במקום אחר שאינו רשות רק חובה, וז"ש לעולם יעסוק שלא לשמה שמתוך וכו', כי צריך שיהיה בכל המדריגות של שלא לשמה גם כן כדי שאם אחר כך יבוא לשמה יעלה גם המדריגות הראשונים ג"כ, וז"ש במקום שבעלי תשובה עומדין אין צדיקים גמורים וכו' (ברכות לד ע"ב) והבן.

At that instant, everything that led to this moment of favor—the hot chocolate, the desire for applause, and the hope for divine reward—all will be uplifted through the *lishmah* and will be transformed in a flash into light and life. The myriad actions that were done for selfish reasons will themselves, suddenly and retroactively, become *lishmah*. And that is truly transformational in a magical way.

"You Broke 'We Will Do,' Be Careful with 'We Will Hear'!"

"Listen to the words of God…" This is like a king who said to his servants, 'Guard for me these two cups' which were *diatreta*.[86] He said, 'be careful with them.' As he was going into the palace, a calf that was at the entrance to the palace butted the servant and broke one of them. The servant stood shaking before the king. He said to him, 'Why are you shaking?' He replied, 'A calf butted me and I broke one of the cups.' The king said, 'If so,

---

86. A rare and expensive roman glasswork.

know and be careful with the second.' So the Holy One said, 'You mixed two cups at Sinai—*we will do* and *we will hear*; you broke 'we will do' by making a calf, be careful with 'we will hear.'

מדרש רבה שמות פרשה כז פסקה ט
שמעו דבר ה' משל למלך שאמר לעבדיו שמרו לי
ב' כוסות הללו והיה דיאטריטא א"ל הוי זהיר בהם
עד שהוא נכנס לפלטין היה עגל אחד שרוי על פתח
הפלטין נגח העבד ונשבר אחד מהם והיה העבד עומד
ומרתית לפני המלך אמר לו למה מרתית אמר שנגחני
עגל ושבר אחד משני הכוסות א"ל המלך א"כ דע
והזהר בשני כך אמר הקב"ה שני כוסות מזגתם בסיני
נעשה ונשמע שברתם נעשה עשיתם לפני עגל הזהרו
בנשמע הוי שמעו דבר ה':

One of the greatest statements of faith we made as a people, and that we can continue to make, is that we are committed to keep the law even if we do not fully understand it. We declare na'aseh ("we will do") even before nishma ("we will comprehend"). In fact, the performance of an act is one of the most important components of our understanding its significance. We learn what Shabbat, or prayer, or charity is through the doing, and develop an appreciation that books alone can never approximate. Na'aseh (acting) done right and combined with an intellectual curiosity will lead to nishma (understanding).

But what should we do if we cannot yet make an honest commitment to one commandment or another? Is there any value in studying the Torah of that commandment without the intention to fulfill that which you are studying? The Midrash seems to say that there is: even if you broke the cup of *action*, hold tight to *study*. Rabbi Chaim Goldvicht, the founding Rosh Yeshiva of Yeshivat Kerem B'Yanveh, taught that ideally a commitment to action precedes the subsequent investigation. Na'aseh should precede nishma. But realistically, in our post-golden-calf reality, there is often an investigation—a curious probing—that must precede the commitment. Such study reveals the exquisite precision and wisdom of Torah thought, and helps us develop a conviction in the commandment's goodness and a confidence in ourselves. That study can slowly lead us to a more careful performance of the mitzvah, which in turn can lead us to an even deeper appreciation of its wisdom: *nishma, na'aseh, ve-nishma*.

Of course, a caveat is in order. While some ulterior motivations are basically harmless, others can be quite toxic. The Tosafot note that studying Torah in order to show off is counterproductive; and studying in order to cynically undermine the tradition is fatally so.[87] But the performance of commandments and the study of Torah out of a desire for heavenly reward, intellectual enjoyment, curiosity, or social reasons are all considered relatively benign, even though they fall short from the ideal. Persevere, and as you slowly internalize the wisdom and values of the Torah you engage, you will most certainly serve from love, delighting in truth because it is true.

---

87. Tosafot to *Pesachim* 50b.

Chapter 18

Purim

Don't Get Drunk, Get "Spiced"!

For a moment, I would like to focus on an aspect of Purim that is often overlooked, that is lost in the celebration and revelry. Purim was a war, among our most famous wars, and as such, it marked a crossroads in the development of the Jewish people.

During wars, lives are lost, communities are overturned, history suddenly switches tracks and heads off into a new direction. When we study history, we often dilate on the wars, not just because they are so dramatic, but because they tend to punctuate larger historical, social, and political processes. Even if the war ends in a strategic stalemate—no territory changed hands, no one emerged clearly as victor or vanquished—still, the cultural and social upheaval remains carved into the flesh of individuals, families, sometimes even nations.

In my life, both Israel and the US have been at war several times, fortunately never with each other. For better or for worse, I've experienced all but one of them solely through the newspapers and electronic media. The one exception, the one I really lived through and experienced in an existential way, was the Gulf War of 1991. At that time I was a student at Kerem B'Yavneh, not far from the Israeli city of Ashdod. KBY is an Israeli Hesder yeshiva, meaning that most of the Israeli students were on active duty in the Israel Defense Forces even while studying in the yeshiva. At that time, I was not yet an Israeli citizen, but instead held an American passport. Like some of you I had come for a year of study abroad. (Actually, I had come for "a year" of study two years earlier—like many of you, my "year" had by then become three years. It would ultimately turn into 18 years.)

My family was back in New York, and as the US built up their military presence on the Saudi-Kuwait border, my parents became increasingly nervous. They were glued to CNN, monitoring every development as the January 14 ultimatum set by the first President Bush approached. In many ways, they were more aware of the impending war than I was in my pure and idealistic yeshiva bubble. As the tension in the region became increasingly palpable, they finally suggested that I return home. I was a tourist; I would not be conscripted to fight, but the threat of chemical weapons left the home front vulnerable as never before, and this (my family reasoned) was enough justification for me to continue my studies in the States.

Torn between my parents and my yeshiva, I had a huge decision to make. To make matters more difficult, Rabbi Shlomo Wolbe, then *mashgiach* of the Mir yeshiva in Jerusalem, remarked at the exodus of American students from the Mir that they were fulfilling the curse of "the land vomiting them out." Rabbi Mordechai Willig of Riverdale and Yeshiva University came to Yavneh and gave a lecture in which he concluded that students did not need to listen to their parents' requests to return home if their learning would suffer. I was, however, older than most of my friends. This was my third year in Israel, and I had already graduated college; while I could easily learn for a while in the US and come back, this would be an acute interruption in my friends' irreplaceable "year in Israel." I decided that I needed to consult with one of the *gedolei ha-dor*, so I went up to Jerusalem to the home of Rabbi Shlomo Zalman Auerbach.

Learning to Grow

Reb Shlomo Zalman listened carefully to my personal situation and told me that I should not refuse my parents' request to return home, so long as I could find some reasonable yeshiva in which to learn. In some ways, I felt crushed; but having my dilemma resolved by such a great personality I also felt relieved. I called home (we still used payphones then, calling via the "International Telephone Exchange") and told them that their request had made its way up to one of the greatest rabbis of the generation, and that he decided that I should listen to my parents' request. I could not refuse them if they demanded that I return, but I asked them to consider one other factor: my roommate was a young Israeli man, and he was in a combat unit; he was Givati. My *chavrusa* (study partner) was also an Israeli, and he too was in a combat unit; he was Golani. They had both tasted battle along the border with Lebanon and if necessary they would be pulled out of yeshiva now as well. They would fight, and risk their lives. How could I turn my back on them, return to the States, and view their battle on television? They are counting on me to keep the study hall alive in their absence, to continue learning while they could not, to pray for them while they are away.

There was a long silence on the other side of the phone. Finally one of my parents said, "Okay, just call home frequently." My parents told me to take good care and to be in contact. We were one people. They never again suggested that I leave.

During that war, my life changed. In retrospect, we know that Israel, miraculously, survived with relatively little damage and loss of life. At the time, however, I and my many friends who remained to face the Scud missiles felt that we were placing ourselves at considerable risk for the sake of our people and our land. Because of this, my love for and commitment to Israel grew as never before, until by the end of the War, which was on the Fast of Esther, I become emotionally committed to settling in Israel, to be the first of my family to return to the land of our people.

Purim

I mention all this as a personal example of what war can do. It changes lives and attitudes. It binds a nation together as one, forces a people to reexamine its right to exist, its purpose and message.

Purim was no different; in fact it was considerably more intense:

And the letters were sent by couriers to all the king's provinces, to destroy, to kill, and to annihilate, all Jews, both young and old, little children and women, in one day, on the thirteenth day of the twelfth month, that is the month of Adar, and to take the spoil of them for plunder.

אסתר ג:יג
ונשלוח ספרים ביד הרצים
אל כל מדינות המלך להשמיד
להרג ולאבד את כל היהודים
מנער ועד זקן טף ונשים ביום
אחד בשלושה עשר לחדש
שנים עשר הוא חדש אדר
ושללם לבוז:

King Achashverosh controlled the entire land of Israel and the vast majority of the Jewish Diaspora. Every significant Jewish community was in his grip, and he decreed total annihilation, on one day, with no escape. The prophets of the time understood that this was no game. God himself had concurred with this ultimate judgment. The curtain was about to fall on the history of the Jews.

Facing potential extermination, the Jews were forced to reflect on their past and to introspect. They asked themselves and each other the basic existential questions: who are we, and for what did we stand; what, in the end, did we contribute? What should we have contributed and what could have been our future? Out of such introspection was born a new sense of meaning and identity, and out of the subsequent miracle of salvation that identity grew wings, expressing a newly discovered purpose and mission.

Learning to Grow

In a way, the Jewish people as it had been did die on that first Purim; and in its place, within the very bodies of its citizens, a new Jewish people with a new awareness and a revolutionary vision of mission was born. The energy of that event continues to permeate the month of Adar. As your long winter term in yeshiva comes to a close, you might well draw on that energy to consider your own accomplishments and plot a course for the future.

Love of the Miracle

Let's pause for a moment and reflect on this war-born revolution in consciousness. What is the unique message of Purim that we have commemorated ever since? Let's read from the Talmud a cryptic passage that contrasts our sense of mission before and after Purim, that contrasts the receiving of the Torah on Sinai with the reacceptance of the Torah at Purim-time.

"And they stood beneath the mountain..." (Ex. 19:17) Rav Avdimi the son of Chama the son of Chasa said: This teaches that God overturned the mountain upon them like an [inverted] barrel, and said to them, "If you accept the Torah all is well; and if not, there will be your burial." Rav Acha bar Yaakov said, "this provides a strong protest against the Torah." Rabbah said: Nevertheless, they re-accepted it in the days of Achashverosh, as is written, 'The Jews confirmed and accepted': they confirmed what they had previously accepted.

תלמוד בבלי מסכת שבת דף פח עמוד א

ויתיצבו בתחתית ההר, אמר רב אבדימי בר חמא בר חסא: מלמד שכפה הקדוש ברוך הוא עליהם את ההר כגיגית, ואמר להם: אם אתם מקבלים התורה - מוטב, ואם לאו - שם תהא קבורתכם. אמר רב אחא בר יעקב: מכאן מודעא רבה לאורייתא. אמר רבא: אף על פי כן, הדור קבלוה בימי אחשורוש. דכתיב קימו וקבלו היהודים, קיימו מה שקיבלו כבר.

Purim

If we Jews have any mission in the world, it is to herald ultimate moral truths, eternal principles woven into the fabric of creation, revealed to the Jewish people by God himself. We are charged to be a light unto nations, to illuminate the world through exemplary behavior. The Talmud relates that this mission, both in the way we received it, and in terms of our commitment to it, changed radically during the year of the Purim story. Let's think analytically for a moment and try to understand this passage.

The simple understanding of the opening verse is clearly that the Jewish people stood at the foot of the mountain. The Rabbis, listening carefully to the exact language of the verse, heard a hint to a deeper understanding: this experience of standing together to receive the Torah was somehow forced—the world's greatest example of religious coercion—and that the object that threatened them was the mountain itself.

This perspective on the Sinai experience is difficult to accept for several reasons. For one, the Jews had already declared, na'aseh ve-nishma, "we will do and we will hear!"; having already stated their desire to receive the Torah, what purpose does the coercion serve? More philosophically, we must admit that a coerced acceptance of faith is no acceptance at all—as the Rabbis say, "God desires the heart" (Sanhedrin 106b).

In response to these questions, Rabbi Meir Simcha ha-Kohen of Dvinsk explained in his commentary on the Torah, Meshech Chochmah, that at Sinai God revealed himself in an unprecedented prophetic event. The Torah describes how the people, in a heightened state of consciousness, began to experience synesthesia, in which the boundaries between the senses blur as the awareness of an overarching unity becomes intensified. The Torah records, "All the people saw the sounds" (Ex. 20:18). The Talmud explains, "They saw that which would normally be heard and heard that which would normally be seen." The more physical a thing is, the more bounded

Rabbi Meir Simcha ha-Kohen (1843–1926) was the rabbi of Dvinsk. His *Or Sameach* is one of the most important commentaries on the Rambam's *Mishneh Torah*. He worked on his Torah commentary, *Meshech Chochmah*, for several decades. Deeply philosophical, it was published only posthumously.

it is. Our physical bodies, for example, will live for only a certain amount of time, while our spiritual souls will live forever. The Jewish people were experiencing spirituality with an awareness that we normally have only for physical things. Just as we can clearly perceive the hardness of the floor on which we stand, and the softness of the chair on which we sit, so did the Jews at Sinai perceive the truth of the laws and principles that God communicated. In such a state, value judgments become irrelevant. A moral, ethical or "religious" law is just as much a part of the fabric of reality as a law of physics. For them, the commandments existed as truths that can brook no breaching.

Given such an understanding of the law, there was no real room to question if, for example, the commandment forbidding work on the Sabbath was good or bad, pleasant or unpleasant, sweet or sour. I could just as well ask you if the law of gravity is pleasant. At best, the question is academic; at worst it is absurd and irrelevant. Just as the mountain, if dropped on their heads, would bury them, good or bad notwithstanding, so too a violation of any commandment was clearly perceived as a breaking with a basic truth. The result of that break would be a parting, a separation, from the Commander, the Source of life. The result would be death.

This intellectual "coercion" was the ultimate religious coercion, far more severe than imposing an action on a person while his mind remains free. Here, the mind itself was forced to accept the irrefutable truth of the Torah. Free will evaporated as God pulled back the curtain and revealed His majesty.

The Torah we received at Sinai was therefore a Torah that radiated great light, but little warmth. The Jewish people related to the Torah much in the way we relate to the law of gravity, to be considered very carefully, always, but not really celebrated. After all, who celebrates gravity? No one. Who has a feeling of satisfaction every time we witness the playing out of a physical law? Again, no one. If the law of gravity were to be suspended, we would all be doing back-flips and lobbing jellybeans at each other with little sentimental attachment to the law we had lost.

This, therefore, was a strong protest against the Torah. Because unless we can taste the sweetness in the commandments, unless we can say that the law is not only categorical, but is also good, then we can never fully internalize the law, relate to it emotionally, in any way that makes us feel fulfilled and that gives our lives meaning. Note that a classical word for "sweet," ערב, is the same word as to become "mixed-in," like in the word "תערובת": one only mixes something into his personality if he can taste the sweetness, while overpowering brightness can drive you away; you need to turn down the light to enjoy the experience, like we do in the evening, ערב.

In short, at Sinai the brilliance of the Torah was bright, and its truth was as undeniable as gravity. But no one sacrifices himself to proclaim the truth of a physical law. Gravity is not worth dying for.

Learning to Grow

As the Sinai experience receded into history, our clear intellectual perception of the truth of the law receded as well. And since we had never developed an internalized emotional connection to the goodness of our tradition, we were left with a dangerous moral vacuum. With every passing generation, our perception of the Torah's absolute truth became increasingly fuzzy; and the one thing that might substitute—a feeling that the Torah was good and beautiful—never fully developed. That disconnect ultimately climaxed in the destruction of the first Temple: a strong protest against the Torah indeed.

This relationship to the tradition changed radically during the Purim miracle. In the years following the destruction, the Jews had been exiled from their land, seemingly cast away by God. They were deep in exile, assimilating and intermarrying (as we see from Ezra in the period that followed). God had hidden His presence to such a degree that no divine name is mentioned, even once, in the entire Megillah, leading the Talmud to find a hint in the Torah for the name of our story's most central character, Esther, in the verse, "And I will surely hide [*hasteir astir*] my face."[88] We Jews tend to be somewhat ethnocentric, and yet the Megillah does not refer to its era as the days of Mordechai or the days of Esther; the Megillah begins quite pointedly by calling these the "Days of Achashverosh." He held the power, and we were a small, scattered minority. The Jewish people had reached the opposite extreme of the Sinai experience: if Sinai was typified by almost excessive and obvious Divine intervention, Purim was typified by apparent Divine abandonment.

This was an environment in which free will was wide open, in which the entire future of the Jewish people could be attributed to Haman's roll of the dice, as much as to Divine Providence. God's hand was hidden, spiritual truths were clouded, moral imperatives were blurred. In such circumstances the intellectual terms "true" and "false"

---

88. *Chullin* 139b.

seem unsuited to matters of ethics. Instead, everyone had to look within to find—if not the absolutely true—the Good and the Sweet.

The apparent sequence of "coincidences" that led to the Jews' salvation easily could have been attributed to fate or to political intrigue. Instead, the Jews of Shushan recognized a profoundly hidden miracle. That determination was not, and could not, have been based on intellect alone, since any number of plausible explanations could have described the situation. The miraculous nature of the events could not be demonstrated by logical proof. Instead, the Jews felt inside, emotionally, that they had never been abandoned after all. The intellect was, for a moment, neutralized by competing explanations; perhaps for the first time, the Jews had to turn to their emotions to find a plausible explanation for what had transpired. There, deep in their hearts, they recognized that God loved them and was with them and had saved them. They responded in kind and re-accepted, this time with their hearts, the commandments that that they had once known as only cold dry truths. As Rashi teaches, they re-accepted the Torah in the days of Achashverosh, "out of love for the miracle that was done for them."

Here, the commandments were not accepted because the intellect demanded them, but rather because the heart cherished them. The commandments provided an emotional connection to their commander, who had become the Jews' beloved savior. They had discovered that the law was not only engraved on cold stone, but that it was etched into the heart of each and every Jew. Their discovery was of a tradition that was sweet and pleasant: "Good" and not just "True." This time the intellect was useless and irrelevant. This time the law was accepted with love, in love.

An Emotional Acceptance

Every year, just as we commemorate the intellectual acceptance of the Torah on Shavuot, so too we celebrate this emotional re-acceptance of the Torah on Purim. This is a time in which we must quiet our over-worked intellects for a day, and reflect on how nice it is to be a Jew, how good are our people, how sweet are our customs, how dear is our God. With a bottle of wine we hush the mind and open our hearts, ready to embrace our tradition, and to embrace each other. Because just as a Torah scroll cannot lack one letter, so we cannot accept the Torah unless we are united as a people in common affection, despite all the petty faults and disagreements that consume us when we are more sober.

> Rava said, "A person must become 'spiced' on Purim, until he doesn't know the distinction between 'cursed is Haman,' and 'blessed is Mordechai.'"[89]

The term to become drunk is לביסומי, to be "spiced." We must become spiced on Purim: we must taste the flavor, the sweetness in all that we have in common as Jews. Few of us choose our meals based on nutritional value alone; want delicious food, bursting with flavor. On Purim we embrace Torah not because it is necessary, not because of a mountain over our heads, but because it is delicious. Our minds stop discriminating, and our hearts reach out to everyone.

Once again, we unite like the Jewish of Sinai who accepted the Torah, as we are told, "like one person, with one heart." But now, we are uniting not out of necessity, forced by prophetic intellection, but out of love for God, His Torah, and His people. And if we macho individualists need a bit of wine to become uninhibited enough to tap into the pure emotional joy of being Jewish—to hug each other and sing together and dance in a circle—then take out the wine, because this is the holiday of celebrating being Jewish.

As Esther said to Mordechai, "Go, gather together all the Jews," because only then can we truly confirm our respect for each other

---

89. *Megillah* 7b.

and for the tradition. This command echoes through the rituals and customs of the day:

- Gather together the Jews: give gifts of food and drink to friends and neighbors.
- Gather together the Jews: give money to the poor so that they too can celebrate.
- Gather together the Jews: have a festive meal with family and friends.
- Gather together the Jews: come together as a community to read about the hidden miracles that God performed for our ancestors, and for us as well.

If we relate to our tradition with our hearts and not just our heads, then our lives as Jews will be enriched and not just "correct," and we will connect with other Jews to celebrate (and, when necessary, to mourn). We have to learn how to relate to the sweetness in every mitzvah, the *ta'am* of the mitzvah. The history is important and the details of the law may be essential, but no less essential is the emotion that we should be brave enough to express without macho inhibition.

Going Deeper: Testing the Body on Autopilot

The particularly Jewish year begins in the spring with the month of the Exodus and the birth of the Jewish people. The Purim miracle and subsequent celebration take place in the twelfth month, at the very end of the annual cycle. At the Exodus, we were confronted with the obvious assertion of theological truths, in our physical world and in history. Every year we attempt to relive the experience of the Exodus, as if it happened to each of us personally, in order to acquire an unmoving conviction in the existence of the Almighty, who cares for His people and performs miracles on our behalf.

Rabbi Yeruchom ha-Levi Levovitz (1873–1936), was the famous *mashgiach ruchani* at the Mir yeshiva in Belarus. He was a disciple of the Alter of Slabodka and the Alter of Kelm as well as the Chofetz Chaim. Some of his better known disciples include Rabbi Shlomo Wolbe, Rabbi Chaim Shmuelevitz, Rabbi Dovid Povarsky, Rabbi Abba Berman, Rabbi Zelik Epstein and Rabbi Shimon Schwab.

At times of such clarity, it is relatively easy to behave properly. The overwhelming intellectual awareness of God's providence helps us restrain our lower passions and desires, and helps motivate positive actions, even while our untrained and animal-like bodies might prefer baser pleasures and unproductive sloth. But as we have discussed, we are hardly at our most efficient when our minds and bodies are pulling in different directions. In addition, we give relatively little honor to our Creator if only our minds can recognize the truth of the Torah. It is when our bodies join in proclaiming the beauty, truth, and sweetness of the Torah, that we are demonstrating greater honor for the Torah, saying that it can inform and uplift even the most distant of places. It is easy to behave well in a Jerusalem *beit midrash*; it is far more elusive—and therefore makes a greater statement—to behave with holiness on the streets of New York.

For twelve long months, beginning with Pesach, we Jews work to incorporate the intellectual truths of the Exodus into our spontaneous emotional response system. For twelve long months, we Jew work to train our earthy bodies to resonate comfortably and naturally with the ideals, values, and detailed laws of the Torah. The goal is to be able to operate with the clarity of the Exodus, even in the darkness of Shushan, and to do so with conviction and joy.

Rabbi Yeruchom ha-Levi Levovitz, the first *mashgiach* of the Mir Yeshiva, taught that by drinking on Purim, we are testing ourselves to see if we have succeeded in our efforts to bring our intellectual clarity down to our gut reaction. With a bit of wine, we neutralize our often over-active Jewish intellects and allow our bodies to run on autopilot, briefly and in an environment controlled by the sanctity of the day's *mitzvot*. Intellectually, we may no longer "know" the distinction between "cursed is Haman," and "blessed is Mordechai"; nevertheless, our very bodies have been so trained that they will naturally bless Mordechai and recoil from the very thought of Haman's wickedness.

Every year, we witness Jews of all colors greeting and celebrating with Jews of different colors. The distinctions between us seem to melt away as we bask in the warmth of God's miracle. We taste the flavor of the tradition and the sweetness of our lives. Savoring our lot we are hardly drunk at all; rather, we've become spiced.

Chapter 19

Passover

The Month of Spring, the Month of *Chesed*

We are all well aware of the unique structure of the Jewish calendar, according to which the lunar calendar must be synchronized with the solar calendar from time to time. The lunar "year" is slightly less than 355 days (the numerical value of the word, "שנה"!). To prevent the months from slowly slipping backwards in the seasons we add a thirteenth month to the year seven times in each nineteen-year cycle.

Most importantly, we go through this process so that the holiday of Passover should always fall out in the spring.[90] The Torah is emphatic in emphasizing that the Jewish people were redeemed in the springtime, and that we should be mindful of this fact when we celebrate Passover.

Shemot 13

And Moshe said to the nation: remember this day on which you went out from Egypt from the house of slaves, that with a strong hand God took you out from this, and you shall not eat leaven. Today you are going out, in the month of the spring...

---

90. *Rosh Hashanah* 21a.

Rashi: "in the month of the spring" — do they not know what was the month?! Rather, so he said to them: see the kindness with which He treated you that He took you out in a month that was proper for leaving, not too hot, not too cold, and not rainy…

שמות פרק יג
(ג) ויאמר משה אל העם זכור את היום הזה אשר יצאתם ממצרים מבית עבדים כי בחזק יד הוציא ה' אתכם מזה ולא יאכל חמץ: (ד) היום אתם יצאים בחדש האביב: (ה) והיה כי יביאך ה' אל ארץ הכנעני והחתי והאמרי והחוי והיבוסי אשר נשבע לאבתיך לתת לך ארץ זבת חלב ודבש ועבדת את העבדה הזאת בחדש הזה:

רש"י שמות פרק יג
(ד) "בחדש האביב" - וכי לא היו יודעין באיזה חדש, אלא כך אמר להם, ראו חסד שגמלכם שהוציא אתכם בחדש שהוא כשר לצאת, לא חמה ולא צנה ולא גשמים. וכן הוא אומר (תהלים סח ז) מוציא אסירים בכושרות, חדש שהוא כשר לצאת:

Rabbi Chaim Goldvicht found this explanation of Rashi perplexing. After all, the Jewish people had been suffering in Egypt for hundreds of years. They were brutally afflicted by harsh taskmasters, and their babies slaughtered. Do we really think they cared about the weather report on the day of their liberation? Rashi's explanation makes the Jewish people—waiting for a day that is not too cold and not too hot—sound like a pampered Goldilocks. Was it of concern to them that they left Egypt when the flowers were in bloom, and the roads well-groomed? This would be hard to accept under any circumstances, but it is absolutely impossible to believe when set in the context of the Egyptian exile.

Even if we do accept this explanation, it is hard to understand why such a marginal detail was given such a prominent role in Jewish law and custom. It finds expression in establishing the Jewish calendar for generations. And every year, at the Passover Seder, each Jewish family takes a green vegetable to remember the springtime. Do we really understand the importance of this?

Rabbi Chaim Yaakov Goldvicht (1924–1995) was born in Jerusalem, where he was a close student of the Brisker Rav. He later studied in the Slabodka Yeshiva in Bnei Brak, where he became close to the *Chazon Ish*. He founded Yeshiva Kerem B'Yavneh, the first Israeli Hesder yeshiva, and was particularly famous for his masterful teaching of *aggadah*. Many of his teachings have been published as *Asufot Ma'arachot*.

As was his habit, Rabbi Goldvicht took this seemingly difficult passage and used it to introduce an important principle that sheds light on Passover in general, and on the personal *avodah* of yeshiva and seminary students during this season.

Kindness and Mercy

The Rabbis tell us that the Jewish people are notable for having three outstanding character traits: we are merciful, we are bashful, and we are kind.[91] For our purposes, I'd like to focus on "mercy" and "kindness." At first glance, these might seem a bit redundant, since both kindness ("*chesed*") and mercy ("*rachamim*") motivate similar extroverted actions of giving. Why do we need both?

In addition, mercy could be perceived as a poor cousin of kindness given that kindness is one of the most idealistic traits of character. Kindness is filled with dynamic energy. One who is kind overflows to all, to rich and poor alike. God himself, in His infinite kindness, wished to overflow and give to others, and therefore He created the universe. At its most sublime, human kindness is a result of a person, created in the image of God, looking at this divine model and saying: just like God

91. *Yevamot* 79a.

overflows and gives me goodness and life, so I must overflow and give goodness and life. Avraham, the first pillar of the Jewish people, effectively personified kindness and made it part of the Jewish legacy.

Mercy, on the other hand, seems to pale in comparison. One can only be merciful to someone who suffers. Indeed, mercy is sometimes thought of as a weakness of the soul, by which the witnessing of another's pain causes a corresponding pain in the heart of the witness. One who has mercy may be trying to alleviate his own sympathetic suffering as much as he desires to alleviate the original suffering of the victim; mercy, therefore, is tainted with a bit of selfishness. Once the Talmud praises us for a wholly altruistic kindness, why bother mentioning second-string mercy?

The truth is that mercy, attentive to the pain of the victim and powerful in its response, deserves top billing right next to kindness. Mercy is more focused than kindness. True, kindness will surely give to rich and poor alike, but lacking the sympathetic pain that mercy experiences, kindness will be less likely to reveal and address the root cause of the suffering. In addition, and perhaps more importantly, because mercy experiences sympathetic pain, its response will tend to be more urgent and commanding. Mercy viscerally feels the need, and is therefore compelled to relieve that suffering as if it were its own. When mercy sees the suffering it feels the pain, and it will not rest until that suffering is resolved.

That's mercy's advantage. But of course, that's mercy's disadvantage as well, because mercy only reacts to what it sees.

Moshe's Ethical Virtuosity

With what attribute did God save the Jewish people in Egypt? At first glance, the answer seems obvious: He saw our affliction and saved us with His immense mercy. Ultimately this is true, but this is not the whole story. It seems that the sins of the Jewish people in Egypt had corrupted them to such a state that they were on the level that the Rabbis referred to as the 49th level of impurity. They had turned away from God, and subsequently God turned from them. There was, as it were, no Divine knowledge of the people's suffering. Instead, there was "*hester panim*," a hiding of the divine countenance, and therefore no awareness which would trigger mercy in the first place. What was the catalyst that caused God to return and look at the Jewish people?

The Rabbis teach us that while the Jewish people were suffering under intense slavery, Moshe was being raised as the son of Pharaoh, comfortable in the king's palace. Growing up as a prince of Egypt, surrounded by luxury, he was only vaguely aware that his wealth came from the blood and sweat of Jewish bondage. If he was aware of the people's suffering, it was only in the most abstract distant sense. From such a distance, his feelings of mercy remained unengaged. But then Moshe did a magnificent act:

And the child grew up and she brought him to the daughter of Pharaoh and he was to her as a son... And it was in those days that Moshe grew up and he went out to his brothers and he saw them in their burdens (*Shemot* 2:10-11).

Rashi: "and he saw them in their burdens" — he directed his eyes and heart to be pained for them.

שמות פרק ב
(י) ויגדל הילד ותבאהו לבת פרעה
ויהי לה לבן ותקרא שמו משה ותאמר
כי מן המים משיתהו: (יא) ויהי בימים
ההם ויגדל משה ויצא אל אחיו וירא
בסבלתם וירא איש מצרי מכה איש
עברי מאחיו:

רש"י שמות פרק ב
"וירא בסבלתם" — נתן עיניו ולבו
להיות מיצר עליהם:

The beginning of this passage notes that the child "grew up," but the very next verse repeats "Moshe grew up." This repetition is clearly coming to indicate something significant, and the *Midrash Tanchuma* elaborates: the first "growing up" was physical; the second related to the development of Moshe's character. In Hebrew, the word *gadol* is a contraction of *gomel dal* (גמל דל = ג' דל), literally meaning one who gives to a poor person. In other words, *gadol* means a *ba'al chesed*. This definition is based in Kabbalah and finds expression in our daily prayers: for example, when we refer to God as *Ha-Gadol*, we are referring to Divine *chesed*, kindness.[92] The Torah is not just telling us that Moshe grew up; the Torah is telling us that Moshe acquired the attribute of kindness. How do we know that Moshe acquired this attribute? Because he went out to his brothers! Were Moshe only merciful, he would certainly have reacted had the Jews come to his door; but they weren't allowed near the palace. So Moshe drew on his power of kindness to get up off his princely throne and to go out to his brothers, so that he would see them. As Rashi explains, Moshe actively turned his eyes in an extroverted movement of kindness, so that his heart would feel their pain. This is true ethical virtuosity: he drew on his power of kindness so that he would see them, and so that he would then have the even more powerful and visceral mercy.

The mercy he cultivated was so moving that he justly killed an Egyptian officer, even though that act threatened his own secure and comfortable future as a prince of Egypt.

In resonance, God responded in kind:

During that long period, the king of Egypt died; and the children of Israel groaned from their labor and cried out, and their cry because of their labor went up to God. God heard their groaning and he remembered his covenant with Avraham, with Yitzchak and with Yaakov. And God looked at the children of Israel and God knew (*Shemot* 2:23-25).

92. See Rabbenu Bachya on *Devarim* 10:17 and Rashi on *Devarim* 3:24.

Rashi: "and God knew" — He placed on them His heart and did not avert His eyes.

God left His state of *hester panim* and chose to look at the Jewish people, to connect to them (the language of *da'at* is always a language of connection), and to save them. Although it may be

שמות פרק ב

(כג) ויהי בימים הרבים ההם וימת מלך מצרים ויאנחו בני ישראל מן העבדה ויזעקו ותעל שועתם אל הא-להים מן העבדה: (כד) וישמע א-להים את נאקתם ויזכר א-להים את בריתו את אברהם את יצחק ואת יעקב: (כה) וירא א-להים את בני ישראל וידע א-להים:

רש"י שמות פרק ב

(כה) וידע א-להים - נתן עליהם לב ולא העלים עיניו:

true that God had mercy for his people, and that this mercy provoked a divine response to Jewish suffering that overwhelmed the natural order, still the initial motivation that led to the salvation was God's attribute of kindness. Just as Moshe invoked his kindness in order to see, and his seeing awakened his mercy, so too God's kindness brought Him to see and to invoke an even greater mercy.

If you want proof that the divine salvation was initially motivated by kindness, recall in which month the Jewish people were saved: the month of spring, the most comfortable time for the Jews to travel! Had God redeemed us only with mercy, He would have taken care of our needs only in so far as was necessary to alleviate the raw suffering. This would include liberation from bondage, escape from Egypt, and the deliverance into our homeland. But mercy alone would not dictate that we should be saved in the nicest of months. That would only be motivated by unadulterated kindness.

It is for this reason that we are commanded to recall that we were saved in the springtime. We adjust the calendar and eat green vegetables at the Seder in order to remember the attribute with which we were saved, the attribute that Moshe exemplified when he set the spark for our liberation, the attribute of selfless *chesed*. We do this in order to recall and to teach that all liberation comes as a flash from outside, an extroverted turning to look.

Look, Feel, Act

When confronted with the another's pain and suffering we must not avert our eyes; rather, we should actively look (kindness), allow ourselves to feel (mercy) and ultimately, we must act. As you dip your parsley into the salt water this Pesach, know that only kindness can overcome the tears of persecution, disease, and self-destructive behavior. Know that kindness was the central attribute of the Exodus and that we must imitate this attribute in order to care for others, sometimes even liberating them.

In chapter 3, we discussed how the long winter months are a time for us to hold back from action, to gestate our idealism in the quiet of the *beit midrash*. The spring has now come, and with it comes the well-deserved vacation that is traditional in the world of the yeshivas. You certainly deserve a break. At the same time, whether you are going home for the holiday or will be spending it with family and friends locally, now is a time for you to look at others and see how you can show them some kindness. As everyone around you prepares for Pesach, cleaning and cooking, adopt a family (perhaps one that has hosted you frequently this year), and offer your services. From babysitting to heavy lifting, there is some contribution that you can make, if only you are willing to look and find it. The alternative—pulling up to the Seder table without having exerted yourself in significant acts of *chesed*—would be distasteful.

Indeed, more than your newly acquired Torah knowledge, those around you will likely evaluate the success of your year based on the kindness you demonstrate toward others. Such an evaluation would be entirely appropriate. If you have been growing deep roots during these winter months, those roots must find expression in the rich foliage of springtime *chesed*.

That's a practical application of this aspect of Pesach, relevant to your age and your stage in life. Of course, as you continue to mature, this lesson should mature along with you. The world is far from perfect, and many people created in the Divine image continue to suffer at the hands of others, or due to their own mistaken lifestyles, or due to the disasters that are the lot of flesh-and-blood. I would like to believe that we *b'nei Torah* would act with boundless mercy towards those who are suffering outside of the *beit midrash* were they standing before us. I'm confident that each of us would empty our pockets and take the shirts off our backs in order to help these people. The problem is that they are often far away, and of such great numbers that the mind fails to comprehend the reality of their tragedies. If we are aware of such people, we are aware of them in only a distant abstract sense, as Moshe must have been aware of the Jewish people while he was still in the Pharaoh's palace.

The Jewish people remain a minority, sometimes embattled. The Torah world in particular has limited material resources and tremendous needs. For the foreseeable future, we will need to focus the lion's share of our efforts on our own community, so that Torah and those who hold it dear can flourish. We know that we have few real friends and even fewer patrons. As Bilam said, we are a "nation that dwells alone" — that is our blessing and our curse. God and God alone will catch us if we stumble, which gives us comfort, even as we are mindful not to rely on His miracles. So practically, the reach of our *chesed* remains limited. Nevertheless, we must acknowledge our solidarity with the rest of humanity as well, even if only in ways that are largely symbolic. With ethical artistry, Moshe used his power of kindness to get himself up out of his chair, to see his suffering kinsmen, in order to allow his attribute of mercy to be inspired and to drive him towards action. Like Moshe, we should tap into the two quintessential Jewish traits of kindness and mercy on behalf of those who are less fortunate than ourselves, although we may be divided not just by geography and culture, but by sometimes serious differences in theological and political visions. After all, Avraham went to war to save Lot from injustice, even though Lot had turned his back on Avraham, preferring the flesh-pots of Sodom over the company of the Divine presence. Moshe too cared not only about the injustices done to his people, but also about those done to the daughters of the (then) idolatrous Yitro. One who is sensitive to the social fabric of the world does not discriminate when he sees it being torn, when he sees individuals persecuted at the end of a gun or by the ravages of disease.

Long ago, inspired by the *chesed* of Moshe, God once turned His face towards His people and redeemed us from bondage; the *chesed* of your generation may yet inspire Him to turn towards us once again, with *chesed* and with *rachamim*.

Chapter 20

Counting the 2.5 Liters

Working on Our "Measurements"

Vayikra 23

And you shall count to yourselves from the day after the Sabbath, from the day you brought the omer of the wave offering; they shall be seven complete weeks. You shall count until the day after the seventh Sabbath—fifty days; and you shall bring a new meal offering to G-d (vv.15-16).

Rashi:

"From the day after the Sabbath" — i.e., the day after the [first day of the Passover] festival.

"Complete" — this teaches that the counting begins in the evening; for if not, the weeks would not be complete.

"The seventh Sabbath" — as Onkelos translated, "the seventh week."

"You shall count until the day after the seventh Sabbath" — "until," but not including the fiftieth; that is 49 days.

"Fifty days; and you shall bring a new meal offering to G-d" — i.e., on the fiftieth day you shall offer it.

"A new meal offering" — This is the first meal offering to be brought from the new crop. And if you ask, "But surely the meal-offering of the *Omer* has already been offered [on the 16 of Nisan, as mentioned]?!" The *Omer* was unlike all the other m e a l - o f f e r i n g s since it was brought of barley.

Like the ways of God, the words of God are often difficult to appreciate, until we stand confronted by a difficult text and wonder, "What was the Almighty thinking?" As

ויקרא פרק כג

(טו) וספרתם לכם ממחרת השבת מיום הביאכם את עמר התנופה שבע שבתות תמימת תהיינה: (טז) עד ממחרת השבת השביעת תספרו חמשים יום והקרבתם מנחה חדשה לה':

רש"י

"ממחרת השבת" — ממחרת יום טוב: "תמימת תהיינה" — מלמד שמתחיל ומונה מערב, שאם לא כן אינן תמימות: "השבת השביעת" — כתרגומו שבועתא שביעתא:
"עד ממחרת השבת השביעת תספרו" — ולא עד בכלל, והן ארבעים ותשעה יום: "חמשים יום והקרבתם מנחה חדשה לה'" — ביום החמשים תקריבוה. ואומר אני זהו מדרשו, אבל פשוטו עד ממחרת השבת השביעית, שהוא יום חמשים, תספרו. ומקרא מסורס הוא:
"מנחה חדשה" — היא המנחה הראשונה שהובאה מן החדש. ואם תאמר, הרי קרבה מנחת העומר, אינה כשאר כל המנחות, שהיא באה מן השעורים:

we begin the commandment of counting the *Omer*, and read the above passage, I find myself perplexed. In the days of the Second Temple, the Pharisees (i.e., Perushim, from whom we halachic Jews are descended) struggled against the Sadducees in their denial of the Oral Law. The Mishnah tells us that one of the points of controversy was the commandment of the *Omer*.[93] Our oral tradition explains

---

93. *Menachot* 10:3.

that the *Omer* should be brought on the second day of Passover, and the "counting" of the *Omer* should commence on the preceding night. This interpretation is brought by Rashi above and is the basis for our universal observance. The Sadducees, however, read our verses literally. They brought the *Omer* on the first Sunday following Passover ("the day after the Sabbath"), then they counted seven literal "Sabbaths" and celebrated Shavuot on the fiftieth day, always on a Sunday. This is the practice of Karaites even today.

Our Rabbis recognized that the Sadducees' overly simple, literal interpretation might appear attractive to the masses, so they instituted several customs to make fun of it, including the very public harvesting of the barley on the evening following *Yom Tov*. Should that night fall out on a Sabbath, they would announce the unusual Friday night harvest in an exaggerated fashion, poking a finger in the eye of the Sadducees, since such a harvest would be considered a desecration of the Sabbath according to their literal reading of the verses.

And here we are left perplexed. Why did the Torah communicate this commandment in a way that was so ambiguous and that opened the tradition up to such controversy? Instead of writing "the day after the Sabbath" couldn't the verse have been written "the day after *yom tov*," or "on the second day," or some other unambiguous phrase? Similarly, why did the Torah need to command us to count seven "Sabbaths"; couldn't it have written seven "weeks" (שבועות) just as is written in *Devarim* 16?

The Power of Biblical Ambiguity

As we study the Torah we find many verses whose literal meaning might confuse the superficial reader or—more likely—the reader who is looking for a reason to be confused. The Torah was written, however, for those of us who recognize that the oral law interpretation is both necessary and hinted to by the text itself. Knowing that faithful Jews will always hold the oral interpretation sacred, the Torah permitted itself deliberate ambiguity to teach lessons that are less practical, but often strikingly powerful.

Take, for example, the famous verse "an eye for an eye; a tooth for a tooth." The form of justice implied by a literal reading of this verse stood as the brutal logic behind much of Hammurabi's code. Hammurabi was probably a contemporary of Avraham, and among his laws was the following dark ruling: should a man murder his neighbor's daughter, he would be punished by having his own daughter executed. Hammurabi's code is filled with such cruel laws.

It was from such a vicious culture that Avraham escaped, to preach compassion and true justice; the Rabbis of the Talmud, descendants of Avraham, understood that such brutality should be unthinkable in a just society. Based on oral tradition, ethical sensitivity, and some point of legal practicality, they explained "an eye for an eye, a tooth for a tooth" as insisting upon only monetary compensation: the *value* of an eye for an eye; the *value* of a tooth for a tooth. But of course the question remains: why didn't the Torah just teach "money for an eye; money for a tooth"?

The answer gets to the heart of the relationship between the written law and the oral law. As we saw in Chapter 6, the written law is supposed to give us an idealistic vision, something motivating in its clarity, something with an endless depth of possible interpretation. The Oral Law, on the other hand, takes the pure simplicity of the Written Law and makes it practical. Practically, we take money for an eye and money for a tooth. But ideally, we should never entertain the belief that money can be a proper compensation for the loss of an eye. No one should ever think, "Here's your money, now we're even."

To anyone who might be tempted to consider money an adequate restitution, the written, idealistic Torah responds, "In no way are you 'even'; in fact, you deserve to get your own eye taken out! Of course we will never do that to you, but that's how you should feel." Relying on the oral tradition to guide us in practice, the Torah permitted itself an ambiguity that was necessary to teach a painfully deep idea.

"From the Day Following the Sabbath"

Likewise, in the case of *sefirat ha-omer*, the Torah relied on the oral tradition for us practically to begin counting on the night before the second day, and took the liberty to call the first day of Passover a "Sabbath" in order to teach an important lesson. True, this opened the possibility of a dangerous misinterpretation, but the lesson to be learned was so crucial that the Torah deemed it worth the risk. It was desperately important to refer to the first day of Passover as a Sabbath, and particularly in the context of *sefirat ha-omer*.

The first day of Passover celebrates the day of liberation from slavery, from callous, externally imposed labor. It certainly makes sense to refer to that first day as a Sabbath. But that first day is not *always* referred to as a "Sabbath"; why is it particularly important to refer to this day as a Sabbath in this context—in the context of *sefirat ha-omer*?

Maharal explains that by calling the day before *sefirat ha-omer* a "Sabbath"—a day of rest—a contrast was implied, indicating that *sefirat ha-omer* itself should be a time of intense labor, comparable in some ways to the Egyptian slavery that preceded the Exodus. Unlike that slavery, however, the period of *sefirat ha-omer* is a time of labor that is internally motivated and self-actualizing. The Torah emphasizes the laborious nature of *sefirat ha-omer* by referring to the day that precedes it as, in contrast, a "Sabbath," a day of rest.

In what way is the period of *sefirat ha-omer* a time of intense labor? Maharal points out that like the earth (אדמה), we humans (אדם) are fertile, full of potential that can be released and expressed by the "seed" that is planted in us. In the case of the earth, an apple seed transforms the earth itself into an apple tree, and ultimately into sweet ripe apples; in the case of us humans, the body allows the soul and the Torah planted within us[94] to be expressed into the world as holy, beautiful actions.

But there is a caveat: for any plant to grow properly and produce fruit, the earth must be properly plowed and fertile. Permit me to continue the analogy: imagine that you are a farmer and that your country is suffering a terrible famine. You have eaten up most of your food, and all you have left in the house is your seed grain. As you know, farmers select the best grain of their crop to use as the seeds for the next year's planting. Medium quality grain is used for bread; excellent grain is used for cake; but the best grain is always used for the next year's seeds. Now at a time of famine, the children are hungry, and they beg you to please use the seed grain as food. You have to have tremendous self-discipline not to eat the seed grain, because if you do, you will have nothing to plant, and next year's harvest will be completely empty.

So here you have your most preciously guarded seed grain. And then, at the time of planting, you take this most valuable grain, and you throw it on the ground, you cover it with dirt, you pour water on top of it, hoping that it begins to decompose in the ground.

Are you nuts?

Not at all. You know that this is the way a new crop will be produced. At the same time, you will not plant this precious grain indiscriminately; you will only plant your seed grain into earth that you know has been properly plowed, and is open and ready to receive the grain. You will only sow your seeds into earth that you know is fertile, that you have reason to believe will act with integrity, producing wheat when you have planted wheat, producing barley when you have planted barley.

---

94. As we say in the blessing over the Torah, "… who has given us the Torah of truth and has *planted* within us eternal life."

Learning to Grow

The period of *sefirat ha-omer* is the period of preparation before the festival of Shavuot, the festival of acceptance (and re-acceptance) of the Torah. Like the farmer, God is only willing to plant his precious Torah into a fertile person, who is open to receive the Torah with integrity and who will reproduce its ideals in his or her life with fidelity. God doesn't want to give his Torah to someone with biases and prejudices, to someone who will corrupt the Torah in order to rationalize his imperfect lifestyle. Like the hard packed earth, we too need to be "plowed" open, to make ourselves worthy receptacles. To demonstrate that we will be able to reproduce learned Torah in our well-lived lives, we plow ourselves open, by working on our *middot*, our character traits. This idea is as subtle as it is critical, and it requires some elaboration.

The "Measurements"

Why, we should ask, are "character traits" referred to as *middot*, literally "measurements"? Isn't it odd that we have a commandment (as formulated by the blessing we say before it) to "count the *omer*," which is a unit of measurement equal to about two liters? What do "measurements" have to do with character?

One of the great Safed kabbalists, Rabbi Moshe Cordovero (Ramak), in his work *Tomer Devorah*, taught a principle that I would like to communicate with the following analogy. Imagine that you have been studying the concept of kindness, *chesed*. There are many potential motivations for *chesed*, some personal and psychological, some social, and some ethical. Perhaps the highest motivation for *chesed* would be an abstract theological understanding that God created the world with *chesed*: He gave us life without us having done anything to deserve to be created, just because He was so full of perfection and energy that He desired to overflow to others. Avraham perceived this *chesed* of the Almighty and wished to emulate Him, impacting the lives of others so fully that he effectively created them anew, as the verse calls them, "the souls that he made in Haran." Reflecting on this level of *chesed* you might be motivated to give to others as did Avraham. "God," you might pray, "You have given me life; allow me to give life!"

Just then, your roommate walks through the doorway. Brimming over with inspired idealism, you turn towards the countertop and pick up a plate of baked goods. "Please, have a cookie," you offer, seemingly trivializing all the *chesed* of Avraham. How did this happen? How did your abstract and expansive idealism turn into something so compact, and almost trivial—a cookie? In truth, almost any concrete act of *chesed* would be nearly trivial in comparison to such lofty ideals; but lofty *chesed* is worthless if it is not transposed into a concrete action. For spiritual, almost infinite ideals to be meaningful, they must somehow be compressed, given a definite shape at a definite time for a definite person. They must pass from an abstract state that is immeasurable into a physical world in which everything can be measured.

According to the Ramak, the part of the human soul that processes this transposition is what we call the "measurements" or the "*middot*." It is for this reason that the refinement of *middot* is so important; because without good *middot*, we might truly wish to give, but we might be incapable of actually translating our desires into action.

On Shavuot, God is prepared to give us His Torah, the expression of His will, the model for our highest aspirations. But like the farmer, He will not give us that seed if there is a suspicion that, because of our poor *middot*, we will not express that will into the world with integrity. Even worse, unable to find harmony between the Torah's principles and our imperfect actions, we might corrupt the Torah we've been given, recasting it in our base image, rather than purifying ourselves according to its shining ideals.

Without the liberty of the Exodus, we could not work on our character and deserve the Torah. Once freed, we had the opportunity to prove before God that we could be trusted with His precious treasure. And so, for seven weeks we do the hard labor of plowing ourselves open, and polishing our *middot*. The goal is to stand at Sinai and say before God, "Master of the universe, I have worked on myself so that I am now able to be kind when appropriate and able to be tough when appropriate; I am able to focus on my own growth when appropriate and I am able to care for others when appropriate; in Your mercy, please give me Your Torah and teach me what is appropriate and when!"

All the basic agricultural labors can be done by hand. Sowing seeds, reaping stalks, threshing the wheat flowers, and winnowing away the chaff can all be done manually. But there is one exception: when you plow open hard, packed earth, you really want to use a beast of burden. Similarly, working on *middot* is the hardest of personal work. It is for this reason that the offering of the *Omer* is barley—animal fodder—and the period of the *Omer* ("the measurements"!) is referred to as the day *after* the Sabbath. It is correct for us to spend one day appreciating the blessing of our newfound liberty—a Sabbath. But then, immediately, we must direct that freedom through a redoubled effort to build not monuments to Ramses, but a refined personality, worthy of standing at Sinai.

"Complete"

You go into a delicatessen and order a bagel. When you get home, you take the bagel out of the bag and, behold, someone had taken a bite out of it! Understandably upset, you go back to the store and confront the owner. The owner responds, "You asked for a bagel; you didn't specify that it should be a *whole* bagel!"

Of course, such a defense would be absurd. A "bagel" means a whole 360° bagel. Similarly, when God says we should count for "seven weeks," that should mean seven *complete* weeks. Why then did He specify that they should indeed be "complete"? Listening to the text with exquisite sensitivity, the Rabbis realized that this must be coming to teach that not just every *day* must be included, but every minute.

As Rashi teaches, "'Complete' — this teaches that the counting begins in the evening; for if not, the weeks would not be complete." Immediately after celebrating freedom, we must direct that freedom towards a constructive goal. Freedom, like any other blessing, is a tool which can be used for good, squandered on

דרשות המהר"ל - דרוש על התורה

העומר מן השעורים, ויום טוב ראשון מורה על החירות, ואיך יהיו שני דברים הפכיים דהיינו החירות והעמל בזמן אחד יחד כי אין ההפכיים נמצאים... הרי כי האדם צריך שידמה לשור וחמור המיוחדים לפרך העבודה ויט שכמו לסבול עול דברי תורה, וזכר שני המינים המה השור והחמור להוראת שני סוגי עול עבודתו בתורה. כי צריך שיעשה עצמו כחמור למשא שהוא בעל גוף חזק כדכתיב (בראשית מ"ט) חמור גרם שנושא עול גדול והולך ביום ובלילה ואין לו מנוח ונחת מרגוע לגופו כלל רק רובץ בין המשפתים, כן יהיה האדם מצד גופו שישתעבד גופו למשאוי התורה בלי מנוח וכדכתיב (יהושע א) והגית בו יומם ולילה. ועוד נוסף ע"ז ישעבד בה כח הנפשיי אשר לו אל התורה כבחינת השור שכחו גדול. הנה אלו שני דברים הם נגד גוף ונפש האדם שבשניהם יהיה עמל בתורה, אם בגוף עמל וטורח בו בתורה בלי מרגוע או מנוחה כלל אשר ידמה בזה אל החמור הנושא משאוי תמיד באין מנוח, אם בנפש אשר בו יעמול בתורה לעיין בהלכה בעיון קשה ועמוק עד כי יעדה עצמו בזה כשור הזה המשוה בכחו כל תל גבוה ולעקור קרקע קשה לחרוש ולפרר בכח שלו את הכל באשר כח נפשו גדול...

vanities, or misdirected for destructive ends. Unlike other blessings, freedom is uniquely powerful, capturing—if only in microcosm— an attribute that is nothing short of divine. Among all the beings on heaven and Earth, only man has free will, and in this way he reflects his divine source. When you are at liberty, you possess an awesome power, and you are most accurately judged by how you use that liberty.

By counting from the day of our liberty to the day of receiving the Torah, we demonstrate that freedom *from* oppression is most valuable when it is transformed into freedom *to* connect with the highest wisdom and to bring that wisdom into the world. In fact, "freedom from" without a constructive "freedom to" can be disorienting and anxiety-producing. The psychologist Erich Fromm has even attributed the totalitarian movements of the early twentieth century to the erosion of the older religious and cultural systems: liberated, but lacking a sense of meaning, many early moderns fled to alternative authoritarian structures that would relieve them of their new, confusing freedom. Fromm titled his book *Escape from Freedom*, and it captured the notion that, like anything else, freedom is a powerful tool that can be used well or abused.

By counting from the day of our liberty to the day on which our freedom is guided by the Torah towards nobility, we link the two days, and demonstrate that the former is most valuable when directed by the latter.

Sefer ha-Chinnuch 306

... and this is the root and the reason why they were redeemed and exited Egypt, so that they should receive the Torah on Sinai and keep it....

And therefore, since this is the whole root of Israel and for this they were redeemed and ascended to all their greatness, we have been commanded to count from the day after the *yom tov* of Pesach until the day of the giving of the Torah, to demonstrate the great desire we have for that glorious day for which we long, as a slave seeks out shade, and who constantly counts for the time of his longing, when he will go free. Because counting shows that all of his salvation and desire is to get to that time.

Counting immediately, from the very first nightfall, shows that we long for the Torah that directs our freedom, a freedom that helps us transition from an anxiety-producing "freedom from" to a self-actualizing "freedom to." Counting immediately and daily also shows that spiritual growth is hard work that requires consistency.

"The Seventh Sabbath"

Just as the counting of the *Omer* does not always begin on a

ספר החינוך - מצוה שו
משרשי המצוה על צד הפשט, לפי שכל עיקרן של ישראל אינו אלא התורה, ומפני התורה נבראו שמים וארץ וישראל, וכמו שכתוב [ירמיהו ל"ג, כ"ה] אם לא בריתי יומם ולילה וגו'. והיא העיקר והסיבה שנגאלו ויצאו ממצרים כדי שיקבלו התורה בסיני ויקיימוה, וכמו שאמר השם למשה [שמות ג, י"ב] וזה לך האות כי אנכי שלחתיך בהוציאך את העם ממצרים תעבדון את הא-להים על ההר הזה, ופירוש הפסוק כלומר, הוציאך אותם ממצרים יהיה לך אות שתעבדון את הא-להים על ההר הזה, כלומר שתקבלו התורה שהיא העיקר הגדול שבשביל זה הם נגאלים והיא תכלית הטובה שלהם. ועניין גדול הוא להם, יותר מן החירות מעבדות, ולכן יעשה השם למשה אות צאתם מעבדות לקבלת התורה, כי התפל עושין אות לעולם אל העיקר:
ומפני כן, כי היא כל עיקרן של ישראל ובעבורה נגאלו ועלו לכל הגדולה שעלו אליה, נצטווינו למנות ממחרת יום טוב של פסח עד יום נתינת התורה, להראות בנפשנו החפץ הגדול אל היום הנכבד הנכסף ללבנו, כעבד ישאף צל, וימנה תמיד מתי יבא העת הנכסף אליו שיצא לחירות, כי המנין מראה לאדם כי כל ישעו וכל חפצו להגיע אל הזמן ההוא.

Sunday, the festival of Shavuot does not always fall out on a Sunday. Although the *Omer* period will always contain seven "Sabbaths," this is (once again) a potentially deceptive way in which to refer to the counting period as understood by the oral tradition. For lack of ambiguity, it would have been better to refer to this period as seven "weeks" (שבועות), as indeed this period is called in *Devarim* 16:9 and from which the festival receives its name. Why, we need to ask, was it important to refer to this period as a period of שבתות, "Sabbaths"?

ספר יצירה פרק ד

(ג) שבע כפולות בג"ד כפר"ת, שבע ולא שש, שבע ולא שמונה. שש צלעות לששה סדרים כנגד שבע קצוות, מהן שש קצוות מעלה ומטה מזרח מערב צפון ודרום, והיכל הקדש מכוון באמצע, והוא נושא את כולן. ברוך כבוד ה' ממקומו:

(ד) שבע כפולות בג"ד כפר"ת, חקק"ן חצב"ן צרפ"ן שקל"ן והמיר"ן וצר בהן ככבים בעול"ם וימים בשנ"ה ושערים בנפ"ש, ומהן חקק שבעה רקיעים ושבע ארצות ושבע שבתות, ולפיכך חיבב השביעי תחת השמים:

As we know, the physical creation was completed on the seventh day, and so the Sabbath, like so many sevens, represents completion in the physical world. *Sefer Yetzirah* effectively explains that every object in the physical world can be plotted based on the position of its points along six vectors: up, down, east, west, north and south. But what holds all the points together; what connects the dots and gives form and function to the whole? That's the inside: the seven. We sense this lesson every week as we busily build our worlds. Every day is a new task, sometimes a very different activity. What connects my leisure on Sunday to my office job on Monday to my kid's school play on Tuesday? That's the Sabbath, on which I stop building and I reflect on the form and function of a life well lived and a world well formed.

So too during the period of counting the *Omer*. As discussed above, during these weeks we are working on *middot*, the traits of character by which we bring our ideals into the physical world. We are not yet working on the ideals themselves—they are given as a gift on Shavuot to those who are properly prepared to receive them; we are only working on being able to engage the physical world with as little friction, bias, or prejudice as possible. Given that we are working on perfecting our connection to the physical world, it only makes sense that we need to do this for a period of seven. Seven weeks of seven days indicates that we are perfecting every aspect of that physical engagement.

Once these physical facets have been perfected, we can reach for the spiritual. In the case of an infant, his body is wholly in the world after seven days, so he can receive *b'rit milah* on the eighth. More complex is the completion of an adult's character: for that he needs a minimum of seven sevens—seven "Sabbaths"—then he can receive a special spiritual flow on the fiftieth.

"Fifty Days"

Once again, the simple understanding of the text conflicts with the law as we know it through the oral tradition. The verses imply that we count the fiftieth day, Shavuot itself, but our law instructs us to end at 49. Rabbenu Asher (the רא"ש) explains that this is an example of the Torah just using round numbers, as it does in other cases.[95] Rashi explains that this should be read as, "count up to fifty days, not-inclusive." But as we have seen above, when there is an apparent contradiction between the plain meaning of the verse and the practical application, we should investigate what ideal the plain meaning is trying to reveal.

In this case, we should understand that we always need to have the fiftieth day in mind as we work on our character. *Sefirat ha-omer* should not be treated as an exercise in character development for the sake of character development. This is not just "self-help." Rather, this is preparation for something higher; for the fiftieth, for

---

95. רא"ש פסחים פרק י' סימן מ'

the acceptance of the Torah. After all, unless we have some Divinely-directed, objectively holy goal, it is difficult to argue why such hard work is really worth the effort.

Analogously, the Rambam teaches that it is important to be healthy so that we can properly serve our Creator; you can't live a thriving Jewish life if you are sick. This point, he says, is crucial. Because if one were to be concerned with his health as an ultimate good, but only as a personal preference without

שמונה פרקים לרמב"ם פרק ה

ואפשר שתהיה הנהגתו כולה לפי המועיל, כמו שזכרנו, אבל י_שים תכליתו - בריאות גופו ושמירתו מן החוליים בלבד. ואין זה איש מעלה. כי כמו שבחר זה הנאת הבריאות - בחר ההוא הנאת האכילה או הנאת הבעילה, וכולם אין תכלית אמיתית לפעולותיהם. ואמנם הנכון, ישישים תכלית כל הנהגותיו - בריאות גופו והמשך מציאותו על השלימות, כדי שישארו כלי כוחות הנפש, אשר הם איברי הגוף, שלמים, ותתעסק נפשו מבלי מונע במעלות המידות ובמעלות השכליות.

reference to its impact on divine service, well… one person might prefer good health and another might enjoy fatty foods. Without some objective reference, who is to say one is objectively better than the other? This is a surprisingly modern statement for the Rambam to make, and it speaks to the fundamental pillars on which Jewish ethics stand. Closeness to God is an objective good, perhaps the only objective good, and as we labor to perfect our *middot* we do so with the fiftieth day in mind, aware of good character being not an end in itself, but an essential means to a much higher end.

Deeper, and frighteningly so, is the thought that good character may be the worst thing in the world if your ideals are corrupt. We Jews have had many enemies over the centuries. Some have had lousy character, and they were therefore less efficient in their anti-Semitism. You could always bribe them with a fancy gift or a bottle of vodka and they'd leave you alone for a while. We have also faced other enemies who were relatively polished, disciplined, and orderly—and those did us much more serious damage.

As you work on your *middot* during this period, it is important to keep the fiftieth day always in mind, because if you develop good character but remain without proper spiritual goals, you have the potential to zoom smoothly and efficiently, at sixty miles per hour—in precisely the wrong direction. And you may develop the leadership and charisma to take others down with you.

So we need to always keep the fiftieth day in mind. But at the same time, we cannot actually count it in practice, because counting implies some human achievement, and ultimately, as much as we prepare ourselves, Torah will always remain more a gift than an achievement.

What is the meaning of "And from *midbar* [wilderness] to *mattanah* [gift]..."? He said to him, "'If a person makes himself like a wilderness that everyone walks over him, Torah is given to him as a gift" (*Eruvin* 54a).

Rabbi Yitzchak said: If a person says, "I labored and did not find," don't believe him; "I labored and found," believe him. And this is talking about words of Torah (*Megillah* 6b).

תלמוד בבלי מסכת
עירובין דף נד עמוד א
מאי דכתיב וממדבר מתנה וממתנה
נחליאל ומנחליאל במות ומבמות
הגיא. - אמר ליה: אם אדם משים
עצמו כמדבר זה שהכל דשין
בו - תורה ניתנה לו במתנה:

תלמוד בבלי
מסכת מגילה דף ו עמוד ב
ואמר רבי יצחק, אם יאמר לך אדם:
יגעתי ולא מצאתי - אל תאמן, לא יגעתי
ומצאתי - אל תאמן, יגעתי ומצאתי -
תאמן. הני מילי - בדברי תורה:

Maharal points out that Torah is *sechel elyon*, "highest intellect," which is so lofty that it is very difficult for us earthly humans to acquire.[96] One must work hard to study Torah, but that is not enough; one must also work on the kind of humility necessary to receive Torah, and there is no better time for that than during *sefirat ha-omer*. We are promised that this combination will result in the Torah being given, but as a gift, not as earned income. Torah is too rarified to be "earned," but it can be "found," quite by surprise, by someone who works on himself and on it, demonstrating an appreciation for its value, beauty, and power.

I remember my first summer home from yeshiva in Israel. As a 22-year-old *ba'al teshuvah*, that first year had been brutally difficult. I still can open my Gemara from those days and turn to the first Mishnah in *Bava Metzia*. In the margin next to "*shnayim*" is written "2"; next to "*ochazin*" is written "holding"; next to "*be-tallit*" is written "a garment." I chewed through those pages word by grueling word. When I went home for the summer I got a study partner at night to learn Tractate *Megillah*, and quite suddenly it seemed like the heavens had opened: I could learn! It was like God saw I had suffered enough and he gave me the gift of literacy. When I returned to yeshiva the next year I related my experience to my friends and each one slowly nodded in agreement. They had labored as well, making themselves "ownerless like a wilderness," and like a gift, the heavens opened for them too.

"A New Meal Offering"

The first grain to ripen in the holy land is the barley, and the first barley is offered as the *Omer* on Pesach. While wheat is the basic human staple grain, barley is mostly used as animal fodder. The implications are obvious, so long as we have not fully received the

---

96. *Netivot Olam, Netiv ha-Torah*, chap. 2.

Torah, we are not fully complete as humans in the most idealistic Jewish conception of being made in God's image. So long as we have not received the Torah, we need to prepare ourselves for it by doing the donkey-like, barley-eating, grunt work necessary to plow ourselves open, working on our *middot*, becoming as unbiased as possible. In that way we reassure God that we will not abuse His Torah, but will accept it, learn it, contribute to it, and act upon it without prejudice and without hesitation.

Then on the holiday of Shavuot, we receive the Torah as a gift, and we bring two loaves of the new wheat, the human staple, showing that we have the ability to express the kind of excellence God intended when He created us and the world. It was on Shavuot that the heavens open for the Jews at Sinai, and as a year of hard work and growth, this year may be the Shavuot of your life. Working on character is always admirable, but during this time of the year your plowing may, like at no other time, uncover the remarkable human waiting to be discovered under some hard packed earth. As you discover your true, magnificent self, the heavens may even open for you.

Chapter 21

Yom ha-Atzma'ut and the Students of Rabbi Akiva

Fighting for Your Way, Hearing Another

They said: Rabbi Akiva had twelve thousand pairs of students between G'vat and Antipatris and all of them died during one period because they did not give respect one to another, and the

תלמוד בבלי מסכת יבמות דף סב עמוד ב
אמרו: שנים עשר אלף זוגים תלמידים היו לו
לרבי עקיבא, מגבת עד אנטיפרס, וכולן מתו בפרק
אחד מפני שלא נהגו כבוד זה לזה, והיה העולם
שמם, עד שבא ר"ע אצל רבותינו שבדרום,
ושנאה להם ר"מ ור' יהודה ור' יוסי ורבי שמעון
ורבי אלעזר בן שמוע, והם הם העמידו תורה
אותה שעה. תנא: כולם מתו מפסח ועד עצרת.

world was desolate, until Rabbi Akiva came to our Rabbis of the south and taught them: Rabbi Meir, and Rabbi Yehudah, and Rabbi Yosi, and Rabbi Shimon, and Rabbi Elazar ben Shammua. And they establish Torah at that time. It is taught in the Tosefta: and they all died between Passover and *Atzeret* [Shavuot] (BT *Yevamot* 62b).

Yom ha-Atzma'ut and the Students of Rabbi Akiva

In the previous chapter we discussed how the time between Passover and Shavuot is particularly appropriate, and perhaps charmed, for personal work on the kind of *middot* necessary for the acceptance of Torah. We need to demonstrate a certain refinement in all *middot*, because some parts of the Torah might call on us to act with more kindness, while other parts of the Torah might call on us to act with more toughness. As I wrote above, we want to approach Shavuot by saying, "God, I've worked on myself so that I can be kind when I should be, and tough when I must be—please give me Your Torah so that I can better know when to be kind and when to be tough!"

But of all the *middot* necessary to acquire Torah, the most essential one is the *middah* of humility. We saw the statement of the Rabbis that only one who is "ownerless like a wilderness" can receive Torah "as a gift." Moshe was the most humble of people, so he was the most transparent conduit through which to bring Torah into the world, and therefore he was the greatest prophet. When you heard Moshe's Torah, you know it was uncolored and unflavored by his personal biases or prejudices. It was pure and unadulterated. The more we are like Moshe, the higher level of Torah can we receive.

I had been married for only a few weeks when my wife and I were invited for Shabbat dinner at the home of Rabbi Moshe Chalkowski and his wife, Bambi, the legendary midwife of Jerusalem. Rabbi Chalkowski is a master educator and my wife's *rebbe*; he was very close with the great *mashgiach*, Rabbi Shlomo Wolbe, and if I was going to be married to his star pupil, he was going to set me straight. At the time I had been studying at the yeshiva of Rabbi Tzvi Kushelevsky, then only blocks away from the Chalkowski home in Givat Shaul, Jerusalem. Rabbi Kushelevsky was famous for his Friday evening class on the laws of the Sabbath and people from around the neighborhood came to the yeshiva every Friday to pray with the yeshiva and hear this class.

Learning to Grow

Almost as soon as we finished Kiddush, Rabbi Chalkowski turned to me and asked me what Rabbi Kushelevsky had taught. Of course, I expected this turn of events and made sure to listen to the *shiur* extra carefully; in any case, I found the subject fascinating and was fortunate to have had learned that evening's topic previously. (Over twenty years later I still remember it: can you use a salt shaker on Shabbat if there is rice in it to absorb the moisture?) I began to review Rabbi Kushelevsky's argument, adding a bit of my own thoughts into the discussion as I laid out the Rosh Yeshiva's points.

Rabbi Chalkowski cut me short: "I didn't ask you for what you think," he said with a playful twinkle in his eye, "just repeat what the Rosh Yeshiva said as clearly as possible. We can discuss your thoughts afterwards." Rabbi Chalkowski was teaching me a wonderful lesson in how to study Torah properly, indeed, how to study anything properly: first you need to listen carefully and be able to recall all the data without any editorializing. Only then can you be sure that the data is as clean as possible, and only then can evaluation of the data be helpful. Some commentators (Maharal among them in his *Derech Chaim*) teach that the 49 days between Passover and Shavuot, the 49 days of working on *middot*, correspond to the 48 virtues by which the Torah is acquired as listed in chapter 6 of *Pirkei Avot* (plus one, which is the day on which the 48 are synthesized together in a balanced life of moral greatness). Not surprisingly, the first virtue listed there is "study" and the second one listed is "attentive listening." My editorializing while recalling Rabbi Kushelevsky's class gave the appearance of some lack of humility on my part, and that appearance probably had a bit of substance to it as well. It sounded like I was more interested in relating my own opinions than trying to understand the ideas of someone far more learned than myself, setting up Rabbi Chalkowski for marvelous teaching moment at my expense, but also for my benefit.

Torah is bigger than any one human can comprehend. The only way to approximate a grasp of the entire Torah is to join together with other Jews in a struggle, even a battle, for wisdom. That requires passionate study and a vigorous advocacy of your conclusions, but it also requires the intellectual humility to listen to, and really understand, the other side of the argument. The Rabbis teach that the pursuit of truth demands a clash between two people who, by the necessity of their own human

תלמוד בבלי מסכת קידושין דף ל/ב
אמר רבי חייא בר אבא אפי' האב ובנו הרב ותלמידו שעוסקין בתורה בשער אחד נעשים אויבים זה את זה ואינם זזים משם עד שנעשים אוהבים זה את זה שנאמר את והב בסופה אל תקרי בסופה אלא בסופה:

המאירי על מסכת אבות פרק ד משנה יד
שכל שיתקבצו שנים או רבים לשאת ולתת באיזה ענין אם הוא לשם שמים והוא שיכונו כולם להעמדת האמת סופה להתקיים ר"ל סוף המבוקש בקבוציהם מתקיים כי כל אחד יודה לחבירו מה שראוי להודות עליו ואז יתברר האמת ויסכימו כולם להעמידו וכשיהיה לכונת הנצוח לא ישמעו זה לזה והמחלוקת במקומה עומדת ותחתיה תעמוד הברחת ואולי פשה תפוטה הצרעת ובברייתא באבות דר"נ סוף פ"מ אמרו כנסיה שהוא לשם שמים כנסית ישראל בהר סיני ושאינה לש"ש כנסית אנשי דור הפלגה:

limitations, each only possess a partial truth. This will, and should, bring them into a conflict that makes them look like ruthless foes. But when the two are battling for the sake of heaven, they will end as beloved friends. The Meiri explains that when people's egos are overly invested in an argument, then they will not properly listen to the other side; but when people are honestly pursuing truth, each party will listen to the opposing position, and will end up admitting to the aspect of truth discovered by the other side. Understanding that each party correctly grasped only one facet of a greater whole, they will find an ultimate resolution to the argument.

Learning to Grow

An argument for the sake of heaven will end with a resolution; but how can you tell that the argument is for the sake of heaven while it still rages? It seems that the passionate opposition of ruthlessly honest truth seekers will at once create the appearance of bitter enmity, while coexisting with a remarkable capacity for *listening*.

The Meiri teaches that this unity, born from mutual respect for others operating *leshem shamayim* is the operative posture of the Jews at Sinai. Imagine walking through the wilderness on the way to receive God's holy Torah and you arrive at a relatively low mountain. Rather than becoming disappointed by the anticlimactic venue, the Jews took the lesson to heart: we can only accept Torah if we recognize that despite our mountain-like greatness, we must also cultivate humility. While still in the wilderness, the people were referred to in the plural, but when they camped at Sinai they were referred to in the singular, because when they saw the humble mountain they came together "as one person, with one heart."[97] Once again, Torah is greater than any one person, faction, or tribe. Only by coming together as a people could we receive the Torah, admitting that we need each other not despite our differences, but because of our differences.

The capacity for achieving unity through the seemingly impossible synthesis between opposites is hinted to in the very term לשם שמים. We are familiar with the term "for the sake of God," לשם השם, or with the related term "לשמה." Why, in this context, are we told we need to be for the sake of *heaven*, לשם שמים? The kabbalists teach that the word for heaven "שמים" is a conjunction of "אש ומים," fire and water, two opposites that cannot possibly co-exist. But of course, when everything finds its proper place in the unified kingdom of the one God, even fire and water can maintain their seemingly contradictory identities and yet co-exist.[98] When we struggle and fight for truth, the ultimate co-existence of these two essential elements needs to be our model as well.

---

97. Rashi and *Kli Yakar* to *Shemot* 19:2.
98. ספר עבודת הקודש ד:ו.

Yom ha-Atzma'ut and the Students of Rabbi Akiva

What enables a clash of apparent opposites not to descend into baseless hatred? Rabbi Zadok ha-Kohen taught that the power of listening is the key. When Leah felt unloved by her husband Yaakov, she felt alone and alienated. She felt hated. Having a second son made her feel vindicated because "God heard that I am hated," and so she called her second son "Shimon" from word for hearing and listening, "שמע."

> **ספר פרי צדיק ראש חודש אייר - אות ה**
> וגירסת הגאונים בניסן המליך אות ה' בראיה,
> ובאייר המליך אות ו' בשמיעה... דהו' מחבר
> נקרא ו' מלשון ווי העמודים וכן צורת הו' כווי
> העמודים, וכן תמיד אות ו' מחבר התיבות.
> וכן חודש אייר מחבר חודש ניסן וחודש סיון
> שיזכו בסיון בקנין במה שזכו בניסן בראיה.
> וזה שכתוב בניסן בראיה ובאייר בשמיעה,
> שהשמיעה קבלה בלב כענין מה שמצינו
> בגמרא לא שמיע לי כלומר לא סבירא לי,
> וזה שכתוב באייר המליך אות ו' בשמיעה...
> ואייר בשמיעה נגד שמעון כי שמע ה' כי
> שנואה אנכי וגו' שאז זמן השתדלות מצד
> האדם ביראה שלא נהיה שנואה במעשים,
> והשמיעה לתקן שלא נהיה שנואה.

Listening was the attribute of Leah's second son, and similarly that is the attribute, according to one text of *Sefer Yetzirah*, of the second month, Iyar. Not surprisingly, the letter of the Hebrew alphabet associated with Iyar is the letter "*vav*," which as a prefix always means "and," while the word "*vav*" means "hook," a tool which enables the connection of two objects. That's the essential quality of the month of Iyar—this is month to work on preparing to receive Torah by working on connection and co-existence in a world of diversity by knowing your own truth while listening carefully to the very different insights of others.

It seems that for all their greatness, the original students of Rabbi Akiva failed in this area. They each were huge repositories of truth, but they neglected to admit that other, perhaps sometimes contradictory perspectives, also contained insights worthy of qualified respect, and that the advocates of these alternative persectives deserved unqualified respect.

Learning to Grow

We have a tradition through the Geonim that the students of Rabbi Akiva stopped dying on Lag b'Omer. If you examine your *siddur* you will see a kabalistic association between each day of the *Omer* and some kabalistic concept, and the concept associated with Lag b'Omer is called הוד שבהוד, "glory within glory." There are different terms for "glory" in Hebrew, but the word *hod* comes from the same root as the word להודות, "to admit." After a person develops a vision for life and feels fully developed, he will want to project that vision into the world and conquer (note that the concept before *hod* is *netzach*, the root of the word "to conquer"). But soon he will discover that he can't only impose his perspective; he must *admit* that his vision will be incomplete because as developed as he may be, he is still limited. That admission brings him to respect the complementary perspectives of others even as he fervently clings to his own. He gives הוד and he projects הוד.

Being in yeshiva or seminary this year should make you passionate about truth. If you have been fortunate enough to find dedicated teachers who speak your language, you will have developed a perspective on Torah and a vision for life that is inspired and expresses your personality. That's beautiful and rare. But don't allow your vision to prevent you from listening carefully to the opinions of other passionate Jews, dedicated to Torah and comitted to living an authentic life based on its values.

One of the most contentious areas in Torah thought for the past several generations is the value of political Zionism, whether secular or religious. Some devoted Jews have gone so far as to attribute the Holocaust to Zionism, while others have attributed the Holocaust to anti-Zionism. Some argue the the modern State of Israel is "the beginning of our redemption's sprouting," while others see it as one of the greatest threats to the continuity of the Jewish people, and each side has compelling support, both textual and traditional. As we struggle for truth, we have fulfilled the first part of the Gemara in *Kiddushin* cited above, and we have become antagonists; lacking resolution, we have not yet become lovers.

Ironically, the Almighty chose to place the most contentious day of this most contentious issue, Yom ha-Atzma'ut, smack in the middle of *sefirah ha-omer*, right at the time of the death of Rabbi Akiva's students. Undoubtedly, your teachers will have their own Torah-based perspectives on this day and what it represents. Hopefully they will help you develop your perspective as well and as you form your opinions you will join the great debate with all the passion of a connoisseur of truth. The lesson of Rabbi Akiva's students should remind you, however, to maintain respect for those with whom you disagree, and that respect should be expressed in ways beyond polite manners. Real respect demands that you carefully listen to the other side, withholding judgment until you fully understand. Real respect demands that a religious Zionist should read and consider the arguments of the Satmar Rav and Rabbi Elchonon Wasserman; real respect demands that a Satmar *chasid* read and consider the arguments of Rabbi Yissachar Shlomo Teichtel and Rabbi Joseph B. Soloveitchik. Certainly, as you begin considering these matters in a careful, mature, and intellectually-informed way you must study all the perspectives carefully, beginning with those closest to your institution's and teachers' tradition.

Zionism is, in many ways, messianic in its intentions and implications (some would argue falsely messianic) as it aims to unite a diverse nation in its ancestral homeland. Even as our understandings of this phenomenon pull us apart, we should recall the error of Rabbi Akiva's students and listen carefully to those with whom we disagree. In this way, the argument itself can become a catalyst for unity, the kind of unity which is a necessary condition of our 49-day march towards Sinai.

Chapter 22

Lag B'Omer and Going Home

Sensitivity, Tolerance, *Kiddush Hashem*

Akilas, who was Caesar Hadrian's nephew, wished to become a convert but was afraid of his uncle Hadrian. So he said to him, "I want to go into business."

Hadrian: Are you are in need of silver or gold? My treasures are open before you!

Akilas: I want to go into business, to go abroad, to learn how people think, and I'd like your advice on how to go about it.

Hadrian: Any merchandise whose price is depressed, all but sunk in the ground—go and deal in it, for in the end its price will rise and you will realize a profit.

So Akilas went to the Land of Israel and studied Torah. After a while Rabbi Elieazer and Rabbi Yehoshua came upon him, and, noticing a change in his facial expression, they said to each other, "Akilas is studying Torah!"

When he came to them, he proceeded to put many questions to them, which they answered him.

He went up to his uncle Hadrian, who asked him, "Why is your face changed? I suspect that either your merchandise sold at a loss, or can it be that someone has distressed you?!"

Akilas: No... You are my relative. Would anyone dare distress me?

Hadrian: Then why is your countenance changed?

Akilas: Because I have studied Torah. What is more, I have had myself circumcised.

Hadrian: Who told you to do such a thing?

Akilas: It was you I consulted.

Hadrian: When?

Akilas: When I told you that I wanted to go into business, and you said to me, "Any merchandise whose price is depressed, all but sunk in the ground—go and deal in it, for in the end it will rise in value." I went around among all nations and found none held in lower esteem and deemed to be more deeply sunk in the ground than Israel, and in the end they will be exalted...

מדרש תנחומא פרשת משפטים סימן ה

ואלה המשפטים, זש"ה, (תהלים קמו) מגיד דבריו ליעקב וגו' לא עשה כן וגו', עקילס (נ"א אונקלוס) הגר בן אחותו של אדריאנוס היה מבקש להתגייר והיה מתירא מן אדריאנוס דודו, א"ל אני מבקש לעשות סחורה, א"ל שמא אתה חסר כסף וזהב הרי אוצרותי לפניך, א"ל אני מבקש לעשות סחורה לצאת לחוץ לידע דעת הבריות ואני מבקש לימלך בך היאך לעשות, א"ל כל פרקמטיא שאתה רואה שפלה ונתונה בארץ לך עסוק בה שסופה להתעלות ואת משתכר, בא לו לארץ ישראל ולמד תורה, לאחר זמן מצאוהו רבי אליעזר ורבי יהושע ראוהו פניו משתנות, אמרו זה לזה עקילס לומר תורה כיון שבא אצלם התחיל לשאול להם שאלות הרבה והן משיבין אותו, עלה אצל אדריאנוס דודו, א"ל ולמה פניך משתנות סבור אני שהפסידה פרקמטיא שלך או שמא הצר לך אדם, א"ל לאו א"ל אתה קרוב לי ואדם מצר לי, א"ל ולמה פניך משתנות, א"ל שלמדתי תורה ולא עוד אלא שמלתי את עצמי, א"ל ומי אמר לך כך, א"ל בך נמלכתי, א"ל אימתי א"ל בשעה שאמרתי לך מבקש אני לעשות סחורה, ואמרת לי כל פרקמטיא שאתה רואה שפלה ונתונה בארץ לך ועסוק בה שסופה להתעלות חזרתי על כל האומות ולא ראיתי שפלה נתונה בארץ כישראל וסופה להתעלות:

Learning to Grow

We can learn a lot from Akilas on so many different levels. First, we need to admire the way Akilas expressed his transformation in a way that would be as least offensive to his uncle as possible. Rather than framing his conversion to Judaism as a deliberate slap in the face, Akilas preferred to use terms to which his uncle could relate. Effectively he was saying, "Uncle, I've learned many values from you, and I'm continuing them in my own life, albeit in my own way." We can learn from Akilas how to emphasize the common denominators between people whom we love and respect, even as we may disagree.

Second, we can appreciate how honest searchers can achieve significant growth by putting some temporary distance between themselves and the culture that has defined them. This is all the more true when they choose to place themselves in the Land of Israel. As Rabbi Yehudah ha-Levi puts it, the best of grape vines will only produce the finest wines when they are planted in the most appropriate soil and tended with the most appropriate skills. For spiritual searchers, the Land of Israel is our fertile soil and the laws of our Torah are those skills.[99] Akilas made the tough choice to leave the comforts of imperial Rome and to place himself in the rarified spiritual environment of Israel, and he flourished.

Which brings me to my third point, itself more of a question than an observation: what did Akilas' face look like when he began studying Torah in Israel? It seems to me, based both on the reaction of Rabbi Eliezer and Rabbi Yehoshua, and from my own work with spiritually-curious students, that Akilas began to radiate a glow of serenity and delight. After all, he was of Roman nobility, and he was also a searcher. Perhaps he arrived in Israel with an expression of a conflicted soul; perhaps in his first weeks he retained, at least externally, the proud countenance of Roman aristocracy. But as he studied Torah, he slowly developed a welcome humility. He softened and let his defenses drop as he realized that the Land of Israel was,

---

99. *Kuzari* 2:12.

indeed, a safe place for him to explore matters of spirituality. Akilas opened himself to deep discussions and placed himself in the trustworthy hands of his masters. He found inner peace and radiated tranquility. As your year comes to a close, look around you and you might see such faces. You might even see a bit of Akilas when you look into the mirror.

Which makes me wonder what happened to Akilas' face when he went back to Rome. "I suspect that either your merchandise sold at a loss, or can it be that someone has distressed you?" It sounds like Akilas was in emotional turmoil, unhappy and uptight. So what, then, does Torah do to our faces? Does it make us happy and serene, or distressed and uptight?

The answer is, of course, that as much as Torah makes us happy, it also makes us acutely *sensitive*. Without Torah we might bumble through life, missing the importance of almost every encounter and event. Torah teaches us that every moment is a divine gift, pregnant with potential. Torah leads us to celebrate even minute victories and to cringe from even microscopic vulgarities.

Over and over again, the Torah expects us to be exquisitely sensitive. For example, why do we dye one of our *tzitzit* blue? The Rabbis tell us that the string of blue reminds us of the sea, and the blue of the sea reminds us of the sky; the sky reminds us of the heavenly throne and the heavenly throne reminds us of God who sits on the throne. The blue string, therefore, begins a series of associations that ultimately reinforces our awareness of the Almighty and saves us from sin. The assumption is, of course, that Jews won't take such symbols for granted; rather, we are so acutely sensitive that even the slightest reminder will trigger a cascade of meaningful associations that will impact our behavior in a significant way.

Another example: why must the Temple Altar be made of rough, unfinished stones and not of cut stones? The Rabbis teach that cut stones are hewn with iron tools, and iron is the element from which swords are made. Swords are instruments of war and death, while the Altar brings atonement, peace, and life. How, then, could we possibly build an object of life from objects that invoke death? The Rabbis assume that a person bringing a sacrifice to the Temple, looking for forgiveness and blessing, would be startled, perhaps overwhelmed, should he be confronted with an Altar of iron-finished stone.

The implication of these examples is obvious. The Torah wants us to develop heightened sensitivity in which no object, no moment, and no person is trivial. From the clothes we wear, to the way we tie our shoes, and most certainly to the way we speak and do business, we must be alert to the impact of our most subtle actions, and mindful of the impact that the actions of others will certainly have on us.

This heightened sensitivity allows us to experience life in high definition, engaging the full dynamic range of our emotions. This is the reason why otherwise cerebral Torah scholars will often cry the hardest tears at a funeral and dance with the greatest abandon at a wedding. The *middot* of their character may be balanced in a golden Maimonidean equilibrium, but these scholars are hardly stuck in a bland, grey middle. Rather, they are centered, unbiased and unprejudiced, so like virtuoso dancers they are able to jump to one extreme and then to another, only to return back to the middle, all in perfect resonance with the spirit of the moment.

Akilas studied Torah and developed such a heightened sensitivity. He was from the murderous politics of Rome, and embraced by a community of fellow travelers on the road of spiritual exploration and self-development. Akilas blossomed and Rabbi Eliezer and Rabbi Yehoshua saw this on his face. They greeted him and taught him; we can only imagine the degree to which his sensitivities were further refined under the guiding hands of such masters.

Lag B'Omer and Going Home

Akilas became a connoisseur of the moral and the spiritual. And then he returned to Rome.

We should not be surprised, therefore, that when he returned to a city in which gladiators fought to the death for public sport, a city in which political dissidents were fed to the lions in the coliseum, a city in which idolatry was matched only by adultery... well, he seemed a bit distressed and uptight.

Over the past many months in yeshiva and seminary you have developed many noble sensitivities. Shabbat is important to you as never before. You are more aware of the way people should and should not speak of one another. Your own speech and the language you use is more refined. You have a better appreciation for *kedushah* and can attribute some of your growth to having limited your interactions with members of the opposite sex. You enjoy discussing Torah topics spontaneously and feel no need to refer to Torah only within the gilded cage of the Shabbat table *dvar Torah*.

You have flourished and blossomed in yeshiva and seminary and have become connoisseurs of the moral and the spiritual. And now you are going home.

Home, for most of you, is hardly ancient Rome. No gladiators. We don't throw people to the lions anymore. The western world in the 21st century is tolerant of Judaism and relatively open and just. We are living in blessed times and we must be appreciative of that.

Nevertheless, the best cities in the Western hemisphere are hardly incubators of holiness. Pick your favorite vice, and you are likely to find it—from the moment you deplane—being marketed as a virtue on billboards, in movies, and on every page of fashion magazines. Some of the dearest friends and relatives whom you left behind continue to be profoundly affected by the mixed norms of this society. They haven't changed much, but you have. And change is noticeable; just ask Akilas.

So if you've had a successful year, you are likely to seem a bit uptight as you reencounter your old environment with all its old associations. You might seem particularly distressed when Aunt Ethel claims that yeshiva is a waste of time (her son is in business school!), or when a high school buddy tries to bait you into an argument about gay rights, or when Uncle Ichabod asks you with a touch of sarcasm "when did you start wearing ____ [insert: skirts, *tzitzit*, a yarmulke bigger than a dime...]."

It's a good thing that such moments get under your skin. You've cultivated a sensitivity that most people, God bless them all, can't quite comprehend. But you've got to recognize that fact and manage it, otherwise these sensitivities are likely to create a *chillul Hashem*.

Rabbi Shimon bar Yochai and the Cave

Rabbi Shimon bar Yochai, the deep thinker to whom the wisdom of the mystical *Zohar* is attributed, also spent considerable time in a rarefied environment and developed exceptional sensitivities. His story is well known, and worth revisiting at length as you prepare to emerge from your year in yeshiva.

> Once R. Yehudah, R. Yosi, and R. Shimon were sitting, and Yehudah ben Gerim was sitting near them. R. Yehudah observed, "How fine are the works of the Romans! They have made streets, they have built bridges, they have erected baths." R. Yosi was silent; R. Shimon bar Yochai answered, "All that they made they made for themselves: they built market-places, to set harlots in them; baths, to rejuvenate themselves; bridges, to levy tolls from them." Now Yehudah ben Gerim went and related their talk, and the story reached the government. They decreed: Yehudah, who exalted us, shall be exalted; Yosi, who was silent, shall be exiled to Tzipori [Sepphoris];

Shimon, who deprecated us, shall be executed.

He and his son went and hid themselves... So they went and hid in a cave. A miracle occurred and a carob-tree and a water well were created for them. They would undress and sit up to their necks in sand. The whole day they studied; when it was time for prayers they got dressed, covered themselves, prayed, and then took off their garments again, so that they should not wear out. And so they lived twelve years in the cave.

תלמוד בבלי מסכת שבת דף לג עמוד ב

דיתבי רבי יהודה ורבי יוסי ורבי שמעון, ויתיב יהודה בן גרים גבייהו. פתח רבי יהודה ואמר: כמה נאים מעשיהן של אומה זו: תקנו שווקים, תקנו גשרים, תקנו מרחצאות. רבי יוסי שתק. נענה רבי שמעון בן יוחאי ואמר: כל מה שתקנו - לא תקנו אלא לצורך עצמן, תקנו שווקין - להושיב בהן זונות, מרחצאות - לעדן בהן עצמן, גשרים - ליטול מהן מכס. הלך יהודה בן גרים וסיפר דבריהם, ונשמעו למלכות. אמרו: יהודה שעילה - יתעלה, יוסי ששתק - יגלה לציפורי, שמעון שגינה - יהרג. אזל הוא... אזלו טשו במערתא. איתרחיש ניסא איברי להו חרובא ועינא דמיא. והוו משלחי מנייהו, והוו יתבי עד צואראייהו בחלא, כולי יומא גרסי, בעידן צלויי לבשו מיכסו ומצלו, והדר משלחי מנייהו כי היכי דלא ליבלו. איתבו תריסר שני במערתא. אתא אליהו וקם אפיתחא דמערתא, אמר: מאן לודעיה לבר יוחי דמית קיסר ובטיל גזרתיה? נפקו. חזו אינשי דקא כרבי וזרעי, אמר: מניחין חיי עולם ועוסקין בחיי שעה! כל מקום שנותנין עיניהן - מיד נשרף. יצתה בת קול ואמרה להם: להחריב עולמי יצאתם? חיזרו למערתכם! הדור אזול. איתיבו תריסר ירחי שתא. אמרי: משפט רשעים בגיהנם - שנים עשר חדש. יצתה בת קול ואמרה: צאו ממערתכם! נפקו, כל היכא דהוה מחי רבי אלעזר - הוה מסי רבי שמעון. אמר לו: בני, די לעולם אני ואתה. בהדי פניא דמעלי שבתא חזו ההוא סבא דהוה נקיט תרי מדאני אסא, ורהיט בין השמשות. אמרו ליה: הני למה לך? - אמר להו: לכבוד שבת. - ותיסגי לך בחד? - חד כנגד זכור, וחד כנגד שמור. - אמר ליה לבריה: חזי כמה חביבין מצות על ישראל! יתיב דעתייהו.

Then Elijah came and stood at the entrance to the cave and exclaimed, "Who will inform the son of Yochai that the emperor is dead and his decree annulled?"

They emerged. Seeing a man plowing and sowing, they exclaimed, "They give up eternal life and engage in temporal life?" Whatever they looked at was immediately burnt up. At this point a Heavenly Voice cried out, "Have you emerged to destroy My world? Return to your cave!"

So they returned and lived there twelve months, then said "The punishment of the wicked in Gehinom is only twelve months." A Heavenly Voice then said, "Leave your cave!"

So they came out: Whatever R. Eleazar injured, R. Shimon healed. He said to him, "My son, you and I are sufficient for the world."

On the eve of the Sabbath before sunset they saw an old man holding two bundles of myrtle and running at twilight. "What are these for?" they asked him.

"They are in honor of the Sabbath!" he replied.

"But one should suffice you?"

"One is for 'Remember' and one for 'Guard.'"

He said to his son, "See how precious are the commandments to Israel." And their minds were calmed.

Rabbi Shimon bar Yochai emerged from his cave inspired with much of the wisdom that he would soon share with his friends on long walks in the Galilee, wisdom that would eventually form the core of the *Zohar*. Even before he was forced into hiding, Rabbi Shimon had little patience for politics and the vanities of a superficial life; in fact, it was this very intolerance that motivated his frank assessment of the Romans and forced him into exile in the first place. Twelve long years of study, meditation, and prayer only added to his purity of vision and otherworldly attitude. He was a man of uncompromising truth, but like Yaakov Avinu before him (the paradigm man-of-truth) he could sometimes fall into a profoundly counterproductive righteous indignation.

Remember, for example, how Yaakov reacted when his father-in-law Lavan accused him of stealing his idols:

Whomever you find with your gods, he shall not live! Before our brothers determine what is yours and take it![100]

Rachel had earlier taken her father's idols to save him from sin; but not knowing that, and indignant over Lavan's false accusation, Yaakov inadvertently cursed his beloved wife. Rashi's comment on this encounter effectively places the responsibility for Rachel's death on Yaakov. So a love for truth is wonderful, but when is becomes righteous indignation, it can only be destructive.

This is not to say that there is no room for feeling strong emotion when confronted by lies and attacks against God and Torah. A lover of God should be intensely affected when the objects of his love are under assault. According to Ramchal in *Mesillat Yesharim*, however, the operative emotion should not be indignation, anger, or hate; rather, the lover of God will feel *pain*. Pain brings tears to our eyes, not fists in the air. And as Gandhi, Nelson Mandela, and Martin Luther King, Jr., have shown, a quiet demonstration of unjust pain will be far more effective than loud shouts of angry protest.

Rabbi Shimon bar Yochai emerged from twelve years of intense Torah study and reflection and confronted a world of mundane occupations and trivial pursuits. He and his son responded by burning to the ground everything on which they looked while accusing the people of having traded eternal life for the vulgar and superficial whims of this ephemeral world.

---

100. *Bereshit* 31:32.

How might your friends back home respond to a younger, twenty-first-century version of Rabbi Shimon, one who has emerged not from a cave, but from a year in Israel? Perhaps they would say, "Just be normal! Go to a movie; hang out with some of your old friends! Chill out!"

Interestingly, God Himself was strongly displeased with Rabbi Shimon's righteous indignation. But never did the Almighty suggest that Rabbi Shimon should just "chill out" and be normal. Instead his message was, "Get back into your cave! You haven't learned *deeply* enough to realize that all these creatures participate celebrating My creation and give Me honor." Rabbi Shimon returned to his cave and reflected for another twelve months on how he should more healthily—more religiously!—relate to the multifaceted world outside of his pure cocoon, a world which honors its creator despite all its imperfections.

It is likely that Rabbi Shimon came to terms with a deep truth that would later be formulated clearly by the *Chovot ha-Levavot*: if I am a greater scholar than other people, then I am certainly more culpable for my flaws, and those who know less than me are certainly less responsible for theirs.[101]

Most importantly, Rabbi Shimon learned to value the small spiritual gestures that average people make on a daily basis. If even unsophisticated people can find meaning and happiness in preparing for the Sabbath, aren't they showing how essential such rituals are to all of humanity, and how such rituals speak to a truth so obvious that it compels even the simple masses? What's more, common folk—who emphasize physical success, beauty, and power—are more likely to engage diverse parts of physicality in their divine service, while the

---

101. "Gate of Humility" 10.

spiritual elite overlook such opportunities. The scholar prepares for the Sabbath by studying the laws and reflecting on the philosophies; the simpler person arranges flowers on the table. Without a doubt, the former is more crucial and potent, but the latter also contributes an important dimension of *avodat Hashem*, and that should never be underestimated or devalued. Effectively they are asserting that God is so great, His light glows in even the least likely of places. "See how precious are the commandments to Israel!"

That glowing light expresses the energy hidden in the seemingly mundane, and is a major theme of the *Zohar* (which means, after all, "glow"). On Lag b'Omer, the anniversary of Rabbi Shimon's ascent to heaven, we celebrate his deep insight by lighting bonfires. Fire is a powerful symbol as it reveals the energy latent in objects that otherwise appear dull and uninteresting. Say for example, you want to eat a peach. The peach is beautiful and sweet. You pick up the peach and say a blessing on it. But the twig on top just gets in your way. You pluck off the twig and discard it. But if it should fall in a fire, it bursts into flames revealing color and light. Suddenly you realize how much energy is packed into that previously uninteresting scrap of wood.

This past year, you've been learning lots of Torah. The fruit that you've tasted is beautiful and sweet. More mundane pleasures are dull tasteless twigs in comparison. We can learn from Rabbi Shimon that there is tremendous spiritual energy hidden inside almost everything. With that insight, we should avoid all forms of righteous indignation even as we continue to cultivate our sensitivities and hard-earned purity of vision. When confronted by people who may not yet share such clarity, don't burn them down; rather, learn Torah more deeply and reveal to yourself and to them how much light even they radiate.

Chillul Hashem and *Kiddush Hashem*

What constitutes a profanation of God's Name? Rav said: If, for example, I buy meat from the butcher and do not pay him at once... R. Yochanan said: In my case it is a profanation if I walk four cubits without speaking words of Torah or wearing *tefillin*. Yitzchak, of the School of Rabbi Yannai said: If one's colleagues are ashamed of his reputation—that constitutes a profanation of God's Name... Abaye explained: As it was taught: "And thou shalt love Hashem your God," in other words, the Name of Heaven should be beloved because of you. If someone studies Scripture and Mishnah, and attends on the disciples of the wise, is honest in business, and speaks pleasantly to simple people,

תלמוד בבלי מסכת יומא
דף פו עמוד א

היכי דמי חילול השם? אמר רב: כגון אנא אי שקילנא בישרא מטבחא ולא יהיבנא דמי לאלתר... רבי יוחנן אמר: כגון אנא דמסגינא ארבע אמות בלא תורה ובלא תפילין. יצחק דבי רבי ינאי אמר: כל שחביריו מתביישין מחמת שמעתו... אביי אמר: כדתניא, (דברים ו) "ואהבת את ה' א-להיך" - שיהא שם שמים מתאהב על ידך, שיהא קורא ושונה ומשמש תלמידי חכמים, ויהא משאו ומתנו בנחת עם הבריות, מה הבריות אומרות עליו - אשרי אביו שלמדו תורה, אשרי רבו שלמדו תורה. אוי להם לבריות שלא למדו תורה, פלוני שלמדו תורה - ראו כמה נאים דרכיו, כמה מתוקנים מעשיו, עליו הכתוב אומר (ישעיהו מט) "ויאמר לי עבדי אתה ישראל אשר בך אתפאר". אבל מי שקורא ושונה ומשמש תלמידי חכמים ואין משאו ומתנו באמונה, ואין דבורו בנחת עם הבריות, מה הבריות אומרות עליו - אוי לו לפלוני שלמד תורה, אוי לו לאביו שלמדו תורה, אוי לו לרבו שלמדו תורה, פלוני שלמד תורה - ראו כמה מקולקלין מעשיו וכמה מכוערין דרכיו! ועליו הכתוב אומר (יחזקאל לו) "באמר להם עם ה' אלה ומארצו יצאו".

what do people then say concerning him? 'Happy is the father who taught him Torah, happy is the teacher who taught him Torah; woe to people who have not studied the Torah; for this man has studied the Torah—look how fine his ways are, how righteous his deeds!' Of him does Scripture say: "And He said to me: You are my servant, Israel, in whom I will be glorified." But if someone studies Scripture and Mishnah, attends on the disciples of the wise, but is dishonest in business, and discourteous in his relations with people, what do people say about him? 'Woe to him who studied the Torah, woe to his father who taught him Torah; woe to his teacher who taught him Torah! This man studied the Torah—look, how corrupt are his deeds, how ugly his ways!' Of him Scripture says: "In that men said of them, 'These are the people of the Lord, and are gone forth out of His land.'"

Abaye taught that, having studied in yeshiva or seminary this year, you are in a privileged position to make a unique *kiddush Hashem*. Until now, should someone see you do something pleasant or unpleasant they would just attribute it to you: either you're a great guy, or bit of a jerk. But now, like it or not, you are an ambassador of Torah in general and of a yeshiva education in particular. A pleasant word, a sincere smile, the returning of a lost object to a neighbor or some extra change to a shopkeeper are all suddenly opportunities to make people fall in love with God.

Just after the close of the Mishnah, in a world that was seemingly more and more devoid of holiness, the first generation of *Amoraim* in both the Land of Israel and in Babylon were remarkably concerned about how their behavior would be interpreted by others. Rav, Rabbi Yochanan, and Rabbi Yitzchak of the house of Yannai all recognized that their behavior would be interpreted as a reflection not of their own personalities but of the Torah that they represent.

Rav emphasized that not just dishonesty in business, but that even a temporary appearance of impropriety could be devastating for the reputation of Torah; Rabbi Yochanan emphasized that a cultivation of wisdom must lead to a corresponding consistent and public devotion to that wisdom; Rabbi Yitzchak emphasized that Torah wisdom must be reflected in one's own character and personal growth.

But note the order in which these are taught. Simple people don't care about our acquisition of Torah if that wisdom does not affect the way we deal with *them*. Once again, most people are relatively physical, and they want to see how Torah refines our interactions with them and the physical world. A devotion to Torah accompanied by sloppy ethics will only be interpreted (and perhaps rightly so) as hypocrisy. Or perhaps even worse: that same devotion to Torah could be misinterpreted as a self-righteous license to exploit less "spiritually refined" barbarians. Witnessing self-righteous hypocrisy and exploitation, they could only respond, "Woe to him who studied Torah." If, on the other hand, they see that our behavior *towards them* is refined, they will even begin to appreciate the Torah we have learned.

It is at this point that Rabbi Yochanan's advice becomes crucial. I don't expect most people to appreciate, by themselves, the beauty and wisdom contained in the Torah and its sometimes odd-appearing rituals. Like most complex and sophisticated matters, Torah is an acquired taste. The great mass of Jews, not to mention gentiles, do not have the background or the necessary skills to begin appreciating the more esoteric parts of our tradition. Most Jews have never experienced a full 24-hour Shabbat. Even fewer have studied classical Jewish texts. And even fewer have studied them in a sophisticated way, in the original language, with the intention to absorb and live the wisdom they contain. It should not surprise us that most people will find more happiness in sports, hobbies, academic pursuits, and entertainment than in our ancient tradition.

Lag B'Omer and Going Home

You, in contrast, *have* lived and studied in the modern world, but you have also experienced the gravity of our ancient Torah that gives meaning, guidance, and fulfillment even in our increasingly chaotic and confusing modern world. Having spent a year in yeshiva, you are in the 99th percentile of the Jewish people. Embrace that distinction. You should take your precious experience, and project public confidence in your tradition and its divine source. In Rabbi Yochanan's day, there existed many competing religions and ideologies, each of which asserted its own supremacy, sometimes at the edge of the sword. Today, almost everyone recognizes that the discovery of meaning and happiness in life is a real struggle. More than at any other time in history, today we can wear our *tefillin* publicly and with pride, while confidently articulating a path towards a fulfilled and happy life.

On the other hand, should you choose to allow the sensitivities you've developed this past year to fade into an indifferent and distant memory, you will be making a derogatory statement against the Torah that may be worse than all the affronts of our worst enemies. We expect anti-Semites to rail against Judaism, to claim that our tradition is archaic and irrelevant. While we remain vigilantly on guard against anti-Semites, their attacks rarely undermine our faith. After all, these attacks are based on bias, prejudice, and profound ignorance. You, on the other hand, learned Torah and experienced Torah like few in your generation. If you decide to just lead a "normal" life after having tasted the sweetness of the fruit, wouldn't you be admitting that the Torah is archaic and irrelevant? Wouldn't that be a terrible indictment against the Torah? Wouldn't that be a *chillul Hashem*?

Lastly, Rabbi Yitzchak teaches that beyond treating others with dignity and the Torah with respect, our spiritual explorations should make us acutely aware of our own inherent self-worth. Happy, spiritually dynamic people have no interest in vulgar amusements, speech, or behavior. The worst part about engaging in such vulgarities is that it indicates a profound emptiness. Again and again we are taught that Torah should make one happy and fulfilled, that we should rejoice when walking to the house of God, that a life of Torah is precious and sweet. Torah is not intended to cramp our style; rather, it is intended to teach us the fundamentals of life, so that we can be immensely creative. The same way a musician can only be creative after he has mastered rigorous scales, and a chemist can only be creative after she has mastered the periodic table of the elements, so too we social, moral, and spiritual creatures, can only be at our most creative when we have mastered the deep lessons of the Torah. Rabbi Yitzchak teaches us that if someone has studied Torah and then goes on to lead a life of shameful impropriety, he has missed the point of all his learning and disgraces his own dignity.

In summary, as you prepare to go back home, you should be aware of the sensitivities you have developed. These sensitivities permit you to see the world in high definition, to appreciate the nuances in every object and in every encounter. Place yourself, as much as possible, in a place where those sensitivities will allow you to thrive and grow, but keep in mind that sometimes those same sensitivities might cause you to appear a bit uptight. Don't allow that appearance to undermine relationships that are dear to you, or to undermine other people's appreciation for the sweetness of Torah.

Engage an imperfect world by cultivating a keen Torah perspective on those good but imperfect people who have yet to develop such sensitivities. Teach them to appreciate your remarkable experience not by preaching and not by debating, but by making a *kiddush Hashem*. With open eyes, and careful steps, you'll soon hear whispering behind your back as people say, "Happy is the father who taught him Torah, happy is the teacher who taught him Torah." Perhaps from heaven too you will hear a whisper, "You are my servant, Israel, in whom I will be glorified."

Chapter 23

Shavuot

The Two Loaves and the Two Roles of Wisdom

Shavuot recalls the bringing of divine wisdom, the *chochmah* of the Torah, into the world at Sinai. But like every Jewish holiday, this is not just a time of recollection, or even of just celebration; rather this is a time in which the energy of the holiday reappears in the world for us to grasp and bring into our lives. Of course, we are taught in *Avot* (2:6) that on every day a heavenly voice calls out from Sinai, inviting us to reaccept the Torah. Nevertheless, Shavuot offers a special opportunity, appropriately placed at the end of your year in yeshiva, to accept Torah with the unique energy of that original, national acceptance.

Unfortunately, too many people think of Torah study as something cold, analytical, and academic. They think of Torah study as the writing of yet another book. Hopefully, you've discovered this year that Torah study is dynamic and exciting. It was given at Sinai with *shofar* blasts, thunder, and lightning. It was given with tremendous energy, and continues to be given with tremendous energy. As the *Sefat Emet* taught, just like all the prophets received their prophecies as an echo from that original prophecy on Sinai, so in *each and every year* every individual receives on Shavuot all the Torah that he or she will eventually discover and innovate.[102] It is for good reason that we prepare for this awesome day with such intensity: only a well-crafted vessel can properly receive and contain all that energy.

In some ways, one might think that a year in yeshiva should begin on Shavuot: first one accepts the Torah, and then one learns. But in truth, it is only the work you've accomplished this year that empowers

> **ביאור הגר"א אורח חיים סימן תקכ"ט סעיף א**
> לשון הרמב"ם בפ' ל' מהלכות שבת ארבעה דברים
> נאמרו בשבת שנים מן התורה ושנים מדברי סופרים
> והן מפורשין ע"י הנביאים שבתורה זכור ושמור
> ושנתפרשו ע"י הנביאים כבוד ועונג שנאמר וקראת
> לשבת עונג ולקדוש ה' מכובד איזהו כבוד כו' שימנע
> אדם מן המנחה ולמעלה מלקבוע סעודה כו' ור"ל
> עונג הוא בשבת עצמו וכבוד הוא בע"ש וכן כסות
> נקיה ע"ש וז"ש בשבת ענג ובי"כ כבוד לבד וכנ"ל:

you to accept the Torah on Shavuot. Every great mitzvah—in fact any great undertaking—requires adequate preparation. If you are serious about an athletic competition, a job interview, or a parent's birthday, you will best demonstrate that seriousness by preparing carefully for that event. This idea—that preparation is the best demonstration of respect—finds expression in *halachah*: according to the Vilna Gaon, while celebrating Sabbath on the Sabbath itself is an important fulfilment of *oneg Shabbat*, preparing for the Sabbath beforehand demonstrates *kavod Shabbat*—honoring the Sabbath; therefore, all the laws that relate to *kavod Shabbat* deal with actions performed before the Sabbath, in preparation for the Sabbath.

Arguably, you came to yeshiva in order to deepen your appreciation for Torah and to deepen your acceptance of Torah, the great theme of Shavuot. Arguably, your entire year has been one great act of preparation, giving respect to the wisdom of the Torah, leading up to the great climax of the Shavuot festival itself. Now, the flood

---

102. *Sefat Emet* to *Parashat Bemidbar*, תרל"ה.

gates of wisdom are about to swing open, ready to fill whomever has made him or herself a fitting vessel to receive that wisdom. All your studies have made you fitting, and the work that you've done on your character, your *middot*, has made you fitting as well. Now, a deeper study of the special *mitzvot* of Shavuot can add a precision to your focus on this holiday, as they symbolize the specific vessels needed to receive and use divine wisdom.

The Two Loaves

One of the unique Temple offerings on Shavuot was the offering of two loaves of leavened bread. These loaves are described in the *Zohar* on a mystical level in one of its more accessible parts, a section called the *Raya Mehemna*, "The Faithful Shepherd" (a sobriquet for Moshe Rabbenu). This section of the Zohar goes through the 613 commandments according to the order of the Torah portions in which they occur, giving a brief mystical explanation for each one. In *Parashat Emor* the *Raya Mehemna* explains the mystical rationale behind the special "two loaves" offered on Shavuot. They represent, we are told, the upper and the lower *shechinot*, the manifestations of God's presence in the world that are "connected as one."

The seventeenth-century *Shelah* expands on this brief passage, explaining that these two *shechinot* are *Binah* and *Ateret* (the latter sometimes referred to as *Malchut*). In this mitzvah the two become linked "with the letter *vav*," which is

> **Rabbi Isaiah Horowitz** (c. 1565–1630) was born and educated in Prague. He served as a rabbi in Austria, Frankfurt, and as Chief Rabbi for Prague before moving to Jerusalem and then Safed. His most famous work is the שני לוחות הברית, abbreviated של"ה, from which his nickname derives. The של"ה was influential for popularizing otherwise difficult mystical ideas and was profoundly influenced by the Chasidic movement that emerged in the next century.

the letter of connection, meaning "and," and which represents the six *sefirot* between these two *shechinot*.

Without becoming overly technical in matters of Kabbalah, it seems that the thrust of our work on Shavuot is to link two complementary perspectives. One the one hand, we are supposed to look upwards and develop *Binah*: we are supposed to think abstractly, guided by the Torah, to see how in the world of higher thought sometimes disparate intellectual concepts exist in harmony. *Binah* finds relationships and connections between the otherwise isolated and particular subjects of *Chochmah*. By studying Torah deeply, we discover how various intellectual ideas stem from one another and illuminate one another. So that very abstract, rarefied approach to

של"ה מסכת שבת
פרק תורה אור

ואחר כך מצאתי בזהר פרשת אמור (ח"ג דף צ"ח ע"א) וזה לשונו: אוקימנא שתי הלחם תרתי שכינתי, עילאי ותתאי דמתחברין כחדא לגביהון תרין נהמי בשבת מזונא דחד תרין מזוני דעילא ותתא, עכ"ל. פירוש, תרתי שכינתי כו', פירושו שתי הלחם הם סוד השתי שכינות. שכינה העליונה סוד הבינה המתגלת על ידי אות ו' שבתפארת, ולחם התחתון רמז לעטרת שכינה התחתונה, הדבוקה תמיד באות ו' שכינה שהוא ביסוד, והיינו ו' ו'. ולפי ששתי הלחם רומזים לסוד הנזכר, ובליל שבת מתעוררת העטרה כמו שכתבתי, לכן ראוי לבצוע מלחם התחתון שעליה רומז לחם ההוא. וזהו אומרו לגביהון תרין נהמי כו', פירוש כנגד סוד שתי הלחם, אנו עושים שני לחם בשבת כאמור:

wisdom is one facet of Shavuot, represented by one loaf.

On the other hand, we are supposed to look at the lower loaf. We are supposed to look down at the world, to see how the Torah we learn should impact, refine, and elevate that world and all who reside in it. Our ideas should not remain locked in the ivory tower of *Binah*; rather, we should fuse our more spiritualized vision with a perspective that is also focused on the world as it is, with all its needs and blemishes, and then use both perspectives to build a kingdom of God, a *malchut*, right here on earth.

Why, however, is the ritual symbol of that fusion signified by loaves of bread?

Most simply, we need to embrace the idea that Torah wisdom should not remain cold and academic, but should energize our behavior the same way that bread, our basic staple food, gives our lives energy and allows us to act in the world.

More deeply, we need to understand that the fusion to which we aspire will not come easily, as all fusions require energy. The calories contained in bread enable our spiritual souls to fuse with our physical bodies, just like the welding of two plates of steel requires tremendous energy and power. On Shavuot, we climb to the highest levels of abstract knowledge and then turn to infuse the earth with the clarity of our newly found spiritual insight. That welding of the abstract and the concrete, of heaven and earth, also requires energy and power.

This concept of fusion is encoded in the Hebrew word for "bread," לחם, itself: it is formed from the last letter of the first half (the more spiritual half) of the alphabet, and the first letter of the second half (the more physical half) of the alphabet, connected by the חי"ת—representing an idealistic vision above the seven days of the natural week. Not surprisingly, the Hebrew word for "welding," הלחמה, is based on the root of the word for bread, לחם.[103]

For the most part, your vision this year has been directed upwards. This is as it should be. But as you prepare to leave yeshiva or seminary for your next stage of life, be it college or a job, it is time to reflect on how you can use the understanding of Torah that you've cultivated to impact those who have not been privileged to share your experience. In fact, even if you intend to return for a second year in yeshiva, there will be a brand new cohort of "Shana Aleph" students for you to greet in the fall. Closer to them in age and life experience, you can be a positive influence on them in ways that are

---

103. See *Ha'emek Davar* to *Bemidbar* 28:2.

less accessible to your teachers. As you have looked upwards this year, you have been profoundly affected. That's one loaf. Now it is time to fuse that loaf with tremendous energy and power to the second loaf: to look downwards and see whom you can affect.

The Two Faces of *Chochmah*

Using different symbols, Rabbi Moshe Cordovero teaches a very similar lesson.

Now, the attribute of *Chochmah* above has two aspects: the higher aspect faces *Keter* and does not face downwards; rather, it receives from above. The lower aspect faces downwards, overseeing the other *sefirot* to which the attribute of *Chochmah* extends. Likewise, a person should have two aspects: the first aspect should be communion in solitude with his Creator in order to increase and perfect his *Chochmah*; the second should be to teach others the *Chochmah* with which the Holy One, Blessed be He, has endowed him.

ספר תומר דבורה - פרק שלישי
והנה, אל החחכמה שני פנים: הפן
העליון הפונה אל הכתר, ואין אותם
הפנים מסתכלים למטה, אלא מקבלים
מלמעלה; הפן השני, התחתון, הפונה
למטה, להשגיח בספירות שהיא
מתפשטת בחכמתה אליהם. כך יהיה
אל האדם שני פנים: הפן הראשון
הוא התבודדותו בקונו, כדי להוסיף
בחכמה ולתקנה; השני - ללמד בני
אדם מאותה חכמה שהקב"ה השפיע
עליו. וכמו שהחכמה משפעת אל כל
ספירה וספירה כפי שיעורה וצרכה,
כן ישפיע בכל אדם כפי שיעור שכלו
אשר יוכל שאת והנאות אליו לצרכו,
וישמר מלתת יותר משיעור שכל
המושפע, שלא תמשך ממנו תקלה,
שכן הספירה העליונה אינה מוספת
על השיעור המוגבל במקבל:

And just as the attribute of *Chochmah* above extends to each *sefirah* according to its measure and needs, one should disseminate his *Chochmah* to each person in the measure his intellect can grasp, according to what is proper for him and his needs. One should take care not to give more than the mind of the recipient can contain, lest harm result, for the Supernal *sefirah* does not go beyond the limits of the recipient[104] (Rabbi Moshe Cordovero, *Tomer Devorah*, Chapter 3).

On Shavuot, as we express appreciation for Torah wisdom in the hope of receiving more, we need to be aware that true Torah wisdom has these two faces. The lover of truth will continually oscillate between the purity of the *beit midrash* and a world desperately in need of his creative attention. In order to emulate the wisdom of our Creator properly, and in order to merit receiving more wisdom, we all need to embrace both of these perspectives to some degree.

Naturally, each of us has a unique personality, and some of us will be more withdrawn, while others will be more activist. When my *rebbe*, Rabbi Beryl Gershenfeld, taught me this concept, he cited Rabbi Shlomo Freifeld, the charismatic student of Rabbi Hutner and the founder of Yeshivat Shor Yoshuv. Rabbi Freifeld is quoted as saying that the city of Bnei Brak was built by two giants...

One was the *Chazon Ish*, and the other was the *Ish Chazon*— the man of vision, the great Ponevezher Rav. A person should embody both strengths within him, that of the *Chazon Ish*, an awareness of the heights that a lone individual, closeted in his room, can scale, and that of the *Ish Chazon*, a vision of how one Jew can affect the entire nation.

These two great personalities personified the two perspectives that we need to cultivate when dealing with Torah wisdom: one looking up to absorb abstract Torah in all its purity; and one looking down to see how to bring that Torah to life in a world thirsty for wisdom. To

---

104. Translated by Rabbi Moshe Miller.

whatever degree one is able to embody both of these perspectives, he or she truly becomes an agent of fantastic growth and change.

For example, Rabbi Aaron Kotler, the famed founding Rosh Yeshiva of Lakewood, heard his own *rebbe*, the Alter of Slabodka, praise Rabbi Yisrael Salanter for exemplifying precisely this powerful combination.

> I heard from our master the Altar of Slabodka, that the main influence of Rabbi Yisrael Salanter on him was that he studied Torah with deep *pilpul*, making this the total focus of his attention; while the very same time, he paid attention to the general spiritual state of *klal Yisrael*, as Rabbi Yisrael was himself a living example of care for the public welfare, with unprecedented self-sacrifice.

Without exaggeration, it is impossible to imagine what the Jewish world would look like today were it not for the influence of Rabbi Yisrael Salanter, who was able to look heavenward with undistracted intensity, and who was then able to turn his eyes back to earth with a compassion that was as practical as it was visionary. *Chochmah* is often referred to in the kabbalistic works as *Abba* (father), and *Binah* is similarly referred to as *Imma* (mother): just like parents intrinsically care for their children, look down at them, and give them what they need in amounts that they can handle, so too Torah scholars who have cultivated a rare and precious wisdom must look down with compassion at their nation and their world, a world that is desperately in need of patient and wise leadership.

Make no mistake: you may have been studying Jewish wisdom in a Jewish institution from Jewish teachers, but God is the Creator of all, and cares for all. If you have absorbed even a little of His infinite wisdom, then you to must turn your attention with compassion to all of creation. As Ramak continues, this includes "inanimate objects, plants, animals, and humans." In sum, studying Torah should give you a sense of ownership without a sense of entitlement; it should make you feel like a responsible patron, without making you patronizing.

2000 Years of Torah

Some people believe that the greatest form of Torah study is to be an advanced scholar, learning in an elite *kolel*, detached from the responsibilities of more basic education. Sometimes this belief is connected with an attitude that views outreach to the unaffiliated as an important mitzvah, but probably not an obligation, and certainly not an obligation for one who could and should be immersed in more sophisticated forms of Torah study.

As we reflect on Shavuot, the day of the giving of the Torah, a surprising statement of the Rabbis seems to indicate something altogether different.

The world is to exist six thousand years; the first two thousand years are to be null and void; the next two thousand years are the period of the Torah, and the following two thousand years are the period of the Messiah. Through our many sins a number of these have already passed [and the Messiah has not yet come].

תלמוד בבלי מסכת
עבודה זרה דף ט עמוד א
תנא דבי אליהו: ששת אלפים שנה הוי העולם, שני אלפים תוהו, שני אלפים תורה, שני אלפים ימות המשיח, בעונותינו שרבו יצאו מהן מה שיצאו מהן. שני אלפים תורה מאימת? אי נימא ממתן תורה עד השתא, ליכא כולי האי, דכי מעיינת בהו, תרי אלפי פרטי דהאי אלפא הוא דהואי! אלא (בראשית יב) מאת הנפש אשר עשו בחרן, וגמירי, דאברהם בההיא שעתא בר חמשין ותרתי הוה, כמה בצרן מדתני תנא? ארבע מאה וארבעים ותמניא שנין הויין, כי מעיינת ביה מהנפש אשר עשו בחרן עד מתן תורה, ארבע מאה וארבעים ותמניא שנין הויין.

357

Learning to Grow

From when are the two thousand years of the Torah to be reckoned? Shall we say from the Giving of the Torah at Sinai? In that case, you will find that there are not quite two thousand years from then until now, for if you compute the years [from the Creation to the Giving of the Torah] you will find that they comprise two thousand and a part of the third thousand; the period is therefore to be reckoned from the time when Avraham and Sarah "made souls in Haran" for we have it as a tradition that Avraham was at that time fifty-two years old. Now, to what extent does our *Tanna* encroach [on the other thousand]? Four hundred and forty-eight years! Calculate it and you will find that from the time when they "made souls in Haran" until the giving of the Torah there are just four hundred and forty-eight years!

We have a tradition according to which the era of "Torah" lasted for 2,000 years following the era of "null and void." When do the 2,000 years of Torah begin? We would expect from the Sinai revelation, on our holiday of Shavuot; however, the Rabbis point out that this date would have been 448 years too late. If so, the era of Torah actually began during the life of Avraham. But when during that long and rich life did "Torah" begin?

Was it from the time he smashed his father's idols, or from the time he discovered the secret of monotheism? Perhaps it was from the time he had a son to whom he could pass the Torah?

The Rabbis suggest none of these possibilities. Instead, they locate the beginning of the era of Torah in Avraham's reaching out to others, inspiring them with his vision, effectively "making them." Torah, it seems, doesn't begin with one's personal study, discovery, or flourishing. Torah begins with what we today would call *kiruv rechokim*, religious outreach.

This idea is echoed in the Rambam and in Rabbi Yosef Karo's commentary, the *Kesef Mishnah*, when they discuss the religious biography of our first patriarch.

Avraham was forty years old when he recognized his Creator. Once he achieved this, he began to reason with the inhabitants of Ur Kasdim and to argue with them, saying that by serving idols they were not following the way of truth. He broke their images, and began to proclaim that it is not fitting to serve anyone other than God, and to Him it is fitting to bow down and to offer sacrifices and libations, so that all creation will recognize Him. Avraham also proclaimed that it was fitting to break and

רמב"ם הלכות עבודה זרה פרק א
ובן ארבעים שנה הכיר אברהם את בוראו, כיון שהכיר וידע התחיל להשיב תשובות על בני אור כשדים ולערוך דין עמהם ולומר שאין זו דרך האמת שאתם הולכים בה ושיבר הצלמים והתחיל להודיע לעם שאין ראוי לעבוד אלא לאלוה העולם ולו ראוי להשתחוות ולהקריב ולנסך כדי שיכירוהו כל הברואים הבאים, וראוי לאבד ולשבר כל הצורות כדי שלא יטעו בהן כל העם כמו אלו שהם מדמים שאין שם אלוה אלא אלו. כיון שגבר עליהם בראיותיו בקש המלך להורגו ונעשה לו נס ויצא לחרן, והתחיל לעמוד ולקרוא בקול גדול לכל העולם ולהודיעם שיש שם אלוה אחד לכל העולם ולו ראוי לעבוד, והיה מהלך וקורא ומקבץ העם מעיר לעיר וממלכה לממלכה עד שהגיע לארץ כנען והוא קורא שנאמר ויקרא שם בשם ה' אל עולם, וכיון שהיו העם מתקבצין אליו ושואלין לו על דבריו היה מודיע לכל אחד ואחד כפי דעתו עד שיחזירהו לדרך האמת עד שנתקבצו אליו אלפים ורבבות והם אנשי בית אברהם:

destroy all the figures, so that nobody will err on account of them, like those who imagined that there is no god except for their idols did. Since his arguments were convincing, the king sought to kill him, but a miracle was performed for Avraham, and he went to Haran. And he began to get up and proclaim to the whole world that there is just one God in the world, whom it is fitting to worship. He went and gathered people together from cities and kingdoms, until he reached the land of Canaan, where he continued his proclamations, as it is written, "...and called there in the name of the Lord, the everlasting God." Since people were coming to him with questions about this matter, he would answer each person as was fitting so that he would return to the way of truth, until thousands and tens of thousands came to him. These were the people of the house of Avraham....

As always, there is much that we can and should learn from our great-great-grandfather Avraham. Firstly, we can see that his passion for truth was such that he was not satisfied keeping it to himself and his close family; rather, he felt a need to share his truth with others. As we saw above, this is one important way of loving God—you should cause others to fall in love with God as well[105]—and we know that Avraham is referred to as God's beloved,[106] perhaps for this very reason.

Secondly, we see one good way to do *kiruv* and one less productive way to do *kiruv*. Avraham began by debating, breaking idols, and telling people "they were not following the way of truth." Even though his arguments were convincing, we don't see that people followed him; instead, it got him thrown into a furnace, and he needed a miracle to survive. Avraham's approach to *kiruv* seems to have changed after this experience. Instead of debating and breaking idols, he simply started teaching true theology, without polemics or theatrics, and with abundant kindness. My experience teaching Torah on campus to unaffiliated Jews has taught me the same lesson: you don't move people by debating and polemics; you move them by teaching wisdom combined with abundant kindness.

---

105. יומא פו.
106. ישעיהו מ"א

Lastly, and most importantly for our purposes, the Jewish people effectively begin with Avraham. He is the first of our patriarchs, even though there were righteous men who preceded him. We know Shem, the son of Noah, had an academy where students were instructed in monotheism; Ever, Shem's grandson, also had such an academy. Why, then, did the Jewish people not begin with them? Why do we not refer to "Shem Avinu" or "Ever Avinu," although Jews are descended from them both physically and spiritually?

Rabbi Yosef Karo asks this question in his *Kesef Mishnah* on the passage cited above and he answers something illuminating: true, Shem and Ever were righteous, and true, they had students; but they only taught students who sought them out. Rabbi Karo concludes that Avraham engaged in *outreach*, "and therefore his stature became extremely great."

Clearly, there was some Torah study present in the world even before Avraham came on the scene, but those years were still considered the era of "null and void." The era of Torah began with a certain special, Jewish approach to Torah—the approach of outreach.

You have spent this year cultivating a sensitivity towards Torah that is precious and rare. Certainly you need to "fill your own tank" before you can legitimately overflow towards others. Like they say on airplanes: in case of emergency, put on your own oxygen mask before helping your neighbor with his. And indeed, you may not have reached the level where you can successfully overflow to others after only one year in yeshiva or seminary. Still, as the year draws to a close, and on the holiday of Shavuot, it is important to reflect on the nature of that Torah you have cultivated. Ultimately, Torah that is kept for yourself, your family, and even your students, is a Torah from the era of "null and void"; the Torah that we received as Jews, the Torah that began the Jewish people, is a Torah that demands to be shared, without debates or iconoclasm, but with overflowing wisdom and abundant kindness.

Learning to Grow

In your social circles, a year or two in yeshiva or seminary might be quite common. But when you look at the Jewish people as a whole, you must conclude that your experience makes you a member of an elite club. You have gained a literacy, a sensitivity, and a respect for our tradition that is both exquisite and obligating. Your hard work, together with the investment of your parents and your teachers, has put you on a path towards greatness and fulfillment. As you accept the Torah anew this Shavuot and prepare to leave the *beit midrash* for the summer, it is time to reflect on three life-shaping questions that will propel you further down that path: what are the present needs of the Jewish people and the world; what are your unique talents; and what mission excites you the most? If you can answer those questions you will be ready to continue developing your skills in a more focused manner, and make the kind of contribution that your elite status demands.

Attributions

1. Photograph of "Remuh Synagogue, 40 Szeroka street, Kazimierz, Krakow, Poland" by Zygmunt Put. Permission is granted to copy, distribute and/or modify this document under the terms of the **GNU Free Documentation License**, Version 1.2 or any later version published by the Free Software Foundation; with no Invariant Sections, no Front-Cover Texts, and no Back-Cover Texts.